ON WAVE AND WING

ON
WAVE
AND
WING

THE 100-YEAR QUEST TO PERFECT THE
AIRCRAFT CARRIER

BARRETT TILLMAN

REGNERY
HISTORY

Regnery History™ is a trademark of Salem Communications Holding Corporation; Regnery® is a registered trademark of Salem Communications Holding Corporation

Cataloging-in-Publication data on file with the Library of Congress

ISBN 978-1-62157-591-7

Published in the United States by
Regnery History
An imprint of Regnery Publishing
A Division of Salem Media Group
300 New Jersey Ave NW
Washington, DC 20001
www.RegneryHistory.com

Manufactured in the United States of America

10 9 8 7 6 5 4 3 2 1

Books are available in quantity for promotional or premium use. For information on discounts and terms, please visit our website: www.Regnery.com.

Distributed to the trade by
Perseus Distribution
www.perseusdistribution.com

*Dedicated to the memory of Attack Squadron 35 (1934–1995)
and Fighter Squadron 111 (1942–1995), historic three-war carrier
squadrons slain by a soulless naval bureaucracy.*
—**BARRETT TILLMAN,** Honorary Black Panther
and Honorary Sundowner

CONTENTS

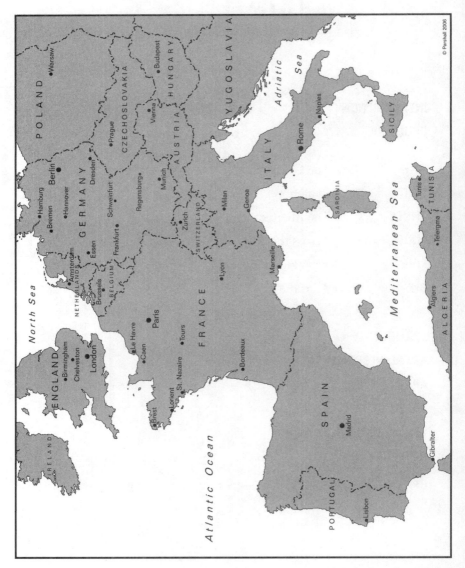

Courtesy Jonathan Parshall

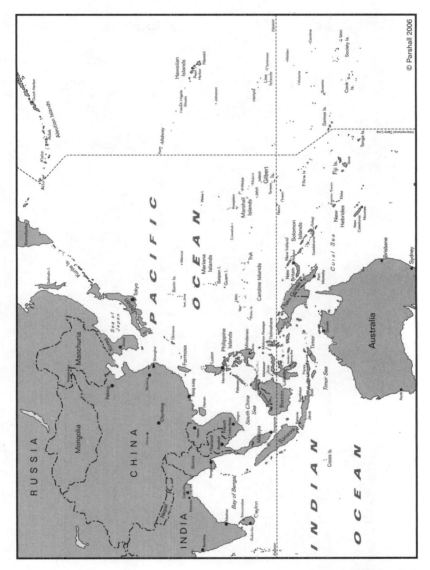

Courtesy Jonathan Parshall

INTRODUCTION

"WHERE ARE THE CARRIERS?"

In time of trouble—real, perceived, or anticipated—U.S. presidents often ask that question. It is no surprise, since an aircraft carrier's flight deck typically delivers four and one-half acres of American sovereignty to the world's oceans, accessible to every continent.

But the aircraft carrier is not an American invention. Its origin dates from Great Britain in 1917, when the battlecruiser HMS *Furious* was rigged with a flight deck to accommodate aircraft during the Great War. In the century since, the carrier has played an increasingly historic role on the world stage. From the first tentative, pioneering efforts during World War I, the fighting flattop emerged fully grown barely two decades later, displacing the battleship atop the pyramid of naval power. Today the carrier retains that pride of place. Yet aircraft carriers are so technically complex, so extremely costly, and so difficult to operate that only three nations have produced them in quantity: Britain, America, and Japan. France trails a distant fourth, while other fleets currently operate single flattops.

However, carrier aviation is far, far more than ships, airplanes, and technology. It is a distinct culture, equal parts cult and guild, melding man and machinery. The blend of the human element with technology has produced worldwide, historic results. Few other endeavors so thoroughly entwine the various technical and human components into a synergistic whole. Human beings are the core of carrier aviation, the fiber binding together wave and wing. Carriers would not exist except for the visionaries, the innovators, the leaders, the risk-takers, the true believers. Together, they have had a dispro-portionate effect upon global events in the past century. Carriers—though thin-skinned, vulnerable ships stuffed with volatile fuel and ordnance—were instrumental not only in the rise and fall of navies, but of great nations and even empires. During the Second World War, carriers were vital to Allied victory in the Atlantic and Pacific. But victory at sea was only a brief blip on history's radar trace, as carrier aviation expanded its influence ashore in Korea, Vietnam, the Medi-terranean, and beyond.

Carrier advocates fought long and hard for their passion, both afloat and ashore. In the 1920s the first generation of carrier aviators paid their tuition in blood, learning the esoteric trade on the narrow wooden decks of ships often hastily modified for the purpose. Land-ing flimsy biplanes on moving platforms that pitched and rolled through oceanic swells called for equal parts courage and skill. Some with ample courage lacked the skill—or the luck—to survive. Yet the pioneer tailhookers believed in the future, and they helped reshape the world's naval structure.

Within four months in 1945 the U.S. Navy helped Britain defeat Nazi Germany's navy (the *Kriegsmarine*) and almost unaided smashed the Imperial Japanese Navy (*Nihon Kaigun*). But in the late 1940s flying admirals and their subordinates had to conduct a years-long battle in Washington, D.C., and in the nation's media to keep what the previous generation had gained. The nation—and the free world—owed them a debt.

The huge majority of fliers and sailors who make carriers function will forever remain anonymous to their countrymen. Only a few stellar figures cross the national firmaments: Admiral William "Bull" Halsey was the jut-jawed seadog who led the task force that launched the 1942 Doolittle Raid against Tokyo, when America's morale needed a boost as never before. Three years later, a fleet commander, he witnessed Japan's surrender in Tokyo Bay.

Japan's foremost admiral, Isoruku Yamamoto, helped build the Imperial Navy's carrier fleet in the 1930s, and in 1941 sent it to Hawaiian waters with stunning consequences. But unlike his U.S. counterpart, Yamamoto perished in the war he initiated.

No comparable figurehead ever caught the public fancy in Britain, despite the Royal Navy's importance in carrier evolution.

Even today the men who actually delivered sea power to their nations largely have come and gone unrecognized. They labored in the bake-oven heat of engineering spaces, providing essential power and propulsion. They sweated on hangar decks, often assuming near-impossible positions while leaning into airframes and engines with screwdrivers or socket wrenches. They strained on "hernia bars" loading bombs on attack aircraft and ammunition into fighters. They dragged heavy hoses to thirsty aircraft, filling fuel tanks for the next launch. They briefed in squadron ready rooms—partly college dormitory hung with flight gear and posters, partly tribal enclave, each with its own esoteric nature. They huddled on the flag bridge where admirals and their staffs pondered the latest intelligence, knowing that it was inevitably incomplete and often inaccurate. All played their essential parts, melding the many into the whole—a potent warship ready to launch violence over the far horizon in service of the state.

Naval aviation also produced the first generation of spacemen. The aviators who rode catapults off carrier decks launched into celestial voyages even to the moon. Approximately half of NASA astronauts wore wings of gold, including the first American in space and the first to orbit earth. Of the twelve men who walked on the moon, seven were naval aviators, including the first and the last.

Today, a century downrange from HMS *Furious*, there is little doubt that carriers will remain the pre-eminent combatants in the world's oceans. The fact that naval warfare no longer exists has not diminished the urgency with which navies and nations acquire ship-based aviation. If there will never be another Midway or Leyte Gulf, there surely will be other Koreas, Vietnams, Libyas, and Iraqs. Thus, the carrier's unique ability to project power ashore will ensure its continued use, "ready on arrival."

Barrett Tillman
June 2016

PROLOGUE

PEARL HARBOR

Shock and Awe, 1941 version. A Nakajima B5N torpedo bomber from the carrier *Zuikaku* over Pearl Harbor on December 7. *Courtesy Tailhook Association.*

IN LATE 1941 THE BATTLESHIP WAS MASTER OF THE WORLD'S oceans. The modern era had arrived at the turn of the twentieth century with all-steel warships capable of firing large-caliber weapons. American battleships scored historic victories over Spain at Santiago, Cuba, and Manila Bay, Philippines, in 1898. Japan was similarly victorious over Russia in Tsushima Strait between Korea and Japan in 1905. The victors in both cases had little reason to doubt that battleships would continue to dominate the world's waterways, despite the arrival of the aircraft carrier.

In America the primacy of the dreadnought was such that the program of the November 29, 1941, Army-Navy Game read, "It is significant that despite the claims of air enthusiasts no battleship has yet been sunk by bombs." Navy won that game 14–6. Eight days later, visiting carrier aircraft played the home team at Pearl Harbor and won, 8–0.

The author of the game's program either was abysmally ignorant or a scandalous liar—no other explanation is possible. He ignored Brigadier General Billy Mitchell's controversially successful test against a captured German battleship twenty years before. Far more conclusively, twelve months previously the British carrier attack on Taranto, Italy, had sunk two battleships and badly damaged another.

Meanwhile, Japan was about to rock the naval world on its stern.

At 6:00 a.m. Hawaii time on Sunday, December 7, 1941, six Imperial Navy aircraft carriers steamed into gray, spume-swept Pacific swells. The ships steadied up directly into the wind and began launching aircraft with a precision born of arduous training.

With practiced skill 183 planes assembled by aircraft type—forty Nakajima B5N torpedo planes, forty-nine B5N level bombers, fifty-one Aichi D3A dive bombers, and forty-three Mitsubishi A6M Zero fighters. Pearl Harbor lay 230 statute miles south. Meanwhile, a scout from the cruiser *Chikuma* snooped the harbor, radioing that the Americans seemed unwary.

Imperial Japan was about to deliver the world a lesson in twentieth-century shock and awe.

PATH TO WAR

The oceanic route to Pearl lay along a tangled path of diplomatic, military, and economic concerns. Japan, increasingly aggressive, began fighting China off-and-on in 1931, going at it full time starting in 1937. Tokyo's aggression continued unchecked, and in 1941 it seemed aimed elsewhere—notably French Indochina and the Dutch East Indies. President Franklin D. Roosevelt took action, ordering an oil embargo in July, and the next month Washington warned the Japanese of possible consequences if they attacked nations beyond China.

Tokyo took little heed. Determined to avoid capitulation to what they considered foreign extortion, the cabinet of General Hideki Tojo opted for war. With less than two years of oil reserves, Tokyo had to act quickly and decisively.

Enter the aircraft carrier.

Admiral Isoroku Yamamoto had risen to command the Combined Fleet in August 1939, days before the new war in Europe. An aviation advocate, he had supported Japan's carrier program and, once committed to war, he backed the Hawaii Plan as preferable to the doctrinal "decisive battle" in mid-Pacific. He knew America well, having served there twice between the wars, and he realized that a pre-emptive strike was essential to Japan's success—if success were possible at all.

Planning had begun in January 1941, when Yamamoto directed a preliminary study with substantial contribution from Commander Minoru Genda, an experienced air operations officer. More details developed from April onward under Rear Admiral Ryunosuke Kusaka, chief of staff of the newly formed First Air Fleet. There was nothing else like it on earth: all six of Japan's large carriers were concentrated under Vice Admiral Chuichi Nagumo.

Intensive training began in late August, affording Nagumo's aircrews barely three months to perfect tactics and techniques. Genda's plan involved a triple blow: high-altitude level bombers, dive bombers, and torpedo planes. The Imperial Navy was well versed in all three, but Pearl Harbor presented a problem: the average depth was barely forty feet, and Japanese torpedoes needed twice as much to recover, rise to the desired depth, and run safely.

Ordnance engineers found an inspired solution. Large wooden surfaces were fitted to the torpedoes' standard fins, providing larger surface areas. Once in the water the wooden fins were released and the Type 91 torpedoes sped on their way. Last-minute tests confirmed the theory.

On the morning of Sunday, December 7, 1941, the aircraft carrier was much like the proverbial musician who works twenty years to become an overnight sensation. When the Imperial Navy stunned the world with the attack on Pearl Harbor, Japan and the United States had two decades of experience operating carriers, perfecting equipment and techniques. Both navies had commissioned their first flattops in 1922, and they had experienced a parallel development.

By 1941, Britain had already used carriers effectively against an enemy naval base. In November 1940 a British carrier launched a successful nocturnal strike against the Italian fleet anchorage at Taranto in the "heel" of the boot. Three major combatants were knocked out of action, altering the naval balance in the Mediterranean literally overnight. But of the world's carrier powers, including Great Britain, only Japan grasped the concept of a unified offensive arm. It was called *Kido Butai* or Strike Force.

The six Japanese carriers bound for Hawaiian waters were arrayed in pairs: the giant sisters *Akagi* and *Kaga* in the First Carrier Division; *Soryu* and *Hiryu* in the Second; and newly commissioned *Shokaku* and *Zuikaku* in the Fifth. They embarked some 420 bombers, torpedo planes, and fighters, while battleships and cruisers operated catapult-launched floatplanes. The carriers were escorted by two battleships, three cruisers, nine destroyers, and nourished by seven tankers. The latter were more important than the fourteen escorts, as the striking force could not reach Hawaiian waters and return without replenishing at sea.

Kido Butai sortied from the Kurile Islands on November 26. Crossing the North Pacific under radio silence, the task force avoided detection during the ten-day transit. Meanwhile, submarines had already departed home waters and bases in the Marshall Islands.

Emperor Hirohito had approved war against the Western powers barely a month before the attack, but he did not grant approval for the Hawaii operation until December 1. Thus, Nagumo's force represented an arrow launched at the heart of the U.S. Pacific Fleet that might have been recalled in flight. Instead, it flew straight to its target.

The first wave was timed to arrive over Pearl about thirty minutes after Japanese diplomats delivered Japan's refusal to accept Washington's demands. But the message from Tokyo took too long to decode, so the mission proceeded as a surprise. The attack precipitated boiling anger throughout America, fueling a surging rage that never abated until V-J Day.

While the leading squadrons winged southward, *Kido Butai* continued as briefed. At 7:15 the second wave of 168 planes lifted off its decks, comprising fifty-four level bombers, seventy-eight dive bombers, and thirty-six fighters.

"TORA, TORA, TORA!"

Leading the first wave over Pearl Harbor was Lieutenant Commander Mitsuo Fuchida, *Akagi*'s senior aviator. Flying as observer in a Nakajima B5N horizontal bomber, he issued the order to proceed with the attack, as described in his memoir:

> One hour and forty minutes after leaving the carriers I knew that we should be nearing our goal. Small openings in the thick cloud cover afforded occasional glimpses of the ocean.... Suddenly a long white line of breaking surf

appeared directly beneath my plane. It was the northern shore of Oahu.

Veering right toward the west coast of the island, we could see that the sky over Pearl Harbor was clear. Presently the harbor itself became visible across the central Oahu plain, a film of morning mist hovering over it. I peered intently through my binoculars at the ships riding peacefully at anchor. One by one I counted them. Yes, the battleships were there all right, eight of them! But our last lingering hope of finding any carriers present was now gone. Not one was to be seen.

It was 0749 when I ordered the attack. [The radioman] immediately began tapping out the pre-arranged code signal: "TO, TO, TO..."

Leading the whole group, Lieutenant Commander Murata's torpedo bombers headed downward to launch their torpedoes, while Lieutenant Commander Itaya's fighters raced forward to sweep enemy fighters from the air. Takahashi's dive-bomber group had climbed for altitude and was out of sight. My bombers, meanwhile, made a circuit toward Barbers Point to keep pace with the attack schedule. No enemy fighters were in the air, nor were there any gun flashes from the ground.

The effectiveness of our attack was now certain, and a message, "Surprise attack successful!" was accordingly sent to Akagi at 0753. The message was received by the carrier and relayed to the homeland.

Mitsuo Fuchida ended the war as a captain. Subsequently he became a Christian evangelist, spending much time in the United States. He died in 1976.

Once Fuchida signaled "*Tora, tora, tora,*" the attack proceeded largely as planned. The first B5Ns over the target were sixteen from *Soryu* and *Hiryu*. Briefed to hit carriers on Ford Island's northwest coast, they went for alternate objectives, destroying the target ship USS *Utah* (née BB-31, re-designated AG-16) and damaging a cruiser.

Akagi's torpedo squadron led a devastating attack. The Nakajimas swept in from the north shore of the harbor, skimming low between Hickam Field and the fuel tank farm, then nudging downward over the water. Making one hundred mph at sixty-five feet, they deployed as per individual briefings and turned onto their attack headings. A quarter mile ahead lay the gray monoliths along Battleship Row.

Of thirty-six torpedoes dropped, probably nineteen found their targets. Hardest hit were *West Virginia* (BB-48) and *Oklahoma* (BB-37) moored outboard at the head of Battleship Row. *California* (BB-44), resting farther ahead of the others, drew further attention and took two hits and slowly settled onto the mud.

Five torpedo planes were shot down, all from succeeding waves as the defenders responded and fought back. After-action reports showed that most ships began returning fire within two to seven minutes.

The high-level B5Ns each carried an 800 kg armor-piercing bomb, designed to penetrate a battleship's thick armor. The ten planes targeting *Arizona* (BB-39) scored four hits and three near misses. One of them found the sweet spot, smashing into *Arizona*'s forward magazine. The 1,760-pound weapon ignited tons of gunpowder, destroying the ship in seconds with three-fourths of the crew.

At 8:40, almost half an hour after the first attack, 167 aircraft of the second wave were led by *Zuikaku*'s senior aviator, Lieutenant Commander Shigekazu Shimazaki. No torpedo planes participated, but fifty-four Nakajima level bombers struck three air bases. The seventy-eight Aichi dive bombers were assigned any carriers in port with cruisers as secondary goals. Nearly three dozen Zero fighters established air superiority over Hickam and Bellows Fields plus Kaneohe Naval Air Station.

Much of the effort was wasted as many dive bomber pilots probably misidentified ship types; perhaps twenty-eight Aichis dove on destroyers or auxiliary vessels.

The brunt of the second dive bombing attack was *Nevada* (BB-36), the only battleship to get underway. Already holed by a torpedo, she took six bombs in a few minutes and developed a list. To avoid sinking, she was beached near the harbor entrance.

When the second wave departed northward, the entire attack had lasted not quite two hours, from 7:55 to 9:45. In their slipstream the Japanese left Oahu stunned, both physically and emotionally.

The attack killed 2,335 U.S. military personnel and 68 civilians.

Arizona was destroyed and *Oklahoma* written off. *Pennsylvania* and *Maryland* were lightly damaged and quickly returned to service, but saw no action until 1943. *Tennessee* and *Nevada* were refitted in 1942 and '43; *California* and *West Virginia* were refloated and fully repaired in 1944. Three cruisers and three destroyers were repaired or rebuilt from 1942 to 1944. Finally, a minelayer was sunk but repaired and operational in 1944.

Combined Army-Navy-Marine aircraft losses were about 175 immediately assessed as destroyed plus twenty-five damaged beyond repair. Some 150 sustained lesser damage.

The Japanese lost twenty-nine aircraft and sixty-five men, mostly aircrew, but including ten sailors in five miniature submarines.

Far at sea, at 11:15 *Kido Butai* began landing the second wave, completed an hour later. The fliers were jubilant. They knew they had inflicted severe damage and were eager to complete the task. But Nagumo opted for prudence. More than one hundred returning planes were damaged to varying extents, and most critically he needed to conserve fuel oil. The Imperial Navy had too few fleet tankers in 1941 and never caught up. Nagumo turned for home, with Second Carrier Division diverting to attack Wake Island.

Pearl Harbor was a rarity in history—a clearly defined day when the old order ended, abruptly, violently, and permanently. Not only had *Kido Butai* initiated a new way of warfare, but it upset the conventional wisdom that naval airpower could not compete with land-based planes. Historian John Lundstrom did not exaggerate when he described *Kido Butai* as "a 1941 atomic bomb."

But retribution was coming.

Of the twenty-nine ships that had departed Japan, one escaped destruction over the next four years. The destroyer *Ushio*, among those diverted en route to shell Midway, survived the Solomons bloodletting and Leyte Gulf and was surrendered at Yokosuka in 1945.

By then, U.S. aircraft carriers had turned the world's greatest ocean into an American lake.

ONE

THE GREAT
WAR ERA

1910–1918

The beginning. Civilian pilot Eugene Ely taking off from the cruiser USS *Birmingham* at Hampton Roads, Virginia, in November 1910. *Courtesy Glenn H. Curtiss Aviation Museum.*

THE FIRST SHIPBOARD AVIATOR WAS A CIVILIAN NAMED

Eugene B. Ely, a native Iowan who came to aviation as an Oregon automobile salesman. Largely self-taught after crashing on his first flying attempt, Ely quickly gained a national reputation working for speed merchant Glen Curtiss, who held U.S. pilot license number one.

In October 1910 Ely became the seventeenth Aero Club member to gain a pilot's license.

The Curtiss Aeroplane and Motor Company was a bitter rival of the Wright brothers, who had mastered powered flight in 1903. But while the Wrights expended much of their effort in patent feuds, Curtiss pressed ahead with technical and—equally important—political matters.

Commander Frederick L. Chapin, the U.S. naval attaché in Paris, watched aviation's often halting but steady progress with interest. The Wrights' impressive 1908 demonstrations set Europe atwitter, with echoes rebounding across the Atlantic. Mating the flying machine to the warship seemed a valid concept, and Chapin submitted a report through channels. Eventually Navy Secretary George von Lengerke Meyer took note and sought a senior officer to observe aviation affairs. In October 1910 he detailed Captain Washington I. Chambers, a battleship man, to observe the international air meet at Belmont Park, New York.

Glenn Curtiss knew an opportunity when he saw one. Though Ely had only gained his license that month, Curtiss took him to meet with Chambers. Asked if they could take off from a platform rigged on a ship, the fliers reckoned that they could not only take off but land aboard as well.

Events accelerated. At Norfolk an eighty-three-foot-long wood platform was erected over the two-year-old cruiser, United States Ship *Birmingham*'s (CL-2) forward deck. The platform was sloped slightly downward to provide a speedier descent on the takeoff run.

On November 14, 1910, the cruiser eased into Hampton Roads with two destroyers as contingency rescue ships. Ely, draped with inner tubes for flotation and sporting a football helmet, climbed into the exposed seat of his Curtiss Pusher. With the four-cylinder engine revving up, he advanced the throttle and began his downhill takeoff.

Ely got off in less than sixty feet and, running off the ramp, he pushed forward on his control wheel. He recovered so low that his wheels dragged in the water, creating a potent rooster-tail spray that cracked his propeller. After wiping saltwater off his goggles, he landed safely on the beach, considering the experiment a failure due to the prop damage. But officialdom disagreed: he received a hefty five hundred dollar reward (worth about $12,500 in 2016) from the U.S. Aeronautical Reserve.

Having proven that a shipboard takeoff was possible, Curtiss and Ely adjourned to California where better weather awaited—along with the 13,900-ton armored cruiser *Pennsylvania* (ACR-4). The ship sported a platform 127 feet long supported above the aft deck. The problem was how to stop an airplane when landing in such a confined space. A circus performer, Hugh Robinson, conceived the notion of using hooks to grapple pendants stretched

After proving that he could take off from a ship in November 1910, two months later Eugene Ely attempted to land his Curtiss biplane on a platform rigged aboard an anchored cruiser. *Courtesy Tailhook Association.*

across the deck, weighted with fifty-pound blocks on each end. With three hooks fitted to the bottom of the Curtiss pusher, Ely was confident of snagging several ropes to drag him to a stop. According to legend, the primitive arresting hooks were grapples obtained during a visit to Fisherman's Wharf.

On January 18, 1911, Ely took off from San Bruno and motored over San Francisco Bay. Forced to land downwind, the aviator dropped the pusher onto the improvised deck and bounced several feet, missing the first ten ropes. But Robinson's hooks snagged several successive lines, dragging the flying machine to a halt. Officers and sailors waved their hats and cheered. Ely's young wife, Mabel—who reputedly had spent the last three years waiting to see him killed—breathed an enormous sigh of relief. Less than an hour later, Ely again revved his plane, returning to shore.

The first trap: on January 18, 1911, Eugene Ely safely landed aboard the armored cruiser USS *Pennsylvania* off San Francisco. Hooks fixed to the landing gear snagged a succession of ropes to stop the aircraft. *Courtesy Tailhook Association.*

The response was mixed. *Pennsylvania*'s Captain Charles F. Pond described Ely's feat as "the most important landing of a bird since the dove flew back to the ark." He was "positively assured of the importance of the aeroplane in future naval warfare." He even suggested constructing "new vessels to serve as floating airfields from which land-type aircraft take off and land." The *San Francisco Examiner* head ined, "Eugene Ely Revises World's Naval Tactics."

However, the British magazine *Aero* sniffed, "This partakes rather too much of the nature of trick flying to be of much practical value. A naval aeroplane would be of more use if it landed on the water and could then be hauled aboard."

Even Captain Chambers had his reservations, despite his patronage of Curtiss. Chambers doubted that flight decks could be installed on warships due to the placement of main-battery gun turrets. He had yet to arrive at the "flat top" concept with a clear, full-length deck unencumbered by other structures. That configuration would only emerge near the end of the First World War.

A later generation would call the Curtiss-Ely combination a "technology demonstrato:." The ability to take off and land safely aboard ship had been proven, but to what end? There the question lingered for eleven years in America's naval twilight zone.

Eugene Ely was killed in a crash at Macon, Georgia, in October 1911, nine months after his shipboard landing. But his pioneering influence stretched farther than even he might have imagined.

BRITISH BEGINNINGS

In May 1912 Britain established the Royal Flying Corps (RFC), originally with separate military and naval wings. Organizational clarity would have to wait.

Meanwhile, Britain's first unassisted takeoff from a ship came fourteen months after Ely's effort in November 1910. The pilot was Acting Commander Charles R. Samson, one of the Royal Navy's first four aviators. In January 1912 he launched from a ramp aboard His Majesty's Ship *Africa*, a battleship anchored in the Medway River. His Short S.27, more resembling a box kite than an airplane, easily made the deck run. Subsequently Samson demonstrated the ability to take off while underway from two other pre-dreadnoughts: HMS *Hibernia* and *London*.

Early infighting between the two aviation branches for funding and equipment was solved at the last minute in July 1914—the month before the Great War erupted. The RFC's naval wing was designated the Royal Naval Air Service (RNAS). The RNAS boasted some 830 personnel and seventy-eight "aeroplanes." That same month Lieutenant Arthur Longmore demonstrated the service's operational potential by successfully dropping a torpedo from a Short Type 81 seaplane.

OTHER PLAYERS

France, Germany, Czarist Russia, and Japan also produced seaplane carriers in the early years. The aircraft either were launched by catapult or were craned into the water for takeoff. In either case they were hoisted back aboard after alighting on the water.

In 1912 the French Navy established an aviation branch (the *Aeronavale*) and converted the sea plane tender *Foudre*, making her the first ship with an aircraft hangar. She demonstrated operational capability in 1913, about the time that HMS *Hermes* briefly became Britain's first seaplane carrier. The French engineer Clement Ader, known to history as the father of French aviation, had published a book five years before *Foudre*'s demonstration predicting the rise of the aircraft carrier of the future. With exceptional prescience he envisioned an unobstructed flight deck, an offset island, and elevators between the hangar and flight decks.

Russia took a significant step in 1913 by experimenting with a Curtiss floatplane aboard the 6,600-ton cruiser *Kagul* in the Black Sea. Boasting the talents of two great aviation pioneers, Igor Sikorsky and Alexander Seversky, the Czarist navy could have become a world leader in naval aviation. Unfortunately, the 1917 revolution upset their momentum.

When the Great War broke over Europe in August 1914, Japan and France briefly employed ship-launched aircraft. That month, Japan commissioned a seaplane carrier, the 7,700-ton *Wakamiya*. Losing no time, the converted freighter deployed to China's Kiaochow Bay supporting the siege of German-held Tsingtao. It was the first use of an aviation ship in combat. A French-designed Farman seaplane successfully launched from the vessel, dropping small bombs and, more importantly, scouting the area. *Wakamiya*'s deployment lasted until year's end when the Kaiser's garrison surrendered.

RULE BRITANNIA

Meanwhile, the Royal Navy continued operating aircraft at sea. The 20,500-ton liner *Campania* was commissioned in 1916 and operated in the Mediterranean and Aegean with as many as ten small flying boats.

The best-known use of a Royal Navy shipboard aircraft occurred during the epic Battle of Jutland at the end of May 1916. Supporting the British battle cruiser squadron, Flight Lieutenant Frederick Rutland and his observer off the 1,700-ton HMS *Engadine* spotted smoke from German screening vessels and radioed a contact report—the first such use of sea-based aviation in combat. (Sadly, "Rutland of Jutland" would be confined in the next war for espionage on behalf of Japan.)

Shipboard operations began progressively, as with this skid-equipped Sopwith Pup aboard HMS *Furious* in 1917. *Courtesy Tailhook Association.*

But something more potent emerged on the nautical horizon. In August 1917 the new nineteen thousand-ton battle cruiser HMS *Furious* conducted deck-landing tests at Scapa Flow. A "flying off" deck replaced the forward eighteen-inch gun turret, and a landing deck was built aft of the superstructure, connected to the forward deck by narrow taxiways. *Furious* received a hangar capable of housing ten aircraft, which could be craned from the hangar to the launch deck. The nascent aircraft carrier of the future was taking shape.

The lead aviator on *Furious* was Squadron Commander Edwin H. Dunning, a twenty-five-year-old graduate of Dartmouth Royal Naval College. Previously a seaplane pilot, Dunning was drawn to shipboard aviation and began proving the concept. Dunning flew a Sopwith Pup, predecessor of the famed Camel fighter. The Pup was among the most popular aircraft of the era: light, agile, responsive. But it lacked an arresting gear such as Eugene Ely had used six years before. Instead, straps were attached to the airframe for crewmen to grasp as the pilot "hovered" just off the deck, nearly stationary in the ship's relative wind.

The first trials were held on August 2, 1917. The combined ship and ambient wind yielded a 47-knot headwind, about the same as a Pup's landing speed. Flying up the starboard beam forward of the island, Dunning adroitly cross-controlled, placing his machine over the original flying-off deck. About ten of Dunning's fellow officers, incongruously clad in blues with winged collars and ties, rushed to grasp the handles and pulled the Sopwith down. It was a risky evolution, as the superstructure forced the pilot to side-slip into position over the deck. The whirling propeller posed a serious risk, and after the first trial Dunning directed his friends to stay clear until the wheels were on deck.

Tuition was paid in blood. Squadron Commander E. H. Dunning died attempting to land his Sopwith aboard HMS *Furious* in August 1917. *Courtesy Tailhook Association.*

Five days later, Dunning tried it again. His first landing had damaged the Pup, so he grabbed another plane and took off. The ship was making 25 knots into a 33-knot wind, producing a substantial 58 knots over the deck. It was far more wind than necessary to operate a Pup, which normally stalled at 32 knots.

Following a self-induced waveoff, either Dunning's engine cut out or he burst a tire, slewing the Pup to starboard. In any case, Dunning went overboard. Though the Pup remained partially afloat, the pilot drowned in the twenty minutes required to get a boat to him.

Furious's log laconically recorded, "Time 1451. Accident, aeroplane plunging into the sea while flying."

Edwin Dunning's father, Sir Edwin H. Dunning, received a laudatory letter from the Navy: "The Admiralty wish you to know what great service he performed.... It was in fact a demonstration of landing an Aeroplane on the deck of a Man-of-War whilst the latter was under way. This had never been done before; and the data obtained was of the utmost value. It will make Aeroplanes indispensable to the Fleet & possibly revolutionise Naval Warfare."

Late that year *Furious* dispensed with the enormous and useless stern turret, receiving a deck for landings linked to the forward launching platform by precariously narrow taxiways on either side of the superstructure. Though two aircraft elevators were added, it was an awkward configuration at best. But it was a beginning.

GETTING OFF *FURIOUS*

Among the pioneers learning the trade aboard *Furious* at Scapa Flow in July 1917 was Sub-Lieutenant Jack McCleery, flying the delightful Sopwith Pup. As quoted in Guy Warner's biography, *World War One Aircraft Carrier Pioneer*, McCleery recalled,

Take-off was assisted by means of a ball welded to a bracket on the Pup's tail skid. This was fixed into a slotted tube mounted on a trestle. The tail was thereby kept up in a flying attitude so that none of the deck available for the take-off run was wasted getting the tail up. The engine was run up and as soon as it was showing satisfactory revolutions the pilot raised his hand and a member of the crew pulled a lanyard to release the cable attaching the aircraft from its mounting and away it went. Landings were made at a small airfield which had been established at Smoogroo Bay on the northwestern side of the Flow. The Pups were returned to *Furious* by picket boats towing little rafts made from old seaplane floats over which planking had been laid.

Eventually the Royal Navy recognized the need for purpose-built carrier aircraft. An early attempt was the 1917 Sopwith Cuckoo torpedo plane, an odd combination with folding wings but no ability to land aboard ship. By November 1918 the type could have flown one-way missions, launching from *Argus* with a half-ton torpedo. Specialized carrier aircraft had to await postwar design and development.

Meanwhile, on April 1, 1918 (April Fool's day, some naval pilots noted), the RNAS was merged with the Royal Flying Corps into the Royal Air Force. The joy of airpower advocates who had sought an independent service was not widely shared in the senior service. Sub-Lieutenant McCleery, the *Furious* survivor, journaled, "RNAS and RFC join together to form the RAF, worse luck. Whole RNAS fed to the teeth, and a good many resignations going in. Will do so myself if they try to interfere with my job."

The organizational change came at an inopportune time. Aside from occurring at the height of the greatest war in history, the "dark blue" airmen of the RNAS (in contrast to the RAF's new light blue uniform) had built to a crescendo, with fifty-five thousand officers and men, almost three thousand airplanes, and about one hundred airships.

Recommissioned after modification in early 1918, *Furious* deployed on anti-Zeppelin patrols. On June 19 she was steaming with a unit of the Home Fleet on a sweep of the North Sea when she was intercepted by several German seaplanes from the Island of Sylt. In response, the carrier launched four Sopwith Camels. The first two were plagued with inoperative guns, but the second element engaged two Friedrichshafen floatplanes and shot one into the water. The crew was captured. It was probably the first time a carrier force came under air attack, portending things to come a quarter-century later.

HMS *Furious*, the world's first operational aircraft carrier, was converted from a battle cruiser in 1917 and launched combat missions in 1918. *Courtesy Tailhook Association.*

One month later *Furious* wrote an entry in the log of naval history that echoes a century later.

Before dawn on July 19, *Furious* reached her planned launch point off the enemy coast. On deck the Camel fighter-bombers revved their engines, awaiting the "go" signal. As the ship's bow rose in the swell, the flight-deck officer waved the first pilot into the dark sky. The target was Zeppelin hangars at Tondern, Germany, in present-day

In July 1918 HMS *Furious* launched the first aircraft carrier combat mission with Sopwith Camels attacking the German airship base at Tondern. Two Zeppelins were destroyed in their hangars. *Courtesy Tailhook Association.*

Denmark. *Furious*, escorted by units of the Home Fleet, approached within several miles of the shore. Seven navalized Camels lifted off, but one aborted with engine trouble.

In two flights, the Great War strike-fighters arrived over the target with timing and surprise on their side. At 4:35 a.m. Captain William D. Jackson's trio dived to attack through the murky dawn, selecting the 730-foot-long "Tosca" airship hangar. The checker-nosed Camels' bombs burst on target, destroying Zeppelins *L.54* and *L.60*, while the second flight burned a captive balloon in its nest.

Despite antiaircraft fire, the raiders got away cleanly, having inflicted substantial damage. But Jackson and two other pilots were forced to land in neutral Denmark, where they were interned. Two aviators stretched their gasoline to reach the task force but ditched in the sea. The final pilot, Lieutenant Walter A. Yeulett, force-landed off Denmark and drowned.

Thus ended the first power-projection mission launched from a ship embarking attack aircraft. Previously, seaplane carriers had deployed floatplanes, which were craned into the water and hoisted back aboard. And though *Furious*'s strike remained the only such operation of the war, it proved the concept of the attack aircraft carrier. The ship's senior aviator, Lieutenant Commander Richard Bell-Davies, said of the Tondern raid, "It finally removed the belief held by many senior officers that attacks by shipborne aircraft on shore and harbour targets were no good."

Though rudimentary in execution, the *Furious*'s realization of ship-launched airpower marked a revolutionary advancement. The potential for aircraft carriers was obvious, and all major navies took note. In barely two decades, flattops would replace battleships in importance, with "battlewagons" subordinated to providing antiaircraft fire to protect carriers. The U.S. Navy's embrace of that role reversal—a concept almost unforeseen at the end of the Great War—would result in a stunning dominance in the Pacific during World War II.

TWO

EVOLUTION

1919–1939

The Royal Navy continued developing carriers and aircraft between the world wars, as with these Fairey III biplanes over HMS *Eagle* in the 1930s. *Courtesy David Reid.*

CONVENTIONAL WISDOM HELD THAT THE GREAT WAR WOULD be "the war to end all wars."

Still, in the intervening years before the outbreak of World War II, the world's navies continued developing fleet aviation, though postwar carrier development was predictably slow, owing to widespread belief that there would be no further world wars.

However, in late 1918 Britain commissioned the 14,500-ton HMS *Argus*, the world's first true aircraft carrier. Lacking a superstructure, she was nicknamed "Flatiron." HMS *Hermes* and *Eagle*, both commissioned in 1924, were carriers in the true sense, sporting "through-deck" designs with islands to starboard. The *Hermes* was the first purpose-built carrier and, with *Eagle*, she served until sunk in 1942.

Following the 1918 amalgamation, the Fleet Air Arm of the RAF was established (not coincidentally) on April 1, 1924, and would remain under Air Force control for fifteen years. Carrier squadrons thus became an anomaly. Now the "light blue" aviators operated hand-in-glove with "dark blue" ships' officers. The arrangement was never tested in combat but seemed to work well enough at the deck plate level. For instance, *Argus*'s 1921 spring cruise was rated "very successful," with only two serious accidents among forty-five landings. It took forty minutes to launch two aircraft and land one, but the amount of time was attributed to balky engines in Parnall Panthers, which resembled two-seat Sopwith Camels.

The British continued experimenting with carrier configurations. *Eagle*, laid down as a battleship, was converted to a carrier, designed

The pioneering HMS *Furious* of 1917–1918 was rebuilt after the Great War, emerging with multiple decks for simultaneous takeoffs and landings. *Courtesy Tailhook Association.*

with islands to port and starboard—a dangerously unworkable arrangement that was scrapped during construction. The next year the modified *Furious* appeared with upper and lower flight decks permitting simultaneous recoveries and launches. But with improved aircraft performance came higher landing speeds, and the lower deck fell into disuse. The ultimate carrier configuration was beginning to emerge, comprised of a single flight deck, usually with a starboard island above a hangar deck.

Hermes offers a representative look at RN postwar carriers. She operated mostly in the Mediterranean and Far East from 1923 to 1925, according to Admiralty priorities. Anti-piracy was a rare mission for carriers, but *Hermes* and *Argus* contributed to Royal Navy efforts in Asia. In September 1927 they conducted operations against pirate bases at Bias Bay (today Daya Bay) on the South China Sea northeast of Hong Kong. The pirate "fleet" of junks and sampans was vulnerable to air attack, but the carriers could not sustain operations long enough to solve the problem.

Britain's fourth carrier, HMS *Eagle*, served much of her time "on China station" in the 1930s, often engaged in anti-pirate patrol. *Courtesy Tailhook Association.*

From 1927 to 1936 *Hermes* frequently summered at Wei Hai Wei to avoid the worst of the Hong Kong heat. Back home for a refit in 1933, she returned to China Station in early 1935. There she resumed anti-piracy operations, launching her Fairey Seals to search for SS *Tungchow*, a British merchant ship with British and American citizens on board. In February three Seals found the missing vessel in the familiar haunts of Bias Bay, and the pirates vacated without harming captives.

Another notable event of the period occurred in 1936 when the Fairey Swordfish (known affectionately as the "Stringbag") entered service. First flown two years earlier, the large, three-seat biplane was conceived as a multi-role carrier type, with torpedo attack, gunfire spotter, and reconnaissance aircraft. The Stringbag was bordering on obsolete at the start of World War II, but it remained invaluable, continuing production into 1944 with nearly 2,400 delivered.

A survivor of the nascent carrier aviators recalled the prewar era in the April 1941 *Naval Review*:

> The business of deck-landing was another that could only be properly learnt on an aircraft carrier, though at certain times the surface of Gosport aerodrome was solemnly marked out with flags to represent the deck, and the aspirants dutifully rumbled in and perched thereon.... The "rumble" or powered approach, which is or was necessary for deck-landing, was always regarded by aeronauts of the old school as a mortal sin, which from the landplane point of view is actually as it is. Mention it to any senior RAF officer and he would be darkly offended.

AMERICAN DEVELOPMENTS

The U.S. Navy's General Board had suggested an aircraft carrier construction program in 1918, but postwar progress was tentative.

"Flying-off platforms" were constructed on some battleships, affording a means of launching spotter airplanes, which would land ashore. However, the wooden platforms on the USS *Texas* (BB-35) and other battlewagons clearly could not substitute for a genuine aircraft carrier flight deck.

The dominant figure in U.S. naval aviation was Rear Admiral William A. Moffett, a forward-looking southerner who had received one of fifty-eight Medals of Honor for Woodrow Wilson's 1914 Vera Cruz expedition in Mexico. Moffett recognized the potential of aviation: during the Great War he commanded Great Lakes Training Center and oversaw a pilot training program. As postwar captain of the battleship *Mississippi* (BB-41), he established an aviation detachment using flying-off platforms atop her twelve-inch gun turrets. The aircraft were all foreign-built Sopwiths, Nieuports, and Hanriots with no capability to land aboard, but the seed had been planted—and it germinated.

In 1921 Moffett was promoted to rear admiral to establish the Bureau of Aeronautics. He was an excellent choice. Though a

Early shipboard operations featured launching wheeled aircraft from platforms on battleship turrets, as in this 1919 evolution aboard USS *Pennsylvania*. However, the aircraft could not return to the ship. *Courtesy Tailhook Association*

non-aviator, the fifty-one-year-old Carolinian was both technically astute and politically capable. Apart from forging an air navy, he waged a successful campaign against Army firebrand Brigadier General William Mitchell, who sought to unify all aviation in one branch.

Moffett also recognized the importance of his service's relationship with America's burgeoning aircraft industry. The fact that no U.S.-built planes had flown from *Mississippi* spurred his support of the Navy's cooperation with manufacturers such as Boeing, Vought, and Douglas.

Moffett's tenure was exceptional. In 1933 he was still chief of "BuAer" after twelve years, having overseen arrival of the first generation of carriers and his pet project, rigid airships. No one else held the position for more than four years. That April he was aboard USS *Akron*, the world's largest airship, when it broke up in heavy weather off the Atlantic coast, killing all but three of the seventy-six people on board.

Moffett was succeeded at the helm of BuAer by Rear Admiral Ernest J. King, who would command the United States Navy during the Second World War.

America's first flattop was USS *Langley* (CV-1), converted from the collier USS *Jupiter* (AC-3) in 1920–1922 as an experimental aircraft carrier. *Courtesy Tailhook Association.*

With the British example before it, the U.S. Navy chose what a later generation would call a proof of concept. In 1920 the collier *Jupiter* (AC-3) began modification with a full-length flight deck, emerging from Norfolk two years later with a new name and designation: the USS *Langley* (CV-1), honoring the Wright Brothers' bitter rival, Professor Samuel P. Langley. On her narrow, 523-foot deck the first generation of tailhook aviators paid their dues, gaining hard-won knowledge and expertise. However, *Langley* remained a noncombatant, eventually proving too small and slow to operate modern aircraft. She was converted to a seaplane tender in 1936.

In 1922, the same year the *Langley* was commissioned, the world's naval powers began allotting permitted combatant tonnage under the Washington Naval Treaty. The signatories agreed to a 5-5-3 ratio of tonnage among America, Britain, and Japan, with smaller quotas for France and Italy. In compliance with the treaty, the top

The U.S. Navy seldom operated more than two carrier together but this 1938 exercise is viewed from USS *Ranger* astern of sisters *Lexington* and *Saratoga*. *Courtesy Tailhook Association.*

three nations scrapped or halted construction on sixty-six major warships, limiting themselves to 135,000 tons of aircraft carriers for the United States and Britain, with eighty-one thousand for Japan. Because conversion of existing ships was permitted, America would gain her first fighting flattops. Two massive thirty-five thousand-ton, sixteen-inch battlecruisers about one-third complete were redesigned as USS *Lexington* (CV-2) and *Saratoga* (CV-3).

Commissioned in late 1927, the "Lady Lex" and "Sara" were matched only by Japan's thirty-six thousand-ton *Kaga*—powerful ships capable of making 33 knots and embarking up to ninety aircraft. Over the next fourteen years, five more carriers joined the U.S. Fleet, including the fifteen thousand-ton *Ranger* (CV-4) in 1934, America's first flattop built as such but limited in size by the Washington Naval Treaty. Most notable were the twenty thousand-ton sisters *Yorktown*

Sisters *Yorktown* (CV-5) and *Enterprise* (CV-6) under construction at Newport News, Virginia, early 1937. They were invaluable in the Pacific five years later. *Courtesy Tailhook Association.*

(CV-5) and *Enterprise* (CV-6) in 1937 and 1938, which would prove crucial to America's war effort in the months after Pearl Harbor.

The *Wasp* (CV-7), which raised her commissioning pennant in 1939, had about the same displacement as the *Ranger* with similar performance: 29 knots and seventy to eighty aircraft. Their wartime careers would be limited: *Wasp* was torpedoed in 1942, and the *Ranger* served mainly as a training platform.

Last of the Yorktown class was *Hornet* (CV-8), which arrived in October 1941, providing the Navy with six operational carriers.

Meanwhile, U.S. Marine Corps squadrons occasionally augmented Navy units aboard carriers. In 1936 about sixty of the 145 "flying leathernecks"—some 40 percent—were carrier qualified, but

Marine Corps squadrons frequently qualified aboard carriers to augment Navy air groups. This Grumman F3F-2 of Marine Fighting Squadron Two upended aboard USS *Lexington* (CV-2) in 1939. *Courtesy Tailhook Association.*

THE FIRST TAILHOOK AIRCRAFT

The first generation of purpose-built carrier aircraft emerged in the early 1920s, appearing in a variety of configurations. Previous carrier planes were adaptations of land-based designs with the addition of a tailhook and sometimes a beefier airframe. For instance, in 1922 the first American planes to "trap" aboard ship were Vought VE-7s, based on a 1917 Army design.

Probably the first airplane designed with a tailhook was Britain's ungainly Avro Bison, a three- or four-man reconnaissance machine first flown in September 1921. Only fifty-five were produced, and though many Bison served with the RAF, they flew from HMS *Furious*, *Argus*, and *Eagle*.

Close behind was the Blackburn Dart a month later, filling a request for "a single-seat deck-landing torpedo bomber." With 118 built, squadron service began aboard *Eagle* in 1923, and the last examples remained in service until 1933. At least five other carrier aircraft entered the British list in 1921–22, although none achieved significant numbers.

After the Vought VE-7, the U.S. Navy acquired more mission-specific carrier aircraft. The Naval Aircraft Factory TS-1, doubling as a floatplane, was introduced late in 1922. Of forty-six built, a handful saw limited service aboard USS *Langley* with Douglas DT-2s.

Based on an Army design, the Boeing FB series entered service in 1925. Two experimental FB-2s were approved for production as FB-5s with hooks fixed to the axle—reminiscent of Curtiss and Ely—rather than an arrestor hook.

Japan entered the race with its Mitsubishi 1MF in 1922. Designed by former Sopwith engineer Herbert Smith working for the Mitsubishi Company, nearly 140 were built, featuring "claw" arresting hooks rather than a conventional tailhook. Smith and his expatriate team also produced the firm's B1M torpedo plane (operational in 1924) and the 2MR recon aircraft of 1922. A Mitsubishi 1MF (Type 10 fighter) logged the IJN's first carrier launch and landed aboard *Hosho* in February 1923.

France's homegrown carrier aircraft left much to be desired. A squadron of Dewoitine D.53s operated from France's only carrier, *Béarn* (commissioned in 1927), but were derived from the original land-based D.1 design.

Fewer than a dozen Levasseur PL.2 torpedo planes were produced. First flown in 1922, they entered service in 1926. More than 200 follow-on models were produced through the 1930s.

A U.S. Pacific Fleet landing signal officer (LSO) waving a plane aboard in 1943; today LSOs are still called "wavers" or "paddlers." *Courtesy Tailhook Association.*

The Royal Navy designated LSOs as Deck Landing Control Officers (DLCOs) but they were commonly called "batsmen" for the "bats" they wielded. *Courtesy Tailhook Association.*

PADDLES AND BATSMEN

Hand in glove with tailhook aircraft were landing signal officers (LSOs) to guide carrier aviators down to safe landings. Because the early LSOs wielded colored paddles, the term "paddles" became generic for the breed, though LSOs often refer to themselves as "wavers."

The origin of LSOs is uncertain. During USS *Langley's* pioneering operations in the early 1920s, reputedly one tyro aviator had trouble getting aboard. Allegedly the executive officer, Commander Kenneth Whiting, grabbed two sailors' white hats and stood aft on the flight deck to motion the junior birdman down.

True or not, the need for specially trained LSOs was obvious. Experienced pilots were selected for the job, though "experienced" was a relative term. During *Langley's* 1925 cruise for Pacific war games, the LSO was Lieutenant D. L. Conley, the only pilot aboard who had made a carrier landing. Another flier, Lieutenant A. W. Gorton, was dragooned into the role and waved his friends in touch-and-go landings until procedures were established. Gorton later confided that the air officer, Commander Charles Mason, watched Lieutenant Del Conley wielding the paddles "until Mason was sure that we knew what the hell we were doing."

Eventually signals were standardized for basic information: high or low, left or right, fast or slow, hook or wheels not down, and the "cut" signal to chop throttle and land the aircraft.

Through much of World War II, the LSO trade was essentially a guild. Likely candidates were selected and mentored by current wavers, learning the business by observation and tutoring. While some junior officers enjoyed the responsibility and prestige, others balked at losing flight time. However, most LSOs were qualified in every type of aircraft aboard their ship, lending variety to the job. Marines also qualified as LSOs, though seldom had reason to perform the role. Meanwhile, in 1941 both Atlantic and Pacific Fleets formed Aircraft Carrier Training Groups that produced some LSOs in the normal course of qualifying pilots. In 1943, a dedicated LSO school was established at Jacksonville, Florida, but it languished postwar. Another school stood up at Pensacola in 1974 moved to Jacksonville, and from there to Norfolk, Virginia, where it remains today.

The Royal Navy mostly did without deck landing control officers (DLCOs), until the verge of World War II. More commonly DLCOs were called "batsmen" for the paddles they wielded. During joint operations with the Americans, as the junior partners the British adopted U.S. LSO signals, which sometimes were opposite of the Royal Navy's. For instance, when a batsman signaled "high" he meant "climb" while his Yank counterpart meant "too high."

Whatever the nationality, LSOs earned a reputation as colorful individualists. James Michener's eccentric character "Beer Barrel" was played to near perfection by Robert Strauss in the movie *The Bridges at Toko-Ri*, showing him sneaking liquor aboard ship in a golf bag. In real life, during the 1980s the senior waver was Commander John "Bug" Roach, who wore a white turtleneck sweater on USS *Ranger's* platform. He added a black bow tie to the ensemble, insisting, "Gentlemen always dress for dinner" while dining on "slider" hamburgers.

Marines would not become a factor in carrier air groups until the end of 1944.

FRENCH ACCENT

France was the only other Western power to build a carrier, but the effort came to naught. Laid down as a battleship in 1914, *Béarn* was named for the province on the Spanish border. She sulked through the Great War and was launched in 1920. Two years later the *Marine Nationale* decided to complete her as a twenty-two thousand-ton carrier, but she was not commissioned until 1927.

France's only prewar carrier was *Béarn*, converted from an uncompleted WWI battleship in 1927. Her operational career was short lived, and she lay idle for most of WWII. *Courtesy Tailhook Association.*

Lacking sufficient carrier aircraft, the *Aeronautique Maritime* looked abroad and purchased export models of Vought's SB2U (later Vindicator) scout-bomber. Enough for two squadrons were delivered on the verge of war in 1939, and though some pilots qualified aboard *Béarn*, all their combat was ashore.

When war broke out with Germany, *Béarn* was assigned to an Atlantic raiding force with two battleships, three cruisers, and a destroyer squadron. She saw no combat, instead transporting much of the French government's gold to Canada after Germany's invasion in May 1940. She spent most of the war laid up in the West Indies. Subsequently she served as an aircraft transport and barracks ship, being scrapped in 1967.

A Boeing fighter of the mid 1920s displays the axle-mounted hooks that engaged longitudinal wires on USS *Langley's* deck, keeping the plane tracking straight. *Courtesy Tailhook Association.*

Ensign John W. Davison's Boeing F4B-3 tailhook snags a wire for USS *Saratoga's* 13,000th arrested landing in January 1929. *Courtesy Tailhook Association.*

ARRESTING SYSTEMS

In the century of conventional carriers, several methods of stopping an aircraft have been tried, evaluated, and ultimately rejected. One became universal.

After the Great War HMS *Furious* was fitted with fore-and-aft wires nine inches apart, elevated fifteen inches over the deck. Landing aircraft were kept straight within the longitudinal wires while hooks on the aircraft snagged the lines laterally. *Argus* used the same system. (For a while she lowered the forward elevator slightly, creating a "trap" for the landing aeroplane's wheels. The system wrecked or damaged one plane in four.) Later in the 1920s *Eagle* received a more advanced version with pendants lowered to about nine inches. Ramps also were tested on *Eagle*.

While effective, the longitudinal arrangement had unavoidable faults. Pilots could not tell if their hooks had engaged, and a skewed arrestment threatened to snag a wingtip on parallel wires. The British abandoned the system around 1927, preferring to do without arresting gear. Then from about 1933 most RN carriers received transverse pendants—essentially the system used today.

In April 1922 the U.S. Navy decreed for *Langley*, "The arresting gear will consist of two or more transverse wires stretched across the fore and aft wires…(leading) around sheaves placed outboard to hydraulic brakes. The plane, after engaging the transverse wire, is guided down the deck by the fore and aft wires and is brought to rest by the action of the transverse wire working with the hydraulic brake."

Commissioned in 1927, *Lexington* and *Saratoga* employed electrically operated longitudinal and transverse arresting gear. However, the original design was modified in 1931 with hydraulically damped cross-deck pendants, a total of eight three years later. Subsequently both ships received another set of transverse wires forward in case flight-deck damage made it necessary to recover aircraft while backing down. Woven-wire barricades could be raised to protect parked aircraft during landing operations.

Japan's pioneer flattop, *Hosho*, largely duplicated Langley's original configuration with fore-and-aft wires supplemented by cross-deck pendants. But the process proved unnecessarily complex, and the longitudinal layout was abandoned.

Often overlooked in carrier development, France took an early lead when *Béarn*, commissioned in 1927, was built with a transverse arresting system. In fact, the French sold their system to Japan, and it was retroactively fitted on *Hosho* and *Akagi* circa 1931.

BEHIND THE ASIAN SCREEN

A third carrier power was building during the decade following the Great War. The Imperial Japanese Navy's experimental carrier *Hosho* ("Phoenix in Flight") was commissioned in 1922—the same year as *Langley*—and Japan forged ahead with two fleet carriers.

The Imperial Navy had a long-established relationship with the Royal Navy, even displaying a lock of the famed British naval commander Admiral Horatio Lord Nelson's hair at the Eta Jima Naval Academy. Japan's twenty-seven thousand-ton Kongo-class battleships were designed by British naval architects, and *Kongo* herself was built in Britain. Therefore, it was not surprising that the Japanese Navy relied heavily upon its English friends for guidance in the emerging art of carrier aircraft.

Only displacing 7,500 tons, *Hosho* nonetheless provided a platform for learning the carrier trade. But the Japanese proceeded slowly and methodically. In early 1923 *Hosho*'s first takeoffs and landings were performed by former RNAS officer William Jordan, contracted to Mitsubishi. Lieutenant Shunichi Kira logged the first landing by an Imperial Navy aviator in March of that year, flying a type 1MF fighter from the Mitsubishi Internal Combustion Engine Manufacturing Company.

Japan's first carrier was the purpose-built *Hosho* ("Phoenix in Flight"), commissioned in 1922, the same year as USS *Langley*. The starboard island was removed two years later, and the slanted portion of the flight deck was straightened. *Courtesy Tailhook Association.*

Hosho's early air group included nine 1MF fighters and six B1M3 torpedo planes. In 1937 the new all-metal Mitsubishi A5M fighter and Yokosuka B4Y bombers dominated, with the A5M (later "Claude" to the Allies) marking the transition to monoplanes.

Like the USS *Lexington*, the near-sisters *Akagi* and *Kaga* were built on incomplete battle cruiser hulls. The *Akagi* was commissioned in 1927 at thirty-six thousand tons, and the *Kaga* two years later at thirty-eight thousand. Modernization in 1935 eliminated their complex arrangement of three flight decks and three hangar decks, while *Akagi* received a portside island so the two could operate side by side without overlapping traffic patterns. Subsequent Japanese carriers adopted a more conventional arrangement: one flight deck and two hangars. The *Soryu* entered service in 1937, and the *Hiryu* in 1939, the only other port-starboard island teammates. The sisters *Shokaku* and *Zuikaku* arrived in 1941, providing six flattops for the Pearl Harbor task force.

Japan's *Akagi* was one of the world's largest carriers before WWII. She and her sister *Kaga*, both sunk at Midway in June 1942, displaced more than 35,000 tons. *Courtesy author's collection.*

Originally, Japan envisioned carrier aircraft mainly for scouting, gunfire spotting, and antisubmarine patrol. However, with more flight decks added in the 1930s, IJN aviators increasingly regarded their primary mission as sinking enemy flattops—an opinion not shared by Tokyo's battleship admirals. The Naval General Staff, though recognizing carrier aviation's growing potential, remained heavily surface oriented, as Japan possessed some of the most powerful battleships and most effective cruisers on earth. Fully integrating carriers into fleet organization as well as combat tactics required hard work and, as in America, a philosophical battle with the "big gun" hierarchy.

Behind the scenes, the Japanese Navy took an early lead with integrating carriers into fleet operations. In contrast to the Americans' emphasis on scouting, the *Nihon Kaigun* formed the First Carrier Division in 1928. That year's fleet exercise tested *Hosho*'s ability to integrate torpedo planes into offensive operations with cruisers and destroyers. The concept proved unworkable mainly due to timing and communication, but far more significant is the fact that the Japanese—widely perceived in the West as backwards and imitative—were thinking on a scale almost unknown in Britain and America.

By early 1932 Japanese naval airmen not only conceived of integrated carrier operations but placed them in combat. The five-week Shanghai Incident, which lasted from January 28 to March 3, involved carrier airpower. The conflict was perpetrated by Tokyo as justification for further Japanese gains in China. Japanese naval infantry clashed with local forces, leading to calls for air support in Shanghai's Chapei District. For the first time, ship-based aircraft clashed with land-based opponents.

The seaplane tender *Notoro* provided combat sorties against military and rail targets, inflicting heavy losses among Chinese civilians—as many as one thousand dead. The large carrier *Kaga* arrived

The odd couple: tiny 7,500-ton *Hosho* and the huge 36,000-ton *Kaga*, which operated together off the China coast during attacks on Shanghai in 1932. *Wikimedia*.

on January 30, followed by the pioneer *Hosho* on February 1. Imperial tailhook aircraft—Mitsubishi B1M3 bombers and Nakajima A1N2 fighters—clashed with Chinese planes, leading to the IJN's first aerial victory, scored over an American-flown Boeing Model 218, a commercial version of the P-12 fighter.

The Japanese carriers continued launching offensive sorties against the Chinese through most of February, including a successful mission against Hang-chou Airfield, which destroyed several Chinese planes on the ground and claimed three in air combat. While tiny *Hosho* and huge *Kaga* appeared unlikely partners, their eighty aircraft coordinated well in the face of Chinese air force defenses at Shanghai. Naval aircraft remained on call after the ceasefire in March.

Other aspects of the Shanghai operation pointed to the future. Much of the planning was conducted by Commander Takijiro Onishi, later the admiral who would command naval kamikaze forces. Many of his subordinates also cut their combat teeth in China. They included fighter pilots who gained air superiority, justifying the value of their rigorous selection process and training, but based on the false premise of unsupportable standards. Typically 65 percent of prewar flight school students washed out, and like all elite forces, they proved vulnerable to inevitable attrition in a prolonged war.

A negative aspect of the Imperial Navy's air campaign emerged thereafter. Whatever the actual numbers, the heavy loss of civilian life in the Chapei District drew attention to the perils of air bombardment. Probably no previous operation had inflicted such a scale of death from the air. Historian Barbara Tuchman described Chapei as "terror bombing" when in fact the carnage likely was as much due to poor visibility in marginal weather and the inherent flaws of 1930s bomb sights.

Nevertheless, Japan's early carrier operations against China demonstrated the Imperial Navy's world leadership in naval aviation. Two aspects stand out: the melding of technical, doctrinal, and operational concerns at a time when no other navy appears to have given them much thought; and the ability of presumably "inferior" sea-based aircraft to compete successfully against land-based opponents.

In 1937 the Sino-Japanese conflict erupted full-blown, not to abate until 1945.

At that time *Nihon Kaigun* (the Imperial Japanese Navy) was caught in a technical and industrial time warp. Ship and aircraft production lagged, as did new flying units, and at that moment the only deployable carrier aircraft were biplanes. Japanese naval aviation, however, was far more than aircraft carriers or seaplane tenders. A growing land-based force on Formosa (Taiwan) was flying new twin-engine Mitsubishi bombers. With the range and payload to strike worthwhile targets more than 400 miles inland, the G3Ms (called "Nells" by the Allies from 1942 onward) lent a view of the future when other naval air groups would fly G4Ms (Bettys) in China skies.

Meanwhile, the Japanese Army—politically the dominant service—forced a renewed conflict with China. In July 1937 the Marco Polo Bridge incident outside Peking (Beijing) gave the militarists the excuse they sought to expand Tokyo's conquests, and again a naval feud brewed up in Shanghai. Chinese planes ineffectually bombed Japanese ships in the Whangpo River, and the Asian mainland erupted in flames.

Consequently, that August Japanese carriers were heavily engaged against Chinese aircraft. On August 16 *Hosho*, *Ryujo*, and *Kaga* operated in the Yellow Sea off Shanghai. Successive days of air combat proved the capability of IJN fighters and the horrible vulnerability of its carrier bombers.

The next day *Kaga* launched twelve Mitsubishi bombers to strike Hangchow's port. Their escorts—nimble, 200-mph biplane Nakajima A4Ns—became separated in the clouds, leaving the B2Ms vulnerable.

Chinese pilots flying powerful Curtiss Hawk III fighters, recently imported from the United States, shredded the Japanese formation, claiming seventeen victories while actually downing at least eight—some sources say eleven. In any case, it was a serious drubbing, as *Kaga*'s two senior aviators were killed.

Facing loss of air superiority, the Imperial Navy took immediate action. *Kaga* raced homeward, quickly taking aboard the next-generation fighter, Mitsubishi's A5M. It was a landmark occasion: the first monoplane carrier aircraft committed to combat. Despite its fixed landing gear, the all-metal Mitsubishi outperformed most contemporary designs, generally dominating China skies within its range.

Meanwhile, the Imperial Japanese Navy's doctrine evolved as operations unfolded. In 1936, five years before the war, IJN tacticians adopted the concept of aircraft-carrier dispersal, operating the ships at extended distances from each other. It was a knowing violation of the Clausewitzian doctrine of mass, accepted against the prospect of an enemy—which could only be the United States—cracking all of Tokyo's eggs in one basket (exactly what would happen at the Battle of Midway in 1942).

CARRIER INTEGRATION

The world's navies now had something else to figure out, aside from the development of carriers, aircraft, and operating procedures: administration. How was aviation to fit into fleet organization?

Britain posed an unusual situation, since the Royal Naval Air Service had merged with the Royal Flying Corps in 1918 to form the Royal Air Force. Its Fleet Air Arm (FAA) was established as a quasi-independent branch six years later, with the RAF providing aircrews and support personnel to Royal Navy ships, both carriers and more traditional types capable of launching floatplanes. This awkward arrangement remained until May 1939, four months before Britain declared war against Germany, when the FAA became part of the navy itself. The RAF also maintained a hand in maritime aviation through its Coastal Command, responsible for helping protect naval supply lines and convoys against enemy submarines.

The British arrangement was not duplicated elsewhere. The American and Japanese navies had long operated their own aviation branches as integral parts of their respective fleets. At the command level the U.S. Navy was profoundly air-oriented. By law, only aviators—so-called "brown shoes"—could command carriers or other aviation vessels such as seaplane tenders. Britain and Japan, on the other hand, permitted non-flying officers to command carriers while relying on qualified staff for aviation expertise. Due to a lack of seniority among aviators, however, some American "black-shoe," or surface-warfare, admirals would lead carrier task forces in 1942.

Brown shoes and black shoes alike struggled for the optimum integration of carriers into fleet doctrine. Fleet Problem V, in 1925, was the first U.S. Navy large-scale interwar exercise to involve an aircraft carrier, the *Langley*. Taking the conn was Captain Joseph M. Reeves, credited with inventing the football helmet at Annapolis (class of '94) and widely known as "Billy Goat" for his white goatee. Another visionary in the Moffett mold, he was designated a naval air observer that year, checking the congressional box requiring airmen to hold aviation commands.

Reeves had commanded USS *Jupiter* in 1913, nine years before she evolved into *Langley*. As commander, Aircraft Squadrons, in the 1925 Fleet Problem, he directed a simulated air attack on Hawaii. The standards and efficiency of deck operations still had a long way to go; during the mock operation, the carrier received a "well done" for launching ten planes in thirteen minutes. On the plus side, flattops would increasingly participate in fleet exercises, both on offense and defense.

Reeves's career flourished thereafter. He retired as commander in chief of the U.S. Fleet in 1936, but was recalled to duty in 1940, remaining throughout the war.

USS *Langley's* (CV-1) deck was full with nineteen aircraft in 1927, probably on the West Coast. *Courtesy Tailhook Association.*

In 1925 *Langley* aviators provided another glimpse of the future. During night practice approaches in February, Lieutenant Harold J. Brow accidentally dropped onto the deck and was dragged to a stop. Two months later four of Brow's shipmates completed intentional night landings in Naval Aircraft Factory TS-1 fighters. For nearly twenty years, round-the-clock carrier operations remained a concept rather than a routine, but *Langley* pointed the way ahead.

In July 1926, the Royal Navy conducted its first night carrier landing, with Flight Lieutenant Gerald Boyce safely landing his Blackburn Dart torpedo plane on veteran HMS *Furious*. Despite successes aboard *Langley* and *Furious*, nocturnal carrier operations remained tentative for almost fifteen years.

The ungainly Martin T4M gave the U.S. Navy a carrier-based torpedo plane in the early 1920s, as this VT-1B aircraft ready to launch from USS *Lexington* (CV-2) circa 1931. *Courtesy Tailhook Association.*

Meanwhile, American aviators and sailors became more proficient cycling the deck. A 1937 study found that France's *Béarn* required more than an hour to recover fifteen aircraft, averaging four and a half minutes between landings. HMS *Glorious* did far better, landing thirty-two planes in forty-two minutes, an average interval of one minute, twenty seconds. In 1935 Japanese *Ryujo* flying Type 94 (D1A1) dive bombers got the landing interval down to about fifty seconds with practice. USS *Saratoga*'s practiced professionals were the fastest, recovering forty aircraft with an average interval of just twenty-eight seconds.

The reasons for the discrepancies were varied, involving pilot and deck crew experience as well as operating techniques. *Béarn*, for instance, placed each landing aircraft on an elevator before accepting the next plane aboard—a time-eating process. In contrast, the *Lexington* installed crash barriers as early as 1934.

Commissioned in 1930, HMS *Glorious* was one of three battle cruisers with *Furious* and *Courageous*, modified into 30,000-ton carriers. She was sunk by German cruisers in 1940. *Courtesy Tailhook Association.*

If there had been an international aircraft carrier census in 1939, it would have revealed considerable growth in the decade preceding World War II. In December 1930, thirteen carriers were in commission worldwide; by August 1939 there were twenty, although a few, such as the *Hosho*, were marginally combat capable.

BIPLANES TO MONOPLANES

Meanwhile, aviation developments kept pace. The United States introduced carrier-based monoplanes in 1937: the Douglas TBD torpedo bomber, later named the Devastator, and the Vought SB2U scout bomber, dubbed Vindicator.

The Royal Navy's transition to monoplanes was glacial, lasting roughly from 1938 to 1944. The two-seat Blackburn Skua, a hybrid fighter and dive bomber, became operational aboard *Ark Royal* in

Fairey Aircraft provided a variety of aircraft to the Royal Navy, including the diminutive Flycatcher fighter, here overflying HMS *Eagle* in 1930. *Courtesy David Reid.*

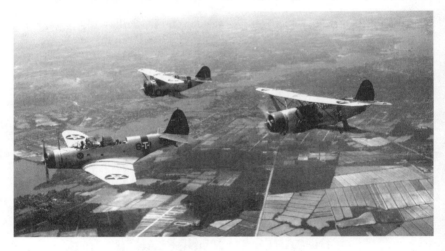

The U.S. Navy was a fleet in transition in 1937 with arrival of the monoplane Douglas TBD, here with a USS *Yorktown* (CV-5) F3F fighter and SBC scout-bomber. *Courtesy Tailhook Association.*

late 1938. The Fairey Fulmar, another two-seat fighter, was introduced in May 1940. Help arrived from America with the first Grumman Martlets (Wildcats) in late 1940, deploying in September 1941.

From 1941 the Fleet Air Arm enjoyed reasonable success with the Hawker Sea Hurricane and the high-performance but relatively fragile Supermarine Seafire, beginning in late 1942. The Fairey Barracua dive and torpedo bomber went operational in early 1943, as did the Grumman Tarpon (née Avenger).

The world's last deploying carrier biplane, the ageless Fairey Swordfish, remained on antisubmarine patrol until late 1944.

The Royal Navy went to war with modern carriers flying obsolescent aircraft, as with these Fairey Swordfish overhead the new HMS *Ark Royal* in 1939. She was sunk by a U-boat in 1941. *Courtesy Tailhook Association.*

Meanwhile, in late 1941, U.S. carrier decks spawned Douglas SBD Dauntless scout bombers and Grumman F4F Wildcats while retaining TBD Devastator torpedo planes. That trio would fight the first six months of the Pacific War.

By 1941 Japan's strike carriers embarked Aichi D3A dive bombers (later called "Vals" by the Allies), Nakajima B5N torpedo planes ("Kates"), and Mitsubishi A6M Zero fighters. Biplanes remained operational well past Pearl Harbor, however, with a few light and

In 1939 Japan prepared to astonish the world with its carrier fleet. At the tip of the imperial spear was Mitsubishi's A6M2 Type Zero fighter, first flown that year. *Courtesy Tailhook Association.*

escort carriers retaining the biplane Yokosuka B4Y attack aircraft well into 1942.

Thus, the new-generation aircraft—flying both from veteran and untried carriers—faced a global conflict never to be repeated.

Britain's Fleet Air Arm had precious little time to prepare for war. Only returned to Royal Navy control in May 1939, the FAA required a great deal of staff work for the increasing likelihood of war. The Naval Air Division recognized two prospects: an "Axis War" against Germany and Italy, and a "Far East War" against Japan. Anticipating greater need for aircraft acquisition, the staff projected 20 percent losses for carrier planes in a given period—well short of reality and less than half the RAF estimate in the far less demanding shore-based environment.

The next world war lurked barely below the horizon.

THREE

THE ATLANTIC

1939–1945

USS *Core* (CVE-13) typified the contribution of escort carriers to winning the Battle of the Atlantic. Her aircraft sank five U-boats between July and October 1943 and shared another with her destroyers. *Courtesy USN.*

IN SEPTEMBER 1939 THE WORLD TEETERED ON A PRECARIOUS fulcrum, dangerously poised between continuing a contentious peace or veering off-balance into the calamitous void of another world war.

The tipping point was passed. That month Germany invaded Poland from the west and Russia attacked from the east. The two totalitarian regimes divided the nation between them, launching Britain and France into war with Germany after years of appeasement to Adolf Hitler's avarice.

That year the world's navies stood on the precipice of a technological revolution. More than half of the U.S. Navy's carrier aircraft were biplanes, and 82 percent of Britain's. But the onset of global war heralded an evolutionary change on carrier decks. Two years later most biplanes were gone, the notable exception being the long-lived Fairey Swordfish, still a potent torpedo plane in a permissive operating environment.

When war broke out in September, the Royal Navy had *Furious*, *Ark Royal*, and *Courageous* in home waters while *Hermes*, previously a training ship, was reactivated. *Eagle* was far afield on China Station, and *Glorious* transferred from the Mediterranean Fleet to the Indian Ocean.

Apart from carriers, the Fleet Air Arm possessed some 230 naval aircraft in twenty squadrons. They included just twenty-seven embarked Blackburn Skua monoplanes, plus six Gloster Sea Gladiator biplane fighters. The FAA tried filling the void with stopgaps such as the Fairey Fulmar, a two-seat fighter rushed into service in 1940, while acquiring Grummans from America.

Within days of hostilities opening, the Royal Navy had carriers at sea, patrolling for U-boats. *Ark Royal*, *Courageous*, and *Hermes* deployed with their escorts, but submarines hunted the hunters. On September 14 *Ark Royal* lookouts called torpedoes inbound, and the twenty-two thousand-ton carrier veered away by the narrowest margin—one torpedo exploded in her wake.

Destroyers jumped on the offending U-boat and depth-charged her to the surface. *U-31* was riddled with gunfire and sank with the crew captured. She was the first U-boat destroyed in the Second World War.

Three days later *Courageous* was patrolling Britain's Western Approaches when *U-29* spotted a biplane. Reckoning that it must be from a carrier three hundred miles offshore, *Kapitänleutnant* (lieutenant commander) Otto Schuhart pressed his hunt. He sighted smoke on the horizon and closed the distance as much as possible. However, airborne planes kept him submerged until the ship turned into the wind to recover aircraft. Ignoring the two escorts, Schuhart set up inside three thousand yards and fired three torpedoes broad on the port beam.

Courageous died quickly, capsizing in fifteen minutes and taking 519 of the 1,260 men on board with her. Schuhart and his boat evaded heavy depth charging to return in triumph, logging forty-one thousand tons on their first war patrol. Unlike most early-war U-boat skippers, Schuhart survived the war.

In response, the British Admiralty pulled the other three carriers out of the Western Approaches until more effective countermeasures could be developed. *Courageous*'s loss demonstrated serious operational problems—inadequate aircraft aloft, no lookouts, and some interior doors were left open. Consequently, the official inquiry produced nearly thirty recommendations based on the first carrier loss.

Ark Royal deployed again in late September, trolling the North Sea. On September 26, her Skuas downed the first German aircraft claimed by British aviation in the war. However, that action gave away the carrier's location, and the Luftwaffe launched thirteen bombers against her. Lacking radar, the British ships had to rely upon eyesight to track the raiders, with antiaircraft guns providing most of the defense. A German Junkers 88 put its two bombs about thirty yards from the target. The dissatisfied pilot, Corporal Carl Francke, returned for a strafing pass before departing.

The aggressive flier returned to Norway, accurately reporting that he had bombed a carrier. Berlin's propaganda machine then took over, claiming *Ark Royal* had been sunk. When the facts became known, Luftwaffe chief Hermann Goering reputedly told Francke, "You still owe me an aircraft carrier!"

1940: GRIEF AND TRIUMPH

The spring of 1940 brought a dirge of defeat in the West. Britain's doomed foray to relieve Norway came shortly after Germany conquered France, but the Royal Navy remained dominant at sea, committing large numbers of ships to Norwegian waters. Assigned to the effort were *Glorious* and *Ark Royal*. However, British fortunes waned in Scandinavia, forcing a withdrawal.

On June 7, seventeen RAF fighters followed *Glorious* aircraft from Norwegian bases to the carrier's position at sea. The risk was judged worthwhile to return fighters to Britain, and all the air force Gladiator and Hurricane pilots safely got aboard—an exceptional feat of airmanship. Amazingly, *Glorious* received permission to return to Scapa Flow to begin a court martial of an aviator who had questioned the judgment of his commanding officer. *Glorious* and *Ark Royal* parted company early in the morning of June 8.

It was a clear day, but *Glorious's* captain, Guy D'Oyly-Hughes, had no aircraft airborne, none on deck, no lookouts posted, and only twelve of eighteen boilers lit—despite embarking with nine Sea Gladiators and six Swordfish. D'Oyly-Hughes had been a distinguished submariner who won his wings, but he had learned nothing along the way. That afternoon, *Glorious* was unable to maintain distance from the powerful German battleships *Scharnhorst* and *Gneisenau*.

The Germans quickly wrecked one destroyer, then shifted fire to the carrier. The second destroyer gamely attacked with torpedoes, hitting *Scharnhorst* before being smothered by gunfire. In barely forty minutes *Glorious* took repeated eleven-inch hits, including to the engine spaces and bridge. She capsized at 6:10, but few survivors were rescued over the next two days. Only thirty-eight of 1,245 carrier men were saved, and one man from each destroyer.

Glorious had suffered some of the same problems that undid *Courageous* nine months before, especially lack of effective air cover. Furthermore, in an eye-watering example of ineptitude, the admiralty only learned of the calamity from a German propaganda broadcast.

However, the potential of carrier aircraft had been demonstrated in early April when Orkney-based Blackburn Skuas sank the cruiser KMS *Konigsberg* at Bergen, Norway, the first major combatant sunk by aircraft in the war. Next the Fleet Air Arm had to prove its capability at sea.

WAR IN THE MED

In the wake of France's capitulation in June 1940, the Royal Navy's attention turned to the Mediterranean, most notably Mersel-Kebir in Algeria, where four French battleships and six destroyers were based. Concerned that powerful French fleet units might join Germany's *Kriegsmarine*, Britain issued an ultimatum to the Vichy naval command: join the Royal Navy; sail to a British port with crews to be repatriated; or steam to a French base in the West Indies for the duration.

The French refused, prompting the Royal Navy to attack on July 3. *Ark Royal* provided Swordfish torpedo bombers and Skua fighter bombers, but air action was brief. *Ark Royal*'s planes mined the harbor and attacked the moored warships, losing a Skua and two Swordfish. Most of the damage was inflicted by British bombardment, destroying one French battleship, damaging two, and inflicting damage on four destroyers, with nearly 1,300 French dead.

The tactical success was largely overshadowed by the political fallout. French public opinion of "perfidious Albion" plummeted, and for a time threatened the nominal Anglo-Franco *entente*.

TARANTO

After Italy invaded Abyssinia in 1935, Admiral Sir Dudley Pound, commanding the Mediterranean Fleet, ordered a contingency plan to attack the *Regia Marina* base at Taranto in the "heel" of the Italian boot. The plan lay fallow for three years until *Glorious*'s skipper, Captain Arthur L. S. Lyster, assumed command of *Illustrious*, the only

DAMAGE CONTROL

The prewar Royal Navy gave insufficient thought to survivability of its carriers and paid the price in combat.

Courageous (September 1939) and *Eagle* (August 1942) succumbed to torpedoes that blew large holes in their hulls, allowing a deluge of water that overcame both ships' compartmentalization. *Courageous* went down in twenty minutes with 519 men among 1,260—a stunning 41percent loss. *Eagle* died even faster. She took four torpedoes and sank in about eight minutes with surprisingly low casualties: 160 of about 1,090 on board.

Glorious (June 1940) and *Hermes* (April 1942) had inadequate hull protection and were sunk by gunfire and bombing, though neither was likely to survive the fatal tactical situations in which it found itself: caught by fast cruisers and overwhelmed by dive bombers, respectively.

Ark Royal (November 1941) was torpedoed east of Gibraltar, sustaining a huge hole at the bilge keel, 130 by 30 feet. Despite better watertight integrity than earlier ships, her damage was compounded by a boiler room fire that interrupted pressure to the operational pumps trying to offset the flooding.

The board of inquiry faulted "Ark's" captain for inadequate damage control and poor state of readiness. A review of warship losses, however, found that *Ark Royal*'s lack of backup power was a design flaw. She capsized about fourteen hours after being hit with only one fatality among 1,488 crew.

Replacing wartime attrition was essential, and the Royal Navy had taken measures by authorizing a class of 30-knot carriers, but prewar treaties limited their size. *Illustrious*, lead ship of four twenty-three thousand-ton carriers, was commissioned in May 1940. She was joined by three sisters—*Formidable*, *Victorious*, and *Indomitable*—over the next year and a half.

carrier in the region. In the next two years the idea was updated and tested until then-Rear Admiral Lyster was confident enough to present a plan—later named "Operation Judgment"—to Admiral Andrew Cunningham, who commanded naval forces in the Mediterranean.

The Taranto concept already had been proven. On July 8 *Hermes* launched six Swordfish against the Vichy French battleship *Richelieu* in Dakar Harbor, French West Africa (now Senegal). The new thirty-five thousand-ton warship was severely damaged by a Mark XII torpedo that blew a large hole in the stern, laying her up until she proceeded to the United States for refit in January 1943. The Royal Navy's ability to launch aerial torpedoes in forty feet of water, as at Dakar and Taranto, was crucial to both operations.

Originally Operation Judgment planned for *Illustrious* and *Eagle* to attack the night of October 21, but *Illustrious* sustained a fire that destroyed or damaged several aircraft. The next feasible time to launch would be in the period from November 11 to 19, which met requirements for the next moon phase and visibility. Judgment was on. Additionally, it would screen several convoys transiting the area.

However, problems still arose. *Eagle* was scratched from the lineup due to lingering damage from air attack three months previously. Five of her Swordfish cross-decked to *Illustrious*, providing twenty-one aircraft for Judgment.

Combining the inner and outer harbors, Taranto was home to a smorgasbord of Italian vessels: six battleships, nine cruisers, eight destroyers, and auxiliaries.

Illustrious launched two strikes of Swordfish late the night of November 11. Lieutenant Commander M. W. Williamson led the first wave of six bombers and six torpedo planes, with some of the bombers doubling as illumination aircraft. Beneath the garish splotches of flares the first wave attacked, torpedoing the twenty-three thousand-ton battleship *Conte di Cavour* and the newer forty-one thousand-ton

Littorio. But resistance was fierce. The Italians fired nearly fourteen thousand rounds of AA ammunition, mostly three-inch or larger. Williamson's deputy was shot down, the crew captured.

HMS *Illustrious* launched Swordfish bombers and torpedo planes against the Italian base at Taranto in November 1940, dramatically shifting the Mediterranean naval balance. *Courtesy Tailhook Association.*

The nine-plane second wave attacked ninety minutes after the first, striking the twenty-seven thousand-ton *Caio Duilio* plus a cruiser and destroyers. One Swordfish was lost with its crew. When the nineteenth remaining Swordfish snagged an arresting wire on board *Illustrious* around 2:30 that morning, Operation Judgment was an unqualified success.

Conte di Cavour, struck by two bombs and two torpedoes, exploded. *Caio Duilio* took three torpedoes and sank in the shallow water. *Littorio* survived three bombs and torpedoes but departed for repairs at Genoa. One destroyer was wrecked, while another destroyer and a cruiser were severely damaged.

In his memoir, Admiral Andrew Cunningham recalled,

The aircrews were in a state of great jubilation. They clamoured to repeat the operation the same night. I agreed at first when Rear Admiral Lyster made the suggestion, though I rather felt that when the excitement wore off and the strain of their ordeal began to tell upon the aircrews, it would be unfair to send them in again. I therefore felt somewhat relieved when a bad weather report automatically put a stop to a second venture.

Of the forty-two fliers over Taranto, only four were decorated soon thereafter. In early 1941 a sympathetic Member of Parliament shamed the admiralty into decorating sixteen more with the balance "mentioned in dispatches," though for some it was too late. The war continued, and besides the crew killed that night, fifteen more died—an overall attrition of 40 percent.

The effects of the Taranto strike reverberated across two oceans. Carrier aircraft had shifted the Mediterranean naval balance in Britain's favor, literally overnight. Reputedly the Japanese naval attaché in Rome paid close attention. There is still argument as to how much influence Operation Judgment exerted upon events in Hawaii a year later, but the similarities are obvious.

AFTER TARANTO

Carriers remained essential to Mediterranean convoys, often sailing beneath clear skies and within range of land-based Axis bombers. Thus, in January 1941 flattops were assigned to Operation Excess, a series of convoys to Malta, Alexandria, and Piraeus (Greece).

The Luftwaffe, anticipating the need to interdict resupply of Allied bases, began transferring *Fliegerkorps* X from Norway. Regarded as an elite unit, the organization's repertoire included dive bombing and torpedo attacks against ships at sea. That month its strength was nearly two hundred bomber and reconnaissance aircraft plus three dozen Messerschmitt Bf 110 fighters.

HMS *Illustrious* escorted a Greece-bound convoy, embarking Fairey Swordfish and Fulmar fighters. On January 10 her Swordfish attacked an Italian convoy, but the British group was soon discovered. *Regia Aeronautica* (Italian Royal Air Force) trimotor bombers approached *Illustrious*, and while her fighters chased the SM.79s, they left the overhead unprotected. Before other Fulmars could be launched, waves of Junkers 87 Stukas descended on the convoy, targeting the obvious prize.

The *Fliegerkorps* X crews were expert at their craft. Nosing into eighty-degree dives, they placed their ordnance with precision, hitting *Illustrious* six times. A follow-up attack yielded another hit, all at the cost of three Stukas. By the time the battered, blackened carrier reached Malta's Grand Harbor, she was steering with her engines. The Germans sensed blood in the water and sent repeated missions to Malta over the next few days, inflicting further damage on the immensely rugged carrier.

Illustrious's condition required dockyard repairs in South Africa and the United States, keeping her out of service until early 1942 when she returned to home waters with *Formidable*, which also enjoyed American hospitality.

The Royal Navy retained other carriers in the Mediterranean, and they were needed in *Illustrious's* absence.

CAPE MATAPAN

In a three-day engagement south and west of Crete in late March 1941, the Italians fielded a battleship, eight cruisers, and seventeen destroyers to prey upon British troop convoys. The Royal Navy responded with three battleships, seven light cruisers, and a similar number of destroyers, augmented by HMS *Formidable*.

On the second day, March 28, "Formid" launched Fairey Albacores (closed-cockpit biplanes) against the Italian flagship, *Vittorio Veneto*, previously damaged at Taranto. The heavy volume of shipboard gunfire kept the Albacore from scoring any bomb hits, but the few defending Luftwaffe aircraft in range proved ineffective against the attackers.

Less known than its stablemate Swordfish, the Fairey company's Albacore was a later design that operated effectively in the Mediterranean. Here an "Apple core" benefits from HMS *Victorious*'s mechanical landing signal device. *Courtesy Tailhook Association.*

At mid-afternoon on March 28, Lieutenant Commander John Dalyell-Stead flew within one thousand yards of the *Vittorio*, putting a torpedo into her port propeller. But she shot the Albacore into the water, killing the three-man crew, though the other carrier planes survived. In a rare opportunity for inter-service cooperation, RAF bombers from Greece kept up the pressure, harassing the Italian armada.

Formidable's third launch of ten Albacore and Swordfish that evening scored another success. Despite smoke and heavy gunfire around *Vittorio*, the biplanes torpedoed the cruiser *Pola*, which coasted to a stop.

With the advantage of radar, part of the British surface force closed to gun range before midnight. The ensuing surface battle was a major British victory: *Marina* lost three heavy cruisers and two destroyers, with *Vittorio* heavily damaged. Lieutenant Commander Dalyell-Stead's crew remained the only RN losses.

THE *BISMARCK* HUNT

Action then shifted to the North Atlantic. In May 1941 Germany's most prestigious warship, the forty-one thousand-ton *Bismarck*, escaped Norway into the North Atlantic with the cruiser *Prinz Eugen*. In a brief gunnery duel off Iceland on May 24, the two German warships engaged four Britons. Though struck in her fuel bunkers, *Bismarck*'s fifteen-inch rifles destroyed HMS *Hood*, and *Prinz Eugen* disengaged to conduct commerce warfare.

With two powerful enemy ships at large among British convoy routes, the admiralty needed more help. Heavy units, including the carrier *Victorious* with battleship *King George V*, were summoned from Scapa Flow. Others from around the map included Force H from Gibraltar with *Ark Royal*. Early in the evening of May 24, one of nine *Victorious* Swordfish put a torpedo on *Bismarck*'s thick armor, inflicting little damage. "Vic" broke off for fuel. *Bismarck* shaped course for Brest, intending to repair her damage and return to sea.

Before sunset on May 26, *Ark Royal*'s Swordfish launched in worsening weather and visibility. They attacked the first large warship they saw—cruiser HMS *Sheffield*, tracking *Bismarck* by radar. Aircrews noted that their "fish" exploded prematurely, apparently the

Though widely considered obsolete in 1939, the Fairey Swordfish remained an effective torpedo plane and reconnaissance bomber for most of the war. *Courtesy Tailhook Association.*

HMS *Ark Royal* underway in 1941. That May her aircraft crippled the German battleship *Bismarck* in the North Atlantic, leading to her sinking. *Courtesy Tailhook Association.*

fault of magnetic detonators. Furthermore, three planes were written off trying to land aboard *Ark Royal*, reducing the number available for a second mission.

Though chagrined, the "Stringbag" crews rearmed, refueled, and the last fifteen took off into gathering darkness. They found the target by radar and deployed to attack.

A single hit settled the matter. Sub-Lieutenant John Moffatt, a twenty-one-year-old Scot, was credited with putting his torpedo into *Bismarck*'s stern. With her rudder stuck to port, she could only circle. It took the British some time to recognize the fact, but at that point the Atlantic predator was doomed. She was overtaken and shot to pieces on May 27.

In two months, carrier-based torpedo planes had played significant roles in actions against two Axis battleships maneuvering at sea. On top of the sensational Taranto attack, there seemed no further room for doubt: naval aviation was a force to count upon.

FIRST OF THE ESCORT CARRIERS

Probably no warship had a more varied career in the Second World War than HMS *Audacity*. Launched in March 1939 as the German cargo liner *Hannover*, she was intercepted in the West Indies in March 1940. Overtaken by Royal Navy warships, her crew tried to scuttle, but the British took her under tow to Jamaica. After repairs she entered British service as *Sinbad*, registered in Kingston, Jamaica. The admiralty saw other uses for a twelve thousand-ton, 440-foot ship, however, and in November renamed her *Empire Audacity*, one of seventeen "ocean boarding vessels" largely devoted to enforcing blockades.

While laid up at Blyth, the German-built vessel underwent another conversion, this time into the first escort aircraft carrier. When she emerged in June 1941 she bore yet another name, as the admiralty preferred simply *Audacity*. She was a rudimentary carrier with no hangar deck, meaning her few aircraft had to be stored and maintained on the flight deck despite weather conditions.

Traditionally superstitious, sailors have long held that it's bad luck to rename a ship. That certainly applied to HMS *Audacity*, which deployed under her fourth name. She embarked eight Grumman Martlets—Royal Navy versions of the F4F Wildcat—on her first convoy escort in September 1941. The fighters were intended to protect ships from air attack, but on convoy OG 74 from the United Kingdom to Gibraltar, Focke-Wulf 200 Condor bombers sank one ship while U-boats destroyed four more.

Then in late October, protecting OG 76 to Gibraltar, *Audacity*'s fighters downed four Condors, a record. One Martlet fell to the FW's heavy return fire, but Sub-Lieutenant Eric "Winkle" Brown became the champion Condor killer with two victories on the cruise. Thereafter *Audacity* was marked for destruction by the U-boat command.

HG 76 left Gibraltar on December 14, with *Audacity* embarking just four Grummans, supported by three destroyers. The convoy drew a U-boat wolfpack while *Audacity*'s planes downed two more Condors but lost one in an attack on a surfaced submarine. *U-131* was damaged and scuttled.

More action came the night of December 21. Ten U-boats stalked the convoy, four actually attacking. Silhouetted under flares, *Audacity* appeared in the periscope of *U-751*'s *Kapitänleutnant* Gerhard Bigalk, a former merchant officer. In two approaches he put three torpedoes into her, igniting aviation gasoline and severing her bow. Sub-Lieutenant Brown, later the world champion carrier aviator, had just moments to order his priorities. Given a choice between saving pajamas recently purchased for his fiancée or his logbook, he did what any pilot would do—he wrapped up his log and abandoned ship.

Audacity sank in little more than an hour.

Additionally, the convoy lost two merchantmen and an escort while Admiral Doenitz wrote off three boats. It was a lesson for both sides in attrition warfare at sea.

SINKING *AUDACITY*

Kapitänleutnant Gerhard Bigalk logged his approach and attack on HMS *Audacity* the night of December 21, 1941:

> Very dark night, overcast…moderate swell.… Spread of four, enemy speed 10 knots, inclination 80°, bows left, depth 3 m, range 1,200 m. After running time of 3 min. 20 sec. we see a detonation against the stern of the enemy—this also turned out to be clearly audible in the forward compartment.
>
> Enemy alters course away from us to port. The light produced by some extremely bright starshell reveals her beyond all doubt to be an aircraft carrier. Now I understand why I got her range and speed so wrong.
>
> I withdraw somewhat to reload torpedoes, keeping a close watch on the carrier.… After her course alteration to port (south) the carrier slows to a halt.… The first torpedo hit must have shattered her rudder and propellers because carrier seems powerless to manoeuvre [sic] herself out of an unfavorable position beam to wind. [Actually her engine room was flooding.] With just a single torpedo—all that remains loaded in my stern tube—there's little chance of my sinking her. I'll have to wait until at least two bow tubes have been reloaded.…
>
> The shadow is so monstrously large that its breadth covers at least two periscope glass widths. Line of bearing 0°, range 800 m, enemy speed=0. Running time 50 sec,

depth 4.5 m. Twin salvo from Tubes I and III. Tube I hits 25 m from the stern. Tube III 10 m forward of midships. Shortly after these hit there is a third powerful detonation accompanied by flames and a substantial quantity of smoke.... Carrier is firing red distress signals. Two destroyers approach at high speed. As one of them heads straight towards me I am forced to withdraw.

Bigalk and his submarine were lost to British bombers in July 1942.

THE END OF *ARK*

Throughout 1941 a series of British convoys ran the Mediterranean gantlet to keep the beleaguered Malta garrison supplied, as it sustained almost daily air attack. Most of the convoys encountered German and Italian bombers from Sicily and Sardinia, requiring Fairey Fulmars and Hawker Sea Hurricanes to defend the ships.

However, the successful Malta reinforcements came at a price. On November 13 *Ark Royal* was approaching Gibraltar from a Malta run when *Kapitänleutnant* Friedrich Guggenberger's *U-81* speared her with one torpedo. The explosion blew a huge hole at the bilge keel, nearly four thousand square feet.

Despite having better watertight integrity than previous carriers, *Ark*'s damage was compounded by a boiler-room fire that interrupted pressure to the pumps trying to offset the flooding. Listing alarmingly to eighteen degrees, she was abandoned but stabilized enough to permit a salvage team aboard. However, her condition deteriorated and she sank early on November 14. Remarkably, there was only one fatality among 1,488 crew.

The board of inquiry faulted Captain Loben Maund for inadequate damage control and a poor state of readiness. A review of warship losses, however, found that *Ark Royal*'s lack of backup power was a design flaw.

In 1943, with another command, Guggenberger was sunk by American patrol planes and sent to a prison camp in Arizona. There he made two unsuccessful escape attempts in 1944. He would subsequently rise to a senior position in NATO.

ANGLO-AMERICAN OPERATIONS

The U.S. and Royal Navies conducted joint operations for the first time in 1942. America's first carrier in European waters was USS *Wasp* (CV-7), dispatched to aid British flattops in reinforcing Malta. In April *Wasp* loaded forty-seven Supermarine Spitfires at the fleet base at Scapa Flow north of Scotland and steamed to the Mediterranean. There she launched the RAF fighters on April 20. The carrier returned to Scapa Flow without encountering opposition and prepared for a repeat performance.

Anglo-American naval operations included some unusual "cross-deck" evolutions including Royal Navy Sea Gladiator biplanes landing aboard USS *Wasp* during joint Atlantic operations. *Courtesy Tailhook Association.*

On May 9 *Wasp* and HMS *Eagle* merged in a joint operation, ferrying a total of sixty-four Spitfires. *Wasp* dispatched forty-seven fighters, though one splashed on takeoff, and another experienced fuel feed problems. The Canadian pilot of the latter elected to try to land aboard, guided by the skilled hands of the landing signal officer, Lieutenant David McCampbell. Pilot Officer Jerry Smith got aboard on his second attempt, receiving naval aviator wings for his feat. Later he disappeared chasing German bombers, while McCampbell became the U.S. Navy's leading fighter pilot.

Twice in April and May 1942 USS *Wasp* ferried Royal Air Force Spitfire fighters to Malta, sustaining the beleaguered Mediterranean garrison against Axis air attack. *Courtesy Tailhook Association.*

Upon return to Britain, CV-7 was hailed by Winston Churchill who famously quipped, "Who said a wasp can't sting twice?"

PROTECTING "PEDESTAL"

During the summer of 1942 the FAA was increasingly concerned with fighter direction in multi-carrier operations. Early in August *Eagle, Victorious, Indomitable, Furious,* and *Argus* trained together, anticipating further operations in support of Malta. That month *Eagle, Furious,* and *Indomitable* joined Convoy WS 21S for Operation Pedestal, sending fourteen freighters and tankers to Malta.

Supported by battleship *Nelson* and battle cruiser *Renown*, it was one of the most powerful units yet deployed to "the Med." *Furious* embarked Spitfires for Malta, but the other two carriers had protective Sea Hurricanes and Fulmars.

On August 10 the convoy was spotted by Axis aircraft that alerted U-boat Command. *Eagle* had escaped an Italian submarine in July, but on August 11, south of Majorca, *U-73* slipped past the destroyer screen and fired a devastating spread of torpedoes. All four slammed into *Eagle*'s twenty-four-year-old hull, sending her down in less than eight minutes. Destroyers rescued 1,160 men of 1,291 aboard.

Furious launched her fighters for Malta, then reversed helm, mission accomplished. But Pedestal turned into a slugfest. Throughout August 12 the Luftwaffe and Italian *Regia* hammered at the convoy, pressing repeated bombing and torpedo attacks.

In a daylong attack against the convoy, Axis aircraft were relentless in their effort to sink the merchant ships bearing essential supplies. The FAA fighter pilots met each threat with skill and determination, claiming thirty enemies against thirteen losses while ships' gunners accounted for a dozen more. The stellar performance was posted by *Indomitable*'s Lieutenant Richard Cork, a Sea Hurricane pilot who had flown with the RAF in the Battle of Britain. He wrote:

> The sky at first sight seemed filled with aircraft. The enemy kept in tight formation and our fighters snapped at their heels, forcing them to break in all directions. One Junkers turned away from the main group and I led my section down towards it. I was well ahead and fired when it filled my sight. Smoke poured from its wings and it disappeared below me into the sea. A few minutes later I saw another Ju 88 out of the corner of my eye, heading along the coast

of North Africa, so I set off in pursuit by myself. At 1,000 feet I came within range and fired. It seemed to stagger in the air, then dropped into the sea with a big splash.

Cork flew three more sorties that day, claiming three more victims. He became the FAA's top fighter ace with thirteen victories, but died flying a Corsair at Ceylon in 1944.

That afternoon a *Staffel* of Stukas got past the depleted combat air patrol and dived on *Indomitable*. They hit her twice and scored three damaging near misses. One of her Sea Hurricane pilots, Sub-Lieutenant Blyth Ritchie, launched at the last moment. Latching onto the retiring Stukas, he splashed two. "Indomit" shaped course for the East Coast of the United States for full repairs.

Without effective air cover, WS 21S was battered that night and the next day. Axis bombers and torpedo boats sank eight ships, leaving five to reach Malta, two barely afloat. Two light cruisers and a destroyer also were lost, but the twenty-nine thousand tons of supplies offloaded meant that Malta would survive.

The Luftwaffe and *Regia* had launched some 330 sorties against Pedestal, sustaining about 12 percent losses, demonstrating the efficacy of a combined fighter and AA defense.

A TORCH TO VICHY

As the Guadalcanal campaign peaked in the Pacific, American carriers prepared for a major Allied offensive in North Africa. Operation Torch landed on the shores of French Morocco on November 8, 1942, with *Ranger* (CV-4), *Suwanee* (ACV-27), *Sangamon* (ACV-26), and *Santee* (ACV-29) supporting U.S. forces north and south of Casablanca. In all, the four flattops embarked 109 Grumman F4F-4 fighters with sixty-two Douglas SBD-3 and Grumman TBF-1

COMBUSTIBLE, VULNERABLE, AND EXPENDABLE

Among the miracles of production in the Second World War was America's escort carrier program. For scale and efficiency, few industrial achievements could match it.

When the United States abruptly faced a severe shortage of flight decks in December 1941, a quick fix was found. Merchant ship hulls could be converted to "baby" or "jeep" carriers capable of operating as many as thirty aircraft. The British had pioneered the concept, but could not meet the numbers required—hence the Royal Navy's reliance on its "rich uncle in America."

USS *Long Island* was the first American escort carrier, originally designated ACV-1 (auxiliary aircraft carrier). Commissioned in June 1941, she was capable of 17 knots and proved the merchant conversion concept, but saw little combat.

The next four escorts were the Sangamon class, converted from oilers to flattops in as little as six months. They were 11,600-ton ships with two elevators to operate twenty-five planes.

Next came the Bogue class, ten serving in the U.S. Navy and thirty-four with Britain as the Attacker and Ruler classes. They were small, usually less than five hundred feet in length, but weighed as much as 14,400 tons and proved highly versatile. Most entered service between early 1942 and early 1944.

Finally, the immensely successful Casablanca class produced fifty ships in twenty-one months. More remarkably, they were commissioned in the year between July 1943 and July 1944. It was a stunning accomplishment, as Henry Kaiser's Vancouver, Washington, shipyard built not only escort carriers, but turned out Liberty transport and cargo ships in as little as ninety days.

Small and lightly armored, "baby flattops" lent themselves to grim sailors' humor. Some insisted that CVE stood for "combustible, vulnerable, and expendable." Others said they were "two-torpedo ships" because the second torpedo would pass over the flight deck.

LANDLOCKED FLATTOPS

Immediately after Pearl Harbor, the U.S. Navy faced a severe shortage of carriers to train tens of thousands of budding tailhook aviators. The fleet carriers were far too few to sideline even temporarily for the purpose, and months would pass before any CVEs could be devoted to the role.

But the Navy looked inward—literally and geographically—and found a solution in a most unlikely place.

Two Great Lakes excursion ships became available for modification: the *Seeandbee*, of 1913 vintage, and *Greater Buffalo*, nine years newer. As coal-fired paddle-wheelers they were odd candidates for conversion to flattops, but they filled a critical void. Not only were they land-locked, but their Chicago base was seven hundred statute miles from Norfolk and 1,700 from San Diego.

Converted Great Lakes excursion steamers were converted to training carriers as USS *Wolverine* and *Sable*. Here, *Sable* launches a Wildcat fighter in 1944. *Courtesy Tailhook Association.*

Seeandbee, acquired in March 1942, was commissioned in August as USS *Wolverine* (IX-64). The IX designator indicated a miscellaneous vessel. Her partner emerged as *Sable* (IX-81) in May 1943, both displacing about seven thousand tons as carriers. Because they were based at Chicago's Navy Pier, their lack of a hangar deck was of little concern.

Wolverine's flight deck measured five hundred feet in length, while *Sable*'s was 535, both about ninety-eight feet wide. Thus, their decks were shorter than a Casablanca-class CVE (476 x 80) but somewhat wider.

Wolverine began qualifying carrier pilots in September 1942, and by war's end she and *Sable* were credited with producing 17,820 aviators who logged nearly 120,000 landings. (Originally pilots needed eight landings to qualify, later reduced to six.) In those three years the ships also trained forty thousand flight deck crewmen—essential supporting players in the carrier aviation cast.

Pilots reported to NAS Glenview from around the country, regardless of their ultimate carrier assignment. Retired Captain Chuck Downey recalled his experience as an eighteen-year-old "nugget" aviator in 1943. "We were only there for about three days. We spent a couple days working with an LSO, practicing carrier approaches at a training field, and then when he felt we were ready, he sent us out to the carrier."

However, unavoidable complications arose. Inevitably the smoke from coal-burning engines wafted ashore, depositing sooty residue over the urban area, including laundry hung out to dry. Beyond that, when operating within view of shore, the carriers caused major traffic jams as motorists slowed or stopped to take in the Navy air show.

Some 140 carrier aircraft sank in the Great Lakes, with eight known fatalities. A few planes survived well enough in fresh water to be retrieved and restored for museum display, a reminder

Training accidents were inevitable. An aspiring Hellcat pilot nearly went overboard trying to land aboard USS *Sable* in 1944. *Courtesy Tailhook Association.*

of the U.S. Navy's innovative approach to problem solving during the greatest war of all time.

bombers. Torch was assembled and launched so quickly that many pilots had little opportunity for training. Some had not flown in two weeks—an inordinately long layoff for carrier aviators.

The Casablanca landings were opposed by Vichy French forces allied with Germany. The defenders counted about two hundred aircraft, including American-built Curtiss fighters and Martin bombers.

Things began poorly. On November 8 a flight of seven *Santee* Wildcats got lost and ran low on fuel. One ditched and five crashlanded ashore with one pilot lost. *Ranger*'s Fighting Squadron Four lost six planes on its first mission, though *Sangamon* F4Fs claimed four shootdowns without loss. Later that day eighteen *Ranger* SBDs attacked harbor facilities including the thirty-five thousand-ton battleship *Jean Bart*, whose fifteen-inch guns posed a threat to Allied ships. She was partly sunk at her mooring while a submarine was destroyed.

When a French surface force steamed out to engage the U.S. warships, Dauntlesses and Wildcats descended to bomb and strafe. A light cruiser and two destroyers were damaged enough to be run aground to prevent their sinking.

On November 9, *Ranger* SBDs were back over Casablanca Harbor where Vichy antiaircraft batteries still posed a threat. Dauntlesses hit *Jean Bart* again, knocking out her remaining AA mounts. Meanwhile, Curtiss P-40s took off from *Chenango* (ACV-28), flying ashore to newly captured airfields. It was a precursor of other joint Army-Navy operations throughout the war.

Operation Torch provided a laboratory for carrier aviators to perfect their trade. They flew support missions for ground troops, sank a Vichy submarine at sea, and engaged in air combat. Some of their opponents were combat veterans of the 1939–40 campaign. A *Ranger* pilot, Lieutenant (jg) Charles A. Shields, bailed out of his riddled F4F, and a Frenchman flying a Hawk buzzed him as he parachuted to earth, "wagging his wingtips and waving and laughing like hell." Still, the tailhook fighters downed twenty-five Vichymen against five Wildcats lost in dogfights.

Losses were stiff, however, amounting to nearly 25 percent by the time the fighting ended on November 10. Ground fire and operational losses were by far the greatest causes, forcing planners to allot more aircraft to future operations.

AVENGER AND DASHER

A catastrophic carrier loss occurred in Torch's wake. On November 15 the American-built HMS *Avenger* was en route to Gibraltar for engine repairs when she crossed paths with *U-151*, which had already sunk seven ships that month. Once more a single torpedo destroyed an RN carrier, although all but twelve of her 528 crew survived. She was *Kapitänleutnant* Adolf Piening's twenty-second victim.

On March 27, 1943, the escort carrier HMS *Dasher* was anchored in the Firth of Clyde on Scotland's southwest coast. Though only eight months in commission, she had participated in Operation Torch, Mediterranean ferry missions, and a convoy escort. An internal explosion inflicted catastrophic damage that destroyed the 8,200-ton ship in about three minutes. As Britain's last carrier loss she was, in English terminology, an "own goal." *Dasher* lost 378 of 528 men aboard, or 71 percent—an extremely high mortality rate for a ship at rest. No definite cause for the explosion was determined, but opinion tended toward the fuel system. In an eerie postscript, wood from the flight deck washed ashore at nearby Ardossan in 1999.

Another CVE expedient was the Empire class of converted grain and oil carriers, merchant crewed with RN airmen, maintenance and support personnel, and shipboard gunners. Ten ships were delivered beginning with *Empire MacAlpine* in April 1943, but the four ex-tankers had no hangar deck. Mostly flying Swordfish, the Empires often carried cargo in addition to the small FAA "air party."

WINKLE'S WAY

The world champion carrier aviator was Captain Eric M. "Winkle" Brown, RN, who logged 2,407 shipboard landings in his lengthy career. He also flew a record 487 aircraft types, excluding variants (i.e., various marks of Seafires, etc.). In 2011 he explained his carrier landing technique to the author:

> As to the subject of deck landings (DLs). I have records of the top "scorers" in the Fleet Air Arm, and besides myself we had one other, Lieutenant Commander "Bill" Bailey,

The most experienced carrier aviator of all time was Royal Navy Lieutenant (later Captain) Eric M. Brown who logged 2,407 carrier landings in his thirty-year career. *Courtesy author's collection.*

who just exceeded 2,000 deck landings which he acquired during three years as a "clockwork mouse" (demonstrating landings to endless courses of wartime recruited naval pilots). However, after this there is a big gap down to 600 with very few in that bracket.

I started my score in 1941 and really piled them up in 1942 and '43 when I was graded as an escort carrier specialist and proofed all the new "Woolworth carriers" coming over brand new from American shipyards, and some also from UK shipyards. I proofed twenty carriers in all, and this involved flying four types of aircraft (two torpedo bombers and two fighters) into each of normally eight arrester wires twice each with each type of aircraft, followed by an accelerated takeoff.

At first I had three pilots to assist me, but they were soon withdrawn because their trap rate on a selected wire was too low and the process took far too long. When on my own my trap rate on a selected wire averaged about 80 percent without a LSO, which I dispensed with largely because he was replaced too frequently or none was readily available in wartime.

I employed a standard deck landing technique of never letting my approved speed creep above 1.1 Vs (stall speed) then aiming for the wire beyond the one that was my target, and cutting the throttle as it disappeared from my forward view.

In 1943 I was mainly engaged in deck landing various models of Seafire while in the Navy's Service Trials Unit, and logged over 500 traps in that somewhat tricky aircraft.

After 1941 I also became heavily involved in catapulting trials, particularly at Farnborough where we had every type of new catapult installed. In fact, my total catapult launches (2,721) exceeds my total traps because so many were made ashore.

Brown retired as a captain in 1970, having flown a record 487 types of aircraft. He died in 2016, age ninety-seven.

OPERATION LEADER

After Torch almost a year passed before an American carrier participated in a European combat operation. In October 1943 *Ranger* joined a British Home Fleet task force for Operation Leader, attacking German shipping in Norway, above the Arctic Circle.

Bodo ("Budu") Harbor succored German and Axis merchant shipping, drawing Anglo-American attention. On October 3 the veteran flattop launched two attack waves: twenty SBDs followed by ten TBFs, both escorted by F4Fs. Trolling the rocky coastline and pouncing on the harbor, the bombers sank six vessels and damaged three, losing three planes. There was no air opposition, although *Ranger*'s fighters were vectored onto two snoopers and splashed a Heinkel and a Junkers recon aircraft. Sharing the two victories was

Lieutenant (jg) Dean "Diz" Laird, later the only U.S. Navy ace with kills against German and Japanese aircraft.

Thereafter *Ranger* returned to more mundane chores, largely serving as a training carrier and occasionally ferrying Army aircraft for the rest of the war.

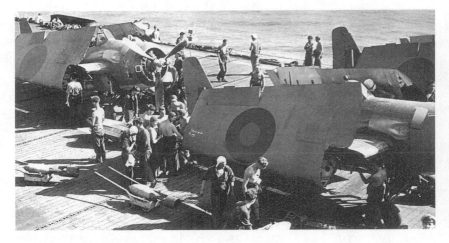

In early 1944 the British Home Fleet launched a series of air strikes against the German battleship *Tirpitz* in Norway. Here Wildcats aboard the escort carrier HMS *Pursuer* are being armed for one of the missions. *Courtesy Tailhook Association.*

HUNTER-KILLERS

The escort carriers' vital role in the Atlantic plugged the four-year "black hole" of the mid-ocean gap, beyond range of land-based aircraft. Therefore, the U.S. Navy formed dedicated antisubmarine units, hunter-killer groups combining flattops with destroyers. *Bogue* (ACV-9) inaugurated the concept in February 1943, when U-boats sank 600,000 tons of Allied shipping. The early hunter-killers learned their trade on the job, eventually finalizing the standard escort carrier loadout of Wildcat fighters and Avenger bombers.

Bogue escorted three Atlantic convoys through April 1943 without any submarine contacts. On May 21, while making the run from Britain to Nova Scotia, Composite Squadron Nine (VC-9) encountered

U-231. The squadron commander, William M. Drane, executed the attack, damaging the submarine's bridge and forcing it to return to France to be repaired. The next day, Lieutenant (jg) William F. Chamberlain dropped four depth bombs from his Avenger onto *U-569* before it submerged. When the sub had to resurface, Lieutenant Howard Roberts straddled it with his bombs, inflicting mortal damage.

In retrospect, May 1943 marked the critical month, as merchant shipping losses plummeted. Victory over the U-boats meant that the buildup to D-Day in Normandy could proceed over the next twelve months.

Bogue made two more kills in June, by which time the Battle of the Atlantic was on the road to victory.

A lesser concern arose in July when the auxiliary carrier designation (ACV) was changed to escort carrier (CVE).

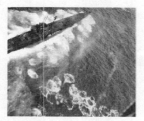

In 1943–1944 British and American escort carriers made a strategic contribution to D-Day, ending the U-boats' sanctuary in the mid-Atlantic gap beyond range of land-based aircraft. Thus, the "baby flattops" opened the oceanic road to Normandy. *Courtesy Tailhook Association.*

By the end of the year, CVEs had destroyed twenty-three U-boats. Only nine more were sunk by carrier planes during 1944, but the effect on the sea war was just as significant as before. Submarines had difficulty closing on convoys without being seen, either by day or night. Radar-equipped Avengers were a constant threat to surfaced subs, and it is unknown how many attacks were thwarted by the carrier planes' presence.

In May 1943 the U-boat command issued a "fight back" order urging surfaced submarines to engage Allied aircraft in gun duels. After heavy losses the order was rescinded in August. *Courtesy Tailhook Association.*

Off the Cape Verdes on March 19, 1944, a *Block Island* (CVE-21) team jumped a surfaced U-boat that opened fire. While the Wildcat strafed, the Avenger sank the sub but ditched with battle damage. The TBF pilot and gunner were lost, but the observer, Ensign Mark Fitzgerald, deployed a rubber raft. He ended up taking on three of the U-boat survivors, all of them wounded. Fitzgerald hauled them aboard and bandaged their wounds. One submariner exclaimed, "You good fellow. Damn war!" The German was *Oberleutnant* Günther Leopold, skipper of *U-1059* on its first war patrol.

However, it was not all one-sided. On May 29 *U-549* torpedoed *Block Island* off the African coast. She had two kills to her credit but was the only American carrier sunk in the Atlantic, with all but six of her 957 men being saved. She was immediately avenged by her escorts. *Block Island* was honored in her namesake, CVE-106, commissioned at year-end.

THE SAGA OF *U-505*

In June 1944 USS *Guadalcanal's* (CVE-60) hunter-killer group scored a spectacular coup off the African coast. The CVE skipper, Captain Daniel Gallery, was an innovative, outspoken leader who had pioneered night flying from escort carriers. On his third outing, with three kills to his credit, "Cap'n Dan" sought something more. He trained his force to maximize the possibility of capturing a U-boat, and got the chance on June 4. *U-505* was depth-charged by destroyer escorts, forced to the surface, and strafed by Avengers and Wildcats. The crew abandoned ship after opening scuttling vents.

Gallery's boarding team descended into the vacated sub and stopped the flooding. *Guadalcanal* herself rigged a line and towed the U-boat until a tug arrived. In the meantime, *Guadalcanal's* LSO,

Off the Azores in June 1944 USS *Guadalcanal's* hunter-killer group captured U-505. The ship's landing signal officer, Lt. Jarvis Jennings, became the only LSO to "wave" landing aircraft while towing a submarine. *Courtesy Tailhook Association.*

Lieutenant Jarvis "Stretch" Jennings, became the only "paddles" to wave planes aboard while towing a submarine. *U-505* was delivered to Bermuda, a priceless intelligence coup.

Bogue, first of the successful hunter-killers, also logged the last U-boat sunk by CVE planes. On August 20 her Avengers slew *U-1229* on its first patrol.

HUNTER-KILLER SUMMARY

More than 750 German submarines were lost to all causes in World War II. Those sunk by Allied carrier aircraft represented a small share of the whole, but the influence of escort carriers cannot be diminished. Their mere presence deterred innumerable attacks, and carrier planes such as Avengers and Swordfish located hostile subs for surface forces to pursue.

The success of the jeep carriers was proven every time a convoy arrived intact at its destination.

From 1940 through 1945 British carrier-based aircraft sank fifteen Axis submarines (eleven and one-half by Swordfish) and shared thirteen more with surface units. Although the Battle of the Atlantic peaked in May 1943, Fleet Air Arm carrier squadrons, alone and with ships, accounted for just three U-boats that year but sixteen in 1944, including those shared with ships and land-based aircraft. HMS *Fencer* set the RN record with four U-boats, three in one Arctic convoy during May 1944.

American CVEs were heavily engaged from 1942 onward, with their carrier planes sinking thirty-one enemy subs (one French and one long-ranging Japanese) while splitting four with destroyers. The most successful hunter-killers were *Bogue*'s (CVE-9) group with twelve confirmed sinkings and *Card*'s (CVE-11) with eleven. In the Pacific, CVEs notched seven submarines, including two shared with escort vessels.

TO THE RIVIERA

After Operation Leader, American carriers endured another lengthy wait before returning to European seas. In August 1944 two escort carriers supported Operation Anvil-Dragoon, the Allied invasion of Southern France. The frigid Arctic environs of Leader stood in stark contrast to the balmy weather of the French Riviera, where F6F-5 Hellcats supported Anvil-Dragoon from USS *Kasaan Bay* (CVE-69) and *Tulagi* (CVE-72). They served alongside two Royal Navy escort carriers, HMS *Hunter* and *Stalker* operating forty-seven Seafires, while a separate all-British task group embarked 129 Seafires, Wildcats, and Hellcats in five other ships, all American-built vessels.

HMS *Hunter* was representative of the RN contribution. Her Seafires logged 307 sorties, including dive bombing, armed reconnaissance, and photo recon. She wrote off four fighters with eleven damaged in landing accidents.

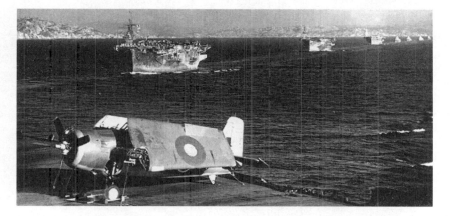

British and American escort carriers supported the invasion of Southern France in August 1944. Five Royal Navy carriers operated independently with four visible here. *Courtesy Tailhook Association.*

The two American squadrons were VF-74, a conventional Hellcat squadron in *Kasaan Bay*, with VOF-1 in *Tulagi*. Lieutenant Commander William F. Bringle's observation unit was unique in the Navy

U.S. Navy pilots seldom encountered German aircraft but Ensigns Alfred Wood and Edward Olszewski flew the same Hellcat from USS *Tulagi* to down four Luftwaffe planes during Operation Anvil-Dragoon. *Courtesy author's collection.*

at the time, trained in controlling naval gunfire while retaining the offensive and defensive capability of the Hellcat.

On D-Day South, August 15, the U.S. Hellcats logged one hundred sorties, spotting for shipboard gunners while interdicting German transport well inland. Over the next two weeks the F6Fs not only claimed hundreds of enemy vehicles destroyed but also scores of locomotives, and they downed eight Luftwaffe planes without loss in air combat. Enemy flak was potent, however, contributing to the loss of eleven Hellcats. Reorganized "Stateside," VOF-1 became VOC-1, a composite squadron with FM-2 Wildcats flying in the Western Pacific.

CARRIERS THAT NEVER WERE

Two Axis carriers were begun but never completed. Germany's *Graf Zeppelin*, intended as the first of two, was laid down in December

1936 and launched two years later. Her thirty-four thousand-ton design provided for 33 knots with a varying air group composition of about forty planes. Construction was erratic, however, and she finished the war on the Baltic coast. Though scuttled in shallow water, the Soviets raised her and expended her in ordnance tests in 1947.

Italy's *Aquila* (Eagle) was a twenty-four thousand-ton carrier converted from the passenger liner *Roma*. Work began in 1941, but conversion lagged due to numerous problems including developing catapults and arresting gear, let alone providing suitable aircraft. Germany seized the incomplete vessel at Genoa with the Italian armistice in 1943. Her hulk was scrapped in 1952.

Other than the United States and Britain, no other nation commissioned a new carrier until 1961. By then, the aviation world was almost unrecognizable to anyone who had flown in the Second World War.

FOUR
ACROSS THE PACIFIC
1941–1945

Seapower incarnate, 1944. A fast carrier task group with an Independence class light carrier, Essex class fleet carrier, and battleship escorts. *Courtesy Tailhook Association.*

IN DECEMBER 1941 THE IMPERIAL JAPANESE NAVY ALONE combined ships, aircraft, and doctrine in a unified package that would burst on the global scene in a stunning display of naval airpower. America and the U.S. Navy would have to shake off the shock of that blow, adjust to a new reality, and take the war to the enemy. Only tailhook aviators could do so.

At the end of 1941, the world carrier census stood at twenty-nine. America had eight, including USS *Long Island* (AVG/CVE-1). Japan

JAPANESE NAVY FRONT-LINE AIRCRAFT, DECEMBER 1941 (DERIVED FROM RENÉ FRANCILLON, *JAPANESE AIRCRAFT OF THE PACIFIC WAR*)

CARRIER CAPABLE STRIKE AIRCRAFT	329
CARRIER CAPABLE FIGHTER AIRCRAFT	380
PATROL AND LAND BOMBER AIRCRAFT	300
TOTAL CARRIER AIRCRAFT	709
TOTAL OVERALL	1,009

U.S. NAVY FRONT-LINE AIRCRAFT, DECEMBER 1941 (DERIVED FROM W. T. LARKINS, *U.S. NAVY & MARINE CORPS AIRCRAFT, 1914–1959*)

TYPE	USN	USMC	TOTAL
CARRIER CAPABLE STRIKE	248	85	333
CARRIER CAPABLE FIGHTER	123	75	198
PATROL	137	0	137
TOTAL CARRIER AIRCRAFT	371	160	531
TOTAL	508	160	668

Front-line: assigned to combat-deployable units.

led the field with ten ships, including *Hosho* on training status. Britain deployed ten (two CVEs), and France's *Béarn* lay idle.

In vivid contrast, the global battleship census hung around sixty, including decommissioned and damaged ships, mainly French and Russian. But the ratio was about to turn.

The Pacific Ocean covers some sixty-four million square miles, more than twice the size of the Atlantic and containing nearly half the earth's water. The 2,400 statute miles from San Francisco to Honolulu is 50 percent farther than the direct line from Paris to Moscow. The expanse from Hawaii to Tokyo is nearly three times farther still, making the Pacific the largest combat arena in history.

The oceanic chessboard was defined by squares composed of lines of longitude and latitude. On that strategic surface, aircraft carriers became the leading players—technically marvelous queens with range, mobility, and striking power. In the forty-four months between December 1941 and September 1945, the United States, Britain, and Japan committed immense resources to the naval contest, with the Anglo-Americans dividing their flattops between the Atlantic and Pacific. But

Mitsubishi's Zero fighter, seen aboard the Japanese flagship *Akagi*, was a lethal surprise to U.S. airmen from Pearl Harbor onward. Its range and performance were unrivaled at the time. *Courtesy Tailhook Association.*

the huge majority of carriers of all types were produced in American shipyards. Including escort carriers delivered to Britain, the United States accounted for 71 percent of the world total from 1939 through 1945.

But before the enormous U.S. industrial base could take effect, the sudden war forced its chilling reality upon a marginally prepared fleet.

PACIFIC LEARNING CURVE

Heavy reliance upon aircraft carriers made 1942 a salient year in the history of naval warfare. The emergence of carrier versus carrier battles—four clashes in six months—was unlike anything previous. Whereas steel-hulled, big-gun battleships had slugged it out for decades, and submarines were well proven in the Great War, flattops were new arrivals.

Tokyo possessed two advantages: first, *Kido Butai*'s sophistication of operational technique and doctrine was unprecedented; and Japan had geography in its favor. In the fall of 1941, the Imperial Navy owned nine carriers while the U.S. Pacific Fleet had three, and Britain's lone carrier proved irrelevant. Thus, Franklin Roosevelt's two-ocean navy had to split its forces, with three carriers committed to the Pacific and four in the Atlantic. That ratio was about to change.

Following the stunning blow at Pearl Harbor, the U.S. Pacific Fleet found itself on the strategic defensive, literally overnight. With the battleships sunk or sidelined, Admiral Chester Nimitz had few options for taking offensive action. In fact, he had only one: aircraft carriers.

USS *Enterprise* (CV-6) had been spared a pier-side death on December 7, delaying its return from a ferry run to Wake Island upon receiving news of the Japanese attack on Pearl Harbor. *Lexington* (CV-2) also was at sea that morning, and *Saratoga* (CV-3) was embarking planes in San Diego. But three flight decks were wholly insufficient to counter *Kido Butai*. Therefore, *Yorktown* (CV-5) hastened from the East Coast to bolster PacFleet's lineup. Of the other carriers, *Ranger* was inadequate for Pacific operations and *Wasp* had Atlantic and Mediterranean commitments. *Hornet* (CV-8), last of the Yorktowns, was working up on the East Coast.

Vice Admiral Chuichi Nagumo, who led Japanese carriers from Pearl Harbor through the Indian Ocean to Midway and the Guadalcanal campaign. Though a non-aviator, he became the world's most experienced carrier commander. *Courtesy author's collection.*

Meanwhile, Vice Admiral Chuichi Nagumo's accomplished airmen and sailors embarked on a wide-ranging Pacific tour, sweeping all before them. While land-based Japanese bombers sank the battle cruiser HMS *Repulse* and battleship *Prince of Wales* on December 10, imperial troops landed in the Philippines and Malaya, and seized Hong Kong and Singapore.

Nimitz's carriers could only hit and run. Between February and April they launched strikes against far-flung Japanese garrisons in the Gilberts, Marshalls, and Solomon Islands. But *Saratoga* was quickly removed from the lineup when she was torpedoed in mid-January. She remained sidelined until early June.

HMS *Hermes* arrived at Ceylon in mid-February, the only British carrier east of Suez. Her small air group consisted of Fairey Swordfish, the biplane torpedo bombers that had crippled *Bismarck* nine months previously. But in the Pacific the Swordfish were largely antisubmarine aircraft, possessing limited strike potential.

Meanwhile, Nagumo's carriers bombed Colombo, Ceylon, on April 5, missing *Hermes* but finding cruisers HMS *Cornwall* and *Dorsetshire* southwest of the island. Fifty-three Aichi dive bombers claimed about eighteen hits on the two ships, destroying both. *Hermes* sent her planes ashore and, with her escorting destroyer *Vampire*, steamed southward to avoid the next Japanese attack.

On April 9 a Japanese scout plane sighted the small force. The British, aware of being seen, directed *Hermes* back to Trincomalee where she could receive protection from Hawker Hurricanes. But Nagumo was fast off the mark, launching eighty-two Aichi dive bombers ("Vals") screened by nine Zero fighters from *Akagi, Hiryu*, and *Soryu*. (*Kaga* was laid up for repairs.) Nearly three dozen Vals dived on the two British warships, hitting them with as many as forty bombs in twenty-seven minutes. A dozen land-based Fairey Fulmar two-seat fighters tried to intervene, to little avail. The remaining dive bombers sank three other ships and a corvette, completing a devastating display of competence, for the loss of four bombers. A moderate riposte from the RAF's Blenheim light bombers missed their targets.

Hermes went down with her captain and 307 men, the first carrier aircraft sunk by an opposing flattop. It was an execution rather than a battle. The first true carrier clash was four weeks away.

DOOLITTLE DO'ED IT!

Though the U.S. Army and Navy had a long rivalry for funding and missions, the pressure of wartime welded them into a highly effective team for the First Special Aviation Project. History still knows it as the Doolittle Raid, America's retaliation against homeland Japan for the Pearl Harbor attack.

Ironically, the concept originated with a submariner, Captain Francis Low. While touring Virginia bases in January 1942, he saw a ship's outline on a bombing range and conceived the notion of launching Army bombers from an aircraft carrier. He sold the concept to Admiral Ernest King, chief of naval operations, who in turn approached General Henry Arnold of the Army Air Forces. Carrier aircraft lacked the range to attack Japan and allow the ships to escape, but Army medium bombers could strike from much farther out.

Arnold tossed the project to his ace troubleshooter, Lieutenant Colonel James H. Doolittle. A rare combination of hot hands and cool intellect, Jimmy Doolittle had won every air race worth entering and had earned an aeronautics Ph.D. He determined that the North American B-25 Mitchell was best suited for taking off from a carrier deck, hitting enemy cities, and escaping to safety in China.

Doolittle selected crews from the most experienced B-25 unit and oversaw training on the East Coast. Coached by veteran carrier aviators, the Army fliers mastered the technique of short-field takeoffs in combat-loaded bombers.

Sixteen Mitchells with spare crews flew cross-country, receiving modifications for the mission. Then they alit at Naval Air Station (NAS) Alameda and were loaded aboard USS *Hornet* (CV-8), America's newest carrier. North of Midway *Hornet*'s unit rendezvoused with her sister *Enterprise*. Only then did the aircrews learn, "This task force is headed for Tokyo."

Retribution for Pearl Harbor came on April 18, 1942, when USS *Hornet* (CV-8) launched Lt. Col. Jimmy Doolittle's sixteen B-25 bombers against Tokyo and environs. *Courtesy Tailhook Association.*

The original plan called for launching the B-25s 450 miles offshore, but on April 18 the Americans were sighted by Japanese picket boats. Consequently, Doolittle's men began taking off two hundred miles farther east than expected, cutting deeply into their fuel reserves over China. Short of cancelling, there was no other option.

While the two carriers made a clean getaway, Doolittle led fifteen other Mitchells operating singly against objectives in the Tokyo urban area. One plane diverted to Russia, critically short of fuel, but most of the others successfully bombed their targets despite Japanese interceptors.

Thirteen hours after launch, however, the returning B-25s ran out of fuel over the China coast. The crews bailed out, seeking help from friendly Chinese. Three fliers perished that night, and eight were captured by the Japanese. Four died in enemy hands; the others survived their ordeal to return in 1945.

Doolittle's triumph galvanized the nation. He received the Medal of Honor and was promoted to brigadier general, en route to commanding three air forces in the Mediterranean and European Theaters.

More significantly, the Tokyo raid convinced the Japanese high command that Pacific Fleet carriers had to be destroyed. A plan quickly evolved to force them into decisive combat against superior odds in Hawaiian waters.

INTO THE CORAL SEA

Meanwhile, in early May the Japanese dispatched a convoy to land troops at Port Moresby, New Guinea, where long-range bombers could interdict sea communications with northern Australia, and extend the defensive perimeter for Japan's major base at Rabaul, New Britain. American code breakers learned of "Operation MO" and provided Admiral Nimitz with ample intelligence. He countered with two task forces built around *Lexington* and *Yorktown*. *Hornet* and *Enterprise* were unavailable, just returned from the Doolittle raid.

Nimitz had a good idea of Japanese forces. The Moresby convoy consisted of a dozen transports with escorts including a light carrier, while a covering force included the Fifth Carrier Division's two flattops. A separate unit aimed at Tulagi, with an anchorage just north of Guadalcanal, largest of the Solomon Islands.

The Americans decided to strike Tulagi before turning to face the carrier threat. However, communications concerns prevented *Yorktown*'s Task Force Seventeen under Rear Admiral Frank Jack Fletcher from coordinating with *Lexington*'s Task Force Eleven under Rear

Admiral Aubrey Fitch. Nevertheless, Fletcher proceeded to launch strikes against Tulagi on May 4. In three waves "Old Yorky's" air group swarmed the anchorage, sinking a destroyer and three mine-sweepers while damaging other vessels. The cost was three aircraft with all four fliers rescued. An exuberant news release claimed a major victory, with fourteen Japanese ships sunk. For the moment, the Japanese were forced off-balance.

Knowing the advantage of mass in the military equation, on May 6 Fletcher merged Task Force Seventeen with Fitch's unit and Task Force Forty-Four, a surface force of U.S. and Australian warships. His combined strength was two carriers, eight cruisers, and thirteen destroyers, plus two vital fleet oilers. In addition to some 130 carrier planes, he benefited from long-range patrol bombers in Australia.

The Japanese, in typically complex fashion, deployed five naval forces. They included a covering group with the light carrier *Shoho* and five escorts, and Vice Admiral Takeo Takagi's striking arm: Carrier Division Five with heavyweights *Shokaku* and *Zuikaku* screened by eight escorts. Combined Japanese air strength was 141, with 127 under Takagi and fourteen in *Shoho*.

Mindful of the Moresby-bound force, on the morning of May 7 Fletcher detached Task Force Forty-Four to watch the passage off the east tip of New Guinea. At the same time both U.S. and Japanese carrier forces lofted scout planes, seeking each other. Around 7:30, multiple Japanese searchers, both ship and land-based, reported several sightings. At that point the situation became clouded in the inevitable fog of war.

A *Shokaku* searcher reported an unidentified carrier with escorts nearly two hundred miles south of Takagi's position. With practiced efficiency, *Shokaku* and *Zuikaku* launched seventy-eight planes in fifteen minutes. The aircrews set course, unknowingly targeting the U.S. replenishment unit, oiler *Neosho* and a destroyer.

An hour after the initial Japanese sightings, their ship-based floatplanes found Fletcher. Within minutes it was the Americans' turn as a *Yorktown* scout spotted the force screening the Moresby invasion convoy. The Dauntless pilot erred by encoding his contact report as two carriers and escorts—an early lesson in the importance of sending vital information "in the clear." Fletcher, with no reason to doubt the intelligence, shot his bolt. Both air groups cleared their decks, with ninety-three planes winging outbound just minutes before the SBD pilot delivered a corrected, accurate assessment. About that time, the B-17s found the invasion force including *Shoho*. Fletcher radioed his strike leaders to proceed to the position plotted by the Army aircrews.

In the world's first aircraft carrier battle, planes from USS *Lexington* and *Yorktown* sank Japan's small Japanese *Shoho* on May 7, 1942. *Courtesy Tailhook Association.*

In the far-flung battle both sides began landing blows. Imperial Navy scouts realized that the tiny oiler force had been erroneously reported, and passed the word. Still, the tactical picture remained clouded, and after failing to find the U.S. carriers, Takagi directed an attack on the oiler unit. The two American ships were swarmed by three dozen Aichi dive bombers, which scored ten hits, instantly sinking the destroyer *Sims* and mortally wounding *Neosho*.

Meanwhile, sixty miles to the north, *Lexington* and *Yorktown* squadrons spotted *Shoho*. Her few Mitsubishi A5M and A6M fighters could not prevent a determined attack. Directed by Commander William B. Ault, "Lady Lex's" pilots pummeled the little flattop with half-ton bombs and torpedoes. Next the Yorktowners piled in, savaging the target nearly dead in the water. Struck by as many as thirteen

A *Yorktown* (CV-5) Douglas Devastator halts in the arresting gear, awaiting the signal to taxi clear. Her torpedo squadron attacked Japanese carriers on both days of the Coral Sea battle. *Courtesy Tailhook Association.*

bombs and seven torpedoes, she sank with 630 of her 834-man crew. Reportedly Lieutenant Commander Robert Dixon, heading *Lexington*'s scouts, radioed, "Scratch one flattop!"—though his language may have been saltier.

The ninety remaining American planes returned to the task force, catching arresting wires on the two victorious carriers while Fletcher pondered his options.

The Japanese invasion force, deprived of air cover, reversed helm to await events.

That afternoon more communications complications arose. Japanese searchers reported Task Force Forty-Four, which became confused with the U.S. carriers. *Shokaku* and *Zuikaku* sent twenty-seven dive and torpedo bombers after Fletcher. But American radar proved a huge advantage, plotting the inbound raiders. A combat air patrol (CAP) of Grumman Wildcats clawed for altitude and pounced on the searching Japanese with lethal results. Nine bombers went down, as did three F4Fs. In the milling twilight confusion, some of the surviving Japanese overflew Task Force Seventeen. A few entered *Yorktown*'s traffic pattern but escaped the astonished Americans. The eighteen remaining Japanese bombers navigated 120 miles to their own decks and recovered at the end of a long, confusing day.

At sunset on May 7, 1942, for the first time in millennia of naval combat, a fleet engagement had been fought beyond range of sailors' vision.

More action was due the next day.

JAPANESE TORPEDOES

Captain Kamero Sonokawa was a combat aviator and staff officer throughout the Pacific War. Interviewed for the U.S. Strategic Bombing Survey in 1945, he reported:

Although the ordnance department claimed that the torpedoes could be dropped at an altitude of 500 meters, we found by experience that only 10 per cent would run properly at 200 meters and 50 per cent at 100 meters. Consequently, an effort was made to drop at from 20 to 50 meters. Since the aircraft torpedo was dropped at short ranges, the low altitude also afforded protection because of depressing limit of AA guns. Pilots were instructed to attempt to drop the torpedo in such a manner that it struck the ship immediately after it leveled off at set depth. Of course conditions varied but a standard drop was made from a range of 600 to 400 meters, at a speed of 160 to 170 knots and at an altitude of from 20 to 50 meters. The aircraft torpedo was armed immediately after striking the water. It weighed 800 kg. [1,760 pounds] and had a 145 kg. [320-pound] warhead. The above tactics were used by our carrier planes against your *Lexington*. After the battle of the Coral Sea the size of the warhead was increased to 220 kg. [485 pounds].

CORAL SEA: DAY TWO

As before, Japanese carrier- and land-based aircraft began the day by seeking the U.S. force. Almost simultaneously the Americans lofted eighteen scout-bombers on a two hundred-mile search. Within minutes of 8:20 both sides learned the other's location, nearly 250 statute miles apart. Though the Japanese planes outranged the Americans', both forces turned to engage.

Shokaku and *Zuikaku* combined to launch fifty-one dive and torpedo bombers screened by eighteen Zeroes. In contrast, *Lexington* and *Yorktown* dispatched separate strike groups totaling sixty attackers with fifteen Wildcat escorts. It was a close race as both sides launched within ten minutes of each other.

Mitsubishi A6M2 Zero fighters aboard the Japanese carrier *Zuikaku* in the two-day Battle of the Coral Sea, May 1942. *Courtesy Tailhook Association.*

The Yorktowners arrived first, finding the enemy force partially concealed by clouds. The strike leader, Commander William Burch, orbited his Dauntlesses to allow the Devastators to arrive for a combined bombing-torpedo attack. The SBDs rolled into their dives shortly before 11:00 a.m., opposed by sixteen Zeros. *Zuikaku* was obscured by clouds, so the Dauntlesses concentrated on *Shokaku*, inflicting major damage to the flight deck and forecastle. Two SBDs went down, including Lieutenant Joseph J. Powers who had vowed "to lay one on the flight deck"—and did it. Two Zeros also splashed, but the remaining TBDs missed with their nine torpedoes, leaving *Shokaku* damaged but operable.

Lexington Air Group was thirty minutes behind. By then *Zuikaku* was visible, and a few Lex SBDs split their attack, adding another hit on *Shokaku*. Cloud cover favored the defenders, however, and few Dauntlesses found a target. Again the TBDs were ineffective, scoring no hits with their eleven torpedoes. The Zeroes won a victory of sorts, splashing three Wildcats for no further losses.

Before the last American planes departed the area, their own ships were dodging bombs and torpedoes. At 11:00 Lex's radar "painted" hostile aircraft inbound from the north, distance seventy-five miles—good performance for the equipment. It gave the defenders twenty-five minutes to react.

The Japanese targeted both carriers, about a mile and a half apart, with most attackers getting in above the CAP. *Yorktown* evaded the "fish" aimed at her, but *Lexington*, bigger and less agile, took two torpedo hits. Shipboard gunners downed four attackers before additional damage could be inflicted.

Aichi dive bombers then swarmed both flattops. Attacking from fourteen thousand feet, they committed nineteen on *Lexington* and fourteen against *Yorktown*. "Lady Lex" took two hits, starting fires that proved fatal. *Yorktown*'s attackers scored a serious center hit and perhaps twelve rattling near misses that sprung plates.

Exiting the area, the Japanese encountered Wildcats and Dauntlesses deployed on "inner air patrol." The SBDs were unable to compete with fast, agile Zeroes—three Dauntlesses dropped into the water, and three Wildcats also went down. Japanese losses to U.S. flak and fighters totaled twenty-three aircraft, but *Zuikaku* also pushed overboard a dozen that were badly damaged or took up space for homing aircraft.

Tactically the Japanese won, as *Lexington* was far more valuable than *Shoho*, but strategically the battle was a victory for the Allies: the Port Moresby landing was cancelled.

Coral Sea proved that carrier warfare imposed a high price. Each side lost a flattop. The U.S. Navy lost sixty-seven planes, and Japan lost at least sixty-nine as well as some patrol planes. Thus, the first carrier battle indicated that either side could expect to lose about half its embarked aircraft to combat, accidents, and wastage.

The battle cost the U.S. Navy 611 men from ships companies and thirty-five aircrew.

A *Lexington* SBD pilot, Lieutenant (jg) William E. Hall, survived the inner air patrol on May 8 to receive the Medal of Honor, while

Yorktown's Joe Powers and Lieutenant Milton Ricketts, a *Yorktown* engineer, were posthumously decorated.

Badly damaged, *Shokaku* was forced out of the area, en route to repair in Japan. *Zuikaku* sustained no material damage, but her air group had been depleted, effectively removing Admiral Isoroku Yamamoto's CarDiv Five from the next crucial operation. The ninety prewar aircrew who died at Coral Sea began a slow hemorrhaging for the Japanese that could not be stanched.

"MIDWAY TO VICTORY"

A month before Coral Sea, Admiral Yamamoto had convinced the naval general staff to launch Operation MI, the seizure of Midway Island 1,300 miles northwest of Oahu. Though prudence would have dictated waiting until Fifth Carrier Division with *Shokaku* and *Zuikaku* could join the four ships of CarDivs One and Two, Yamamoto was in a hurry. He wanted to destroy the Pacific Fleet's remaining flattops before America's enormous industrial power came to bear. His self-allotted six-month timetable after the Pearl Harbor triumph was ticking away.

The Japanese knew that the Americans had to defend Midway, thus forcing the Imperial Navy's doctrinal decisive battle. The concept of "a Pacific Jutland" appealed to Tokyo—a titanic engagement based on the 1916 clash between the British and German fleets in the North Sea. Victorious in one conclusive battle, Japan would achieve its strategic aims. With *Akagi*, *Kaga*, *Soryu*, and *Hiryu* against an estimated two U.S. carriers, Operation MI shaped up as a near certainty, even considering land-based aircraft on Midway.

To a large extent, the Battle of Midway was won before the first aircraft launched. Admiral Nimitz's gifted cryptanalysts gleaned the basics and many details of Yamamoto's plan, allowing the PacFleet commander to deploy his forces accordingly. *Enterprise* and *Hornet* in Task Force Sixteen returned to Pearl Harbor, while *Yorktown* with Task Force Seventeen limped home with its Coral Sea bomb damage. In merely three days "Old Yorky" was sufficiently repaired for sea, her weary air group largely replaced by *Saratoga*'s, as "Sara" remained on the West Coast.

Nimitz knew that Vice Admiral Chuichi Nagumo's carriers would approach Midway on June 4, part of a larger scheme involving the invasion force and supporting units, plus submarines. Task Forces Sixteen and Seventeen waited northeast of Midway, aided by long-range Consolidated PBYs from the atoll itself.

The senior American was Rear Admiral Frank Jack Fletcher, who had ridden *Yorktown* since early in the year. A non-aviator, he benefited from an excellent staff. Vice Admiral William Halsey was beached with illness, replaced by Rear Admiral Raymond Spruance, whose cruisers had screened *Enterprise* for months.

With overwhelming surface strength—eleven battleships and sixteen cruisers—Yamamoto was confident of crushing the defenders if it came to a gun battle. He did not know that Nimitz deployed 232 carrier aircraft and 115 ashore, thus outnumbering *Kido Butai*'s embarked squadrons—though the Japanese enjoyed a qualitative edge.

Early on June 4 Nagumo launched 108 planes against Midway, which detected the inbound threat by radar. Marine Corps fighters scrambled to intercept but were badly mauled by combat-experienced pilots flying superior aircraft. Of twenty-five Brewster F2As and Grumman F4Fs, sixteen were shot down with most of the pilots killed. The Japanese lost eleven planes while bombing Midway's facilities.

The defenders responded when Nagumo's location was reported by PBY patrol planes. Between 7:10 and 8:20 a.m., Midway-based Army B-26s and B-17s, Navy TBFs, and Marine SBDs and SB2Us attacked *Kido Butai*. Faced with Zeros and flak, eighteen Marauders, Avengers, and scout bombers were downed without inflicting damage upon the enemy.

After an hour's respite the Japanese faced three carrier-based torpedo attacks. *Hornet*'s VT-8 attacked at 9:20, losing all fifteen Devastators. *Enterprise*'s VT-6 lost ten of fourteen an hour later, shortly followed by *Yorktown*'s VT-3. Two of the latter escaped but ditched en route home. That morning ended the Devastator's career, with four surviving of forty-one launched. Combined with VT-8's detachment ashore, which lost five of six Avengers, the "torpeckers" sustained an 89 percent attrition.

THE SAGA OF TORPEDO THREE

When most of Saratoga Air Group went aboard *Yorktown* before Midway, one of the torpedo pilots was a noncommissioned flier, Chief Aviation Pilot Wilhelm Esders. He had been in the squadron since 1938 and represented the high degree of experience in prewar units. Ten of Torpedo Squadron Three's planes were shot down attacking the Japanese carriers, leaving only Esders's and another Devastator still flying. Esders recalled the incident:

> Four Zeros chased me twenty to twenty-five miles.... The last (one) flew alongside about ten feet off my wingtip. The pilot...raised his right hand...apparently executing a half salute. What he intended to mean I will never know. Possibly "good show," "well done," or perhaps "let me get some more ammunition." Whatever it was, he joined the other three and headed for their fleet.
>
> Soon I was joined by Machinist Harry Corl with his gunner ARM3/c Lloyd Childers, and we headed for

Yorktown. We were both forced to ditch and were later rescued.

Radiomen-gunners were just as dedicated to fulfilling their mission as the pilots. They were not only well trained, but highly motivated, and would shoot their guns (until) they were incapable of carrying out their assignment. This happened to my gunner, Mike Brazier. He was hit at least seven times with 7.7mm ammo and twice with 20mm explosive projectiles. As if the small-caliber wounds were not enough, the 20mms exploded, blowing away all the flesh on his legs between the knees and ankles.

However, despite his enormous wounds, Mike somehow managed to change the coils in the radio receiver and helped me steer closer to the task force, where we ditched.

When I removed Mike from the aircraft I could see the large bones in each leg as I got him into the rubber raft. Of course, he bled to death. Yet this young man was still able to talk to me in the raft, expressing how badly he felt that he wasn't able to perform better or longer.

This was the kind of men we had in Torpedo Three.

Despite grievous losses, the sustained attacks kept Nagumo off balance. He lacked time to follow the day's operations plan, which called for a possible follow-up strike on Midway. When a cruiser-based scout reported *Yorktown*, the same deficit applied. While *Kido Butai*'s sweating ordnance crews slaved to rearm Nakajima bombers with torpedoes, continuing American air attacks compounded the problem.

The three U.S. carriers followed separate routes and fortunes. *Hornet*'s martinet air group commander insisted on seeking nonexistent enemy carriers to the west. His incompetent fighter commander ran all ten Wildcats out of fuel, while most of the SBDs straggled back to the ship or tried for Midway. Only Commander John Waldron's Torpedo Eight found the enemy, breaking formation to hunt to the southwest. He died with twenty-eight of his men.

Enterprise's Torpedo Squadron Six TBD Devastators ready to launch on the morning of June 4, 1942. Four of fourteen returned. *Courtesy Tailhook Association.*

Enterprise put up a strong team: thirty-two SBDs, fourteen TBDs, and ten Wildcats. But the launch dragged on while Lieutenant Commander C. Wade McClusky orbited with his Dauntlesses, burning fuel. Finally, he was ordered to "proceed on mission assigned" and led his two squadrons southwesterly, expecting to find Nagumo 155 nautical miles southwest, heading toward Midway. The TBDs and F4Fs proceeded independently, while the Wildcats mistakenly tagged onto *Hornet's* Devastators.

McClusky had graduated from Annapolis on June 4, 1926, and possessed considerable experience as a fleet aviator. A fighter pilot, he was new to dive bombers, but he was persistent in hunting

The most important tactical decision of the Battle of Midway was made by *Enterprise's* air group commander, C. Wade McClusky, who found the Japanese carriers by following a hunch. *Courtesy Tailhook Association.*

Nagumo. When his formation arrived at the expected interception point, he found only sea and sky, and continued on a few minutes more. He reasoned that his prey could not have advanced past the briefed contact point, so he turned northwesterly, paralleling Nagumo's expected track.

Still finding nothing after twenty more minutes, McClusky finally got a break. He found a Japanese destroyer headed northeast and reckoned it was joining the carriers. Taking his heading from the "tin can," he proceeded on course until a pale break appeared on the horizon. McClusky raised his binoculars and saw the Japanese striking force.

Unknown to McClusky, Task Force Seventeen was also engaged. *Yorktown* retained her scouts for close reconnaissance but launched eighteen SBDs, a dozen TBDs, and six Wildcats. The mission leader was Lieutenant Commander Maxwell F. Leslie, who lost his bomb shortly after departing the force. But he continued as briefed, searching to the southwest, and because he left later than Task Force Sixteen squadrons, he flew a straighter course to the target. As McClusky's Dauntlesses approached Nagumo from the southwest, Leslie closed from the southeast. The result was an historically significant coincidence—an almost simultaneous attack by three SBD squadrons.

Only the Yorktowners managed a nearly coordinated attack. As Lieutenant Commander Lance Massey's TBDs went for *Hiryu* to the north, Leslie's dive bombers selected *Soryu*. Massey died at the head of his squadron, while *Yorktown*'s six fighters fought a lopsided battle. Lieutenant Commander John S. Thach, inventor of the weaving tactic that bore his name, tried to support Massey but could not. One of his F4Fs was downed, but the outnumbered Grummans splashed three or more Zeros.

Between the torpedo planes and Thach's Wildcats, no Zeros intercepted SBDs during the attack. *Enterprise*'s fighters, circling high overhead, did not hear the Devastator squadron's calls for help.

Meanwhile, Leslie, without his bomb, led VB-3 down on *Soryu*. His pilots were good: they scored with three bombs that gutted her and killed nearly two-thirds of her crew. Bombing Three got away clean.

At nearly the same time there was a traffic jam overhead Carrier Division One. McClusky wanted to assign one carrier to his scouts and another to his bomber squadron, but doctrine and communication got scrambled. Marveling at the lack of interceptors, he split his dive flaps, nosed down, and drew a bead on the thirty-six thousand-ton *Kaga* steaming upwind.

Enterprise's biographer, Commander Edward P. Stafford, described the ephemeral moment:

> In a dive bomber's dream of perfection, the clean blue Dauntlesses—with their perforated dive flaps open at the trailing edges of their wings and their bing bombs tucked close and pointing home, the pilots straining forward, rudder-feet and stick-hands light and delicate, getting it just right as the yellow decks came up, left hands that would reach down and forward to release now resting on the cockpit edge, gunners lying on their backs behind the cocked twin barrels searching for the fighters that did not come—carved a moment out of eternity for man to remember forever.

McClusky's bomb missed, but five others struck home, turning the giant into a floating cauldron with more than eight hundred sailors killed.

However, in the confusion nearly thirty SBDs dived with McClusky—all except Bombing Six's skipper, Lieutenant Richard H. Best with two wingmen. Realizing what had happened, he pulled out of his dive and led his bobtailed flight a few miles farther. His target was Nagumo's flagship *Akagi*, which he boresighted. Dick Best claimed he was the best bomber in the Pacific Fleet, and he proved it. Diving broad on the port beam, he put his half-ton bomb within feet of the island. The weapon exploded against a loaded torpedo plane on the hangar deck, igniting uncontrollable fires. Best's two partners got near misses at the least—one possibly struck the hull. In any case, *Akagi* was doomed with one-sixth of her crew.

Then there was only one thing to do: pull in the flaps, shove up the power, and wave-hop through the outraged destroyers and cruisers defending the flattops.

Several SBDs were chased by vengeful Zeros. One managed to wound McClusky, but he escaped. However, *Enterprise* lost eighteen of her thirty-two scout bombers, including two out of action aboard *Yorktown*. "Yorky's" Max Leslie and his wingman ditched safely, while the rest of his squadron recovered aboard The Big E.

While Task Forces Sixteen and Seventeen sorted out who had done what, Japan's remaining flattop vowed to continue the fight.

An SBD scout-bomber narrowly misses USS *Hornet's* landing signal officer in an off-center landing. *Courtesy Tailhook Association.*

RETRIBUTION

Hiryu's crew watched the three pyres on the southern horizon with stunned awe. However, the "Flying Dragon" reacted quickly. Armed with the Americans' location and seeking retribution, she dispatched eighteen Vals with six Zeros. A second wave of ten torpedo planes with six fighters was readied to follow.

The first strike arrived overhead *Yorktown* just before noon. Wildcats and AA gunners splashed thirteen Aichis, but the survivors hit the target three times and scored two damaging near misses—an excellent performance. Admiral Fletcher was forced to transfer to a cruiser, ceding overall command to Spruance in *Enterprise*.

Though brought to a stop, *Yorktown* doused her fires and regained power, working up to nineteen knots two hours later. That was when *Hiryu*'s torpedo planes arrived.

The ten Nakajimas found an alerted CAP. *Yorktown*'s fighters splashed five B5Ns and a Zero, losing three F4Fs. But two Type 91 torpedoes plunged into *Yorktown*'s hull at 40 knots, eliminating electrical power needed to pump water or oil to correct a worsening list. Captain Elliot Buckmaster ordered abandon ship.

Only six planes returned to *Hiryu*, but she doggedly prepared to continue the battle with nine bombers and thirty-one Zeros, including orphans from other carriers.

If *Hiryu* knew where to find *Yorktown*, then *Enterprise* knew where to find *Hiryu*, thanks to a displaced *Yorktown* scout. Big E

After the morning strike by U.S. dive bombers eliminated three Japanese carriers, only *Hiryu* remained. She was destroyed by Douglas SBDs that afternoon, effectively ending the battle. *Courtesy Tailhook Association.*

launched twenty-six SBDs, a mixed lineup of her own and *York-town*'s overflow. They went without fighter escort as a hedge against an attack by another enemy carrier. *Hornet* launched a follow-up strike that trailed the *Enterprise* bombers.

Spruance's planes arrived over *Hiryu* at 5:00 that afternoon, unseen until too late. The strong combat air patrol downed two SBDs but could not prevent the others from pressing their attack. Bombing Six's CO Dick Best got his second hit of the day, followed by three more. Trailing pilots saw the carrier was doomed and switched their dives to a nearby battleship. *Hornet*'s pilots harassed some escorts, and the war-winning Dauntlesses turned for home.

Behind them the sun began its descent into the Pacific's western horizon.

Hiryu lingered until morning, by which time the other three imperial carriers had already sunk.

DAYS TWO AND THREE

That night three air groups of proud and tired U.S. aviators reflected on what they had lost and won. Then their pride turned to incredulity. Admiral Spruance withdrew, following orders to defend Midway rather than pursue a beaten enemy. His prudence was warranted, as a nocturnal surface fight with Japanese battleships and cruisers would only have gone one way.

June 5 passed largely without action as the Americans tried to sort out confusing patrol plane reports, and Spruance pondered his options. Finally, late that afternoon Task Force Sixteen launched fifty-eight scout bombers against a phantom carrier and found nothing. On the return leg thirty-two of the SBDs had a go at the destroyer *Tanikaze*. Having evaded two B-17 attacks already, she escaped damage again while downing an SBD. The other Douglases reached their flight decks, logging the first night combat "traps" in U.S. carrier history.

The third day of the battle, June 6, dawned with another opportunity for Task Force Sixteen. During the night two Japanese cruisers, *Mogami* and *Mikuma*, had collided en route to shell Midway. They reversed course, vainly trying to get out of air range, but were spotted by scouting SBDs. From barely one hundred miles range, *Enterprise* and *Hornet* sent off three powerful strikes totaling eighty-one Dauntlesses, the last three Devastators, and twenty-eight unnecessary Wildcats. In successive attacks *Mogami* was battered with five bombs but survived. *Mikuma* took hits that ignited secondary explosions—fatal damage to the 13,600-ton warship. Two attentive destroyers also were lightly damaged.

But the Imperial Navy was nothing if not persistent. That afternoon, nearly four hundred miles north-northeast of *Mikuma*, the submarine *I-168* penetrated the destroyer screen circling the crippled *Yorktown* and fired four torpedoes. One ripped apart the destroyer *Hammann* (DD-412) lashed alongside to support salvage efforts. Two more torpedoes smashed into "Yorky's" tortured hull, inflicting a death blow. She lingered until dawn the next morning when she capsized and sank. *I-168*'s attack killed some eighty men, though she succumbed to an American submarine a year later.

The Battle of Midway was over.

MIDWAY RECAP

Yorktown's loss hurt Nimitz; she was the most experienced American carrier, arguably with the finest staff afloat. But her sister *Enterprise* more than met the challenge and would prove essential to the Pacific Fleet in months to come.

The weak link in the American team was *Hornet*. Captain Marc Mitscher, a well-regarded early aviator, proved lacking as a carrier captain. In fairness, he lost much-needed training time during the

Doolittle operation, but he relied on unqualified subordinates, and he made some poor decisions, such as launching his short-ranged fighters first. Under a new skipper the ship did far better in the time remaining to her.

For Japan, Midway marked the fork in the victory road. Deprived of four carriers and 110 irreplaceable aircrew, Tokyo lost all its misplaced hope of forcing Washington into a settlement. While the Imperial Navy retained strong, capable players, it lacked America's depth of talent to come off the bench. In football terms, Team America now had possession and would run the ball the length of the field. Chester Nimitz quipped that the epic battle put America "about Midway to victory."

Additionally, Midway removed all doubt that the aircraft carrier had supplanted the battleship as the dominant player on the world's oceans.

GUADALCANAL

Only sixty days after Midway, the strategic balance shifted in America's favor. Following six months of playing defense, the Pacific Fleet launched the nation's first offensive of the Second World War. It occurred in an obscure part of the world few people had ever heard of.

Guadalcanal was the largest of the Solomon Islands, nearly eight hundred statute miles east of New Guinea and bordering the sea lanes from Hawaii to Australia. Japan had already recognized the island's worth, building a seaplane base at Tulagi, scene of the precursor to Coral Sea in May. Now, with an airfield on Guadal's northern plain, the island was an obvious choice for conquest. The First Marine Division was assigned the task, with air cover from *Enterprise*, newly repaired *Saratoga*, and *Wasp* transferred from the Atlantic.

Operation Watchtower kicked off August 7 with seventy-five ships in support. Now a vice admiral, Frank Jack Fletcher commanded the carriers; after Coral Sea and Midway he was the world's leading practitioner of flattop warfare. His planes quickly overcame the meager defenders, but the Imperial Navy took immediate notice. From six hundred miles northwest, the airfields at Rabaul, New Britain, launched twenty-seven twin-engine Mitsubishi bombers (later code-named Bettys) and nine Aichi dive bombers (Vals), escorted by seventeen expertly flown Zeros. The imperial fighters shot down ten carrier planes against two losses, and the bombers mortally damaged a transport while scalding a destroyer.

Combat continued the next day, and while Japanese losses exceeded American, Fletcher was concerned about his dwindling air strength. Additionally, the Marines were slow to unload the transports, exposing the precious flattops to greater danger. Fletcher asked permission of the theater command to pull out of range, and received it. While the Marines viciously condemned his action, clearly it was prudent. *Hornet* was the only other fleet carrier, and America would have no new flight decks until the following summer.

Meanwhile, Japanese surface forces intervened. Though outnumbered two to one, on the night of August 8–9, a powerful IJN cruiser force drubbed the American-Australian warships around Savo Island north of Guadalcanal. Four Allied cruisers were lost, leaving the transports wholly vulnerable. They had no choice but to hoist anchor and depart, still not fully unloaded.

The leathernecks ashore endured frequent bombing for several days until Marine squadrons arrived. On August 20 Wildcats and Dauntlesses landed at Henderson Field—named for the Marine dive bomber who died at Midway—delivered by the escort carrier *Long Island*.

Three days later Admiral Yamamoto set in motion a reinforcement effort. Nearly two thousand Japanese troops were embarked in transports heavily screened by escorts, intending to deliver the soldiers on August 24. Two Imperial Navy carrier forces were involved: Admiral Nagumo with *Shokaku* and *Zuikaku*, recovered from their Coral Sea drama, and the light carrier *Ryujo* operating independently under Rear Admiral Chuichi Hara.

The timing favored Japan. Fletcher, commanding Task Force Sixty-One, had detached *Wasp* for refueling when the crisis broke, again forcing him to fight outnumbered. Nonetheless, *Enterprise* and *Saratoga* turned toward the threat, their 154 tailhook planes opposing about 175 Japanese.

EASTERN SOLOMONS

The Battle of the Eastern Solomons on August 24 was fought over a wide area: Nagumo well to the north of Guadalcanal and Fletcher to the north and northeast. Action began that afternoon with *Ryujo* launching a small strike of Nakajima level bombers against Henderson Field that was intercepted by Marine Wildcats. Both sides lost three planes, but radar plots gave Fletcher a good idea of Hara's location.

Though Frank Jack Fletcher, riding *Saratoga*, had overall command of the U.S. carriers, the *Enterprise* operated semi-independently. Commanding the Big E's Task Force Sixty-One was Rear Admiral Thomas Kinkaid, who led *Yorktown*'s escorts at Coral Sea and *Enterprise*'s at Midway. Though not an aviator, like Fletcher he had Nimitz's confidence.

Both main carrier forces found each other about the same time, but Japanese communications proved superior. Nagumo lofted a strike shortly before 3:00, twenty-seven *Shokaku* and *Zuikaku* dive bombers with fifteen Zeros. Two *Enterprise* scouts nosed into an attack that scratched *Shokaku* but left her intact. Other Big E search teams also found enemy ships and attacked cruisers.

Fletcher stood by to repel boarders as his radar detected Nagumo's bombers inbound. The Japanese encountered fifty-three Wildcats airborne, but some were poorly positioned to intercept. Sara and Big E quickly launched aircraft on deck to reduce the fire hazard, moments before the Aichis rolled in at 4:30. They concentrated on *Enterprise,* which put up a spirited defense, but the Japanese pilots were determined. Two put 550-pound bombs within feet of each other, holing the hull and detonating ammunition. A third bomb struck forward, blowing a ten-foot hole in the flight deck but causing little structural damage.

Four Aichis, thinking the carrier doomed, diverted to attack the escorting battleship *North Carolina* (BB-55). All four were shot into the sea.

Wildcats and AA guns took their toll on the attackers—twenty-six in all. Five F4Fs were also downed, including victims of "friendly" antiaircraft gunners. *Zuikaku* alone lost her entire nine-plane bomber squadron.

AA ACTION AT EASTERN SOLOMONS

Enterprise came under heavy air attack during the Eastern Solomons battle of August 24. The action was described by the Big E's gunnery officer, Lieutenant Commander Elias B. Mott.

> We were absolutely unable to see the planes due to the fact that they were so high and small, and that it was late in the afternoon and the sky was considerably bluer than it would have been earlier.... About 1712 [5:12 p.m.] the first Jap dive bomber commenced its attack.
>
> One of our forward 20mm gunners opened up on him when he was at 10,000 feet, and this was the signal for the formation. Everybody opened up with five-inch and with

automatic weapons. The attack lasted five or six minutes, and during that time they came down one after another starting from the port bow and working around to the starboard quarter. At one time I remember seeing five Japanese dive bombers in line all the way from about 2,000 feet to 12,000...

We had the old 1.1 inchers without power drive and about thirty-two 20mm and of course our eight five-inch guns. Five-inch on local control did very well. They hit several planes on the nose...and the planes disintegrated. The tremendous number of 20mms that we were able to bring to bear on each plane caused them either to miss or to drop in flames.... However, as they worked around toward the stern, where we had little firepower protection, when they came down although we hit them, they were able to take aim and we sustained three hits. One on five-inch Gun Group Number Three; one on the flight deck aft, which penetrated down three decks; and another one just abaft the island structure on the flight deck. This was an instantaneous bomb. The one that hit Gun Group Number Three wiped out the entire group of thirty-nine men.

My impression of the battle was that if we had a little more firepower, it might have been different. It looked to me that if you had enough guns that the enemy planes would be in trouble, would have to swerve off or...the pilot would be killed. However, in a dive-bombing attack, it's not just a case of getting one plane or ten or even fifteen. You've got to get them all, you can't afford to get hit.

Nagumo's second wave, almost equal to the first, might have done severe damage to *Enterprise*, if it weren't for poor Japanese communication. The follow-up strike returned to CarDiv Five minus five planes.

Leading *Enterprise*'s air group was Lieutenant Commander Maxwell F. Leslie, skipper of Bombing Three at Midway. New to the Avenger, he nonetheless navigated to an erroneous contact report (waves breaking over a reef) and back again, reaching *Saratoga* to make his fourth landing in a TBF—his first such landing at night.

Meanwhile, Lieutenant Turner F. Caldwell took eleven orphaned *Enterprise* SBDs to Henderson Field. Designated "Flight 300" in the Big E's air plan, they remained ashore for more than a month, sinking a transport and a destroyer.

The action was not over, however, as Hara's *Ryujo* task force remained the focus of *Saratoga*'s air group, led by the tough, capable Commander Harry Don Felt, who had helped inaugurate the SBD to fleet service. Flying his personal Dauntless, "Queen Bee," he orchestrated a coordinated attack of thirty dive bombers and eight torpedo planes against the enemy force.

Felt directed twenty-one SBDs and five TBFs to hit *Ryujo* while the others went for the large cruiser *Tone*. Attacking from fifteen thousand feet, Bombing Three and Scouting Three contributed to the tonnage dropped, but the Midway-experienced VB-3 did most of the damage. The carrier launched fighters just before bombs began to fall, too late to intervene.

The action report summarized, "Three direct bomb hits and several very close misses were observed. A torpedo hit was observed on the starboard side forward.... The carrier flight deck from amidships aft was smoking fiercely and flames were seen shooting out from the hangar deck. Planes rendezvoused in small groups and proceeded to their base."

Tone dodged the torpedoes aimed at her.

Separately, Sara launched two SBDs and five TBFs responding to a report of a large surface force. Led by Lieutenant Robert M. Elder, one of the finest aviators afloat, the small formation found the battle-ship *Mutsu* with seaplane carrier *Chitose* and four escorts. Dropping out of the late-afternoon sky through heavy flak, the Dauntlesses put both bombs close aboard, opening *Chitose*'s hull and destroying aircraft on deck. She was towed to Truk in the Carolines for repair and eventual conversion to a conventional carrier.

Enterprise reeled from her casualties, seventy-eight killed and ninety wounded. The toll was a shock: in the previous nine months of war she had lost fewer than one hundred dead. Clearly, carrier warfare would continue exacting a price.

The Eastern Solomons battle gained the Marines on shore a valu-able respite from Japanese reinforcement. Most of the Japanese troops stymied in their effort to reach Guadalcanal were delivered later, but lacking many weapons. Meanwhile, action continued at sea.

On August 31 *Saratoga* was sidelined for the second time that year. Another of Japan's ubiquitous submarines caught her off San Cristobal Island and scored with one torpedo, keeping her ineffective almost until year's end.

Meanwhile, carrier squadrons cycled in and out of Guadalcanal, code name "Cactus." Apart from *Enterprise*'s Flight 300, Scouting Three joined the "Cactus Air Force" for six weeks in September and October. *Wasp*'s Scouting Squadron Seventy-One flew up from the rear area to remain from late September to early November. Their presence was important to the perennially shorthanded air garrison.

SANTA CRUZ

The malarial Santa Cruz Islands bear three hundred miles east of the Solomons, and might remain unknown to history but for the fourth carrier battle of World War II's Pacific Campaign, fought nearby in October 1942.

In a rare example of strategic cooperation, the Japanese Army and Navy put aside their bitter enmity long enough to plan a serious effort to end the Guadalcanal campaign. Coordinated with a large Imperial Army offensive ashore, the Japanese Navy sought to defeat America's remaining carriers, depriving the Marines of essential support at sea.

Once again Vice Admiral Chuichi Nagumo headed the Imperial Navy force, sisters *Shokaku* and *Zuikaku* entering their third carrier duel. The twenty-four thousand-ton fleet carrier *Junyo*, recently converted from a liner, nearly matched "Sho" and "Zui" in tonnage, with fewer aircraft. Additionally, the eleven thousand-ton light carrier *Zuiho* faced her first action. In typical Japanese fashion, several surface units were dispersed ahead of the carriers, totaling forty ships.

Commanding the U.S. carriers was Rear Admiral Thomas Kinkaid, a veteran of Eastern Solomons. He was outnumbered as no other U.S. admiral ever would be: *Enterprise* (Task Force Sixteen) and *Hornet* (Task Force Seventeen) against four imperial carriers. *Enterprise* operated the new Air Group Ten, entering its first battle.

The Big E's screen included the new battleship *South Dakota* (BB-57), two cruisers, and nine destroyers. *Hornet* was escorted by four cruisers and six destroyers.

Catalina patrol planes found *Kido Butai* on the morning of October 25, about four hundred statute miles north of Task Force Sixty-One. Kinkaid closed the distance, hoping to strike while daylight permitted. He sent off two dozen planes at mid-afternoon, but Nagumo, knowing he had been spotted, opened the range. *Enterprise*'s abortive strike returned in darkness, losing seven precious aircraft.

That evening, with two more flight decks, Nagumo's air strength overshadowed Fletcher's by 194 operational planes to 137, a 40 percent advantage.

Shortly before 7:00 a.m. on October 26, scouts from both sides found the opposition. Knowing that the first blow was crucial in carrier combat, Nagumo and Kinkaid both cleared their decks, eager to get in the initial strike. In barely forty minutes *Kido Butai* put up sixty-four aircraft led by Lieutenant Sadamu Takahashi, including twenty-one dive bombers, twenty torpedo planes, and a new "tracker" aircraft, designed to pursue any information obtained en route.

Enterprise entered her third carrier battle in the October 1942 engagement off the Santa Cruz Islands. A Scouting Squadron Ten Dauntless enters the pattern before landing. *Courtesy Tailhook Association.*

But the Americans got in the first blow. Two *Enterprise* scouts, having monitored other planes' contact reports, diverted from their assigned sector, first to investigate a battleship report, then the carrier force. The leader was Lieutenant Stockton Birney Strong, one of the most aggressively capable aviators of his generation. During Eastern Solomons he had passed up a shot at enemy carriers to take his information directly to the Big E. He would not be doing that a second time. Together with Ensign Charles Irvine, he pushed his hunt eighty miles beyond his own sector—and his persistence was rewarded.

Zeros were harrying the on-scene scouts, handing Strong and Irvine an unexpected gift: a clear shot at what Strong called "a big carrier," actually *Zuiho*, steaming near the cloud-covered *Shokaku*. The two SBDs rolled into their seventy-degree dives, tracked the target from astern, and expertly put both five hundred-pounders through the flight deck aft. "Auspicious Phoenix" was effectively out of the battle, unable to recover aircraft. Strong and Irvine's gunners shot down a pursuing Zero, then both pilots squeaked back to *Enterprise* on fumes, finishing one of the finest missions ever flown from aircraft carriers.

However, *Zuiho*'s contribution to the first strike was already airborne. So was Kinkaid's first launch, a hasty scramble of twenty-one *Hornet* SBDs and TBFs escorted by eight F4Fs. They were followed by twenty-four more planes, while *Enterprise* put up a fighter-heavy launch of ten bombers with eight Wildcats. The Americans now had seventy-one aircraft outbound, but they lacked *Kido Butai*'s institutional integration.

The opposing air groups crossed paths before 9:00, each side eyeing the other. *Zuiho* Zero pilots hit the *Enterprise* fliers from six o'clock high, knocking down two Avengers and three Wildcats while losing four Mitsubishis. Three other American pilots had to abort with battle damage, reducing the strike to ten planes including the new fighter skipper, Lieutenant Commander James H. Flatley, a Coral Sea veteran. The Big E's fliers found no carriers, so they attacked Rear Admiral Hiroaki Abe's vanguard force and damaged the cruiser *Chikuma*.

Hornet's second strike also came upon Abe, adding one more bomb hit. At that point two-thirds of the U.S. offensive capability was spent.

But the first *Hornet* launch struck gold. The SBDs were led by Lieutenant Commander William J. Widhelm, who had missed the chance to bomb carriers at Midway. He set his sights on the nearest undamaged carrier.

However, *Shokaku*'s newly installed radar revealed the *Hornet* strike at a reported ninety-seven miles—incredible performance for the period, and far better than the Type 2 set's official range of sixty miles on formations. Undoubtedly the atmospherics favored the Japanese with exceptional readings, as "ducting" possibly funneled the beam along an unusually narrow front, possibly yielding inaccurate figures.

No matter: *Shokaku* gained precious time to prepare for action with damage control crews taking precautions. Nagumo's CAP set upon the *Hornet* formation as twenty-three Zeros splashed three escorting Wildcats and two SBDs, including the flamboyant "Gus" Widhelm who ditched nearby and cheered his friends from his raft. The air battle cost Nagumo two fighters before the Dauntlesses began pounding half-ton bombs into *Shokaku*'s ancient pine deck.

Left to lead the attack was Lieutenant James M. "Moe" Vose, who recalled, "I was first to dive. Widhelm's people had joined on mine and I saw three hits on *Shokaku*. As we pulled out we were taking evasive action, under continued Zero attack."

Shokaku took at least four, possibly six, hits, mostly aft. Serious fires erupted, requiring five hours to extinguish, and leaving the deck "looking like an earthquake fault zone." She lost 140 of her crew and more than fifty fliers in the battle.

Meanwhile, Task Force Seventeen knew that trouble was inbound. Alerted by airborne pilots, *Hornet* prepared for action, but U.S. radar only registered the raiders at forty statute miles. Few of the thirty-seven available F4Fs could be vectored onto the Japanese formation, leaving *Hornet*'s main defense to the force's AA guns, which opened fire shortly past 9:00.

Lieutenant Takahashi's sixteen attacking pilots were pros: they hit *Hornet* with three bombs in as many minutes. A fourth plane, obviously crippled, dived into the ship's island, spewing flaming gasoline.

Then the twenty Nakajimas arrived. Expertly splitting port and starboard for an "anvil" attack, they torpedoed *Hornet* twice. She went dead in the water, an easy target for a remaining Aichi that suicided into the hull.

While the cruiser *Northampton* prepared a tow line for *Hornet*, the second Japanese strike rolled in: nineteen bombers, sixteen torpedo planes, and eight fighters. Several Fighting Squadron Ten "Grim Reapers" intercepted, living up to their name. One stellar pilot, Lieutenant Stanley "Swede" Vejtasa, expended all his ammunition on two Nakajimas and five Aichis, an unheard of feat for U.S. airmen. Nevertheless, the dive bombers hit Big E twice and landed a plate-rattling near miss.

Zuikaku's Nakajima squadron bracketed *Enterprise*, seeking to duplicate *Hornet*'s fate. On the bridge was Captain Osborne Hardison, only five days in command. His expert bridge crew neatly dodged nine torpedoes that boiled past the hull, likely an American record.

One heroic Nakajima pilot, his plane aflame, flew into the escorting destroyer *Smith*, setting her on fire. The skipper steered into the battleship *South Dakota*'s wake, dousing the flames. *South Dakota*'s gunners claimed twenty-six shootdowns in the attack—clearly an exaggeration but indicative of the abrupt role reversal of battleships and carriers. The battlewagons now served as high-powered escorts for the flattops.

Nagumo's second strike had taken crippling losses: twenty-one of thirty-five bombers versus six American.

Meanwhile, returning *Hornet* pilots from the *Shokaku* attack drew "friendly fire" from American ships. Lieutenant "Moe" Vose summarized, "This was understandable, as the force had been under severe attack. The *Hornet* was badly hit and unable to take us, and although *Enterprise* was on fire forward with a bomb hit aft, we still

The U.S. task force under attack during the Battle of Santa Cruz in October 1942. Thick antiaircraft fire screens blot the sky against Japanese raiders. *Courtesy USN.*

recovered aboard. On landing, the aft elevator was jammed in the down position so it was necessary to catch the number one wire."

Kido Butai's third launch was seventeen *Junyo* bombers escorted by a dozen Zeros, arriving overhead Task Force Sixteen at 11:20. They near-missed *Enterprise* and hit *South Dakota* and the cruiser

During the Santa Cruz battle *Enterprise's* landing signal officer, Lt. Robin Lindsey, brought dozens of planes aboard the Big E's crowded deck with one elevator stuck in the down position. *Courtesy Tailhook Association.*

San Juan, to little effect. That minimal success cost them eleven planes.

Dozens of TF-61 aircraft remained overhead, gasping for fuel. *Enterprise*'s talented landing signal officer, Lieutenant Robin Lindsey, took aboard pilots from both carriers. He continued landing planes until the flight deck was nearly full. The last pilot in the pattern was Swede Vejtasa, whose trust in Lindsey was justified. The LSO gave him an early "cut" signal, and the new ace skillfully snagged the rearmost wire, "locking" the deck: there was no more room. Sixteen remaining pilots ditched or headed for distant Espiritu Santo.

While *Northampton* was laboriously towing *Hornet*, *Junyo* and *Zuikaku*'s persistent air groups flung three more attacks at the Americans. They totaled fourteen torpedo planes, six bombers, and nineteen Zeros, adding another torpedo and bomb hit, leaving the pummeled carrier without power. There was no option but to scuttle *Hornet*, though she resisted, taking torpedoes and hundreds of shells from her escorts. Finally, two Japanese destroyers put her under in the early morning hours. She sank with 118 crew and twenty-two fliers dead or missing.

Kido Butai had sent 138 sorties against TF-61, more than Nagumo launched at Midway and Eastern Solomons combined. But in exchange for sinking *Hornet* and damaging *Enterprise*, the Japanese incurred crippling personnel casualties, losing 145 experienced pilots and aircrew—even more than at Midway. The attrition could be replaced in numbers, but never in quality.

Unlike Eastern Solomons two months before, Santa Cruz was a clear Japanese tactical victory. But Tokyo's combined Army and Navy strategy failed to end the Guadalcanal campaign, where the bloodletting continued.

The U.S. Pacific Fleet was left with one fast carrier, the battered *Enterprise*, which counted forty-four sailors killed and sixteen fliers missing. Her damage control team again demonstrated its expertise, and she was back in action in two weeks.

Again the high price of carrier combat was evident: Kinkaid lost eighty-one aircraft (59 percent) and Nagumo ninety-nine (50 percent).

As PacFleet's only available big-deck carrier, *Enterprise* was a priceless asset that season. Air Group Ten cycled in and out of Henderson Field on Guadalcanal during the November crisis, contributing to the ultimate defeat of Japan's final effort to retrieve the situation. When Tokyo decided to withdraw its remaining troops in February, the vital six-month campaign reached its sanguinary end.

INTERIM: 1943

In early 1943 only *Saratoga* and *Enterprise* remained available in the Pacific, and Big E was overdue for refit. But help came from an unlikely source: the Royal Navy. Between January and May HMS *Victorious* had received modifications on the East Coast and at Pearl Harbor to accommodate American aircraft and support equipment. The veteran of the *Bismarck* hunt and Mediterranean convoys, codenamed "Robin" in Allied message traffic, filled the breach until new-generation American carriers arrived later that summer.

Saratoga and *Victorious* briefly operated as Task Force Thirty-Six, supporting amphibious landings farther up the Solomons chain, with U.S. and British squadrons sometimes "cross decking" to fill operational requirements, occasionally with U.S. escort carriers. Both navies flew Grumman aircraft—Avenger torpedo planes and Wildcat fighters—but some semantics needed to be thrashed out. For instance, British landing signal officers were "batsmen," catapults were "boosters," and aircraft elevators were "lifts." "Vic" returned to Britain in October, but she would be back steaming alongside her allies before war's end.

NEW BLOOD

That August the wartime generation of fast carriers began arriving in Hawaii. The spanking new *Essex* (CV-9) and *Yorktown* (CV-10) promised much and delivered on that potential. In the next two years they and their ten sisters carried the main burden of PacFleet carrier requirements.

In fact, the Pacific War was waged and won in shipyards as much as in combat. Whereas prewar carriers such as *Yorktown* and *Enterprise* required between three and four years from keel-laying to commissioning, the wartime Essexes typically took sixteen to twenty months. The record was *Franklin* (CV-13), produced by Newport News in only fourteen months.

The Essex class has been called "the DC-3 of aircraft carriers" for versatility and longevity. Twenty-four units were delivered from 1943 to 1950, and it remains the most-produced fleet carrier design of all time, the last being retired in 1991.

The new generation of carriers arrived in Hawaii in the summer of 1943. USS *Essex*, lead ship of the CV-9 class, preceded a dozen of her sisters in Pacific combat. *Courtesy Tailhook Association.*

Although originally conceived as a somewhat larger *Yorktown* when ordered in July 1940, CV-9 possessed increased operability and survivability. As with *Wasp* (CV-7), the midship elevator was moved to port, allowing more flexibility in flight deck operations for a larger air group. The early design envisioned two flight deck catapults and a transverse "cat" to launch planes off the hangar deck—an option seldom used. Defensive measures included additional armor, greater compartmentalization, and much increased antiaircraft armament. Standard displacement rose from 19,800 in the Yorktowns to 27,100 for early Essexes.

The first three ships were laid down before Pearl Harbor, becoming *Essex*, *Lexington* (CV-16), and *Bunker Hill* (CV-17). Orders for ten more were placed before January 1942.

The Essexes proved near-perfect weapons for the Pacific Theater. They displaced one-third more than the Yorktowns, possessing excellent range and room for nearly one hundred aircraft. More and better radars with a fully integrated combat information center gave task force fighter directors a 360-degree perspective almost from sea level to about thirty thousand feet. Combined with new four-channel VHF radios, the fast carriers' 1943–44 air defense capability exceeded anything previously deployed.

Meanwhile, a hasty program to convert cruiser hulls to light carriers (CVLs) was producing results. The Independence (CVL-22) class got a head start with light cruiser hulls, the first five laid down by New York Shipbuilding of Camden, New Jersey, in 1941. They were commissioned at the rate of almost one a month through 1943, requiring a median eighteen months for conversion and completion.

When delivered, the CVLs displaced about 14,700 tons, operating thirty or more aircraft. Capable of 31 knots, they could steam with their Essex-class teammates.

The same month that *Essex* and *Yorktown* reached Pearl, *Independence* and *Princeton* (CV L-23) went operational. They were followed by *Lexington*, *Bunker Hill*, and three more CVLs through year-end.

NEW PLANES FOR NEW SHIPS

With new ships came new aircraft. The TBF Avenger bomber, deployed aboard carriers since Guadalcanal, remained for "the duration." Big, long-ranged, and versatile, with its three-man crew it excelled at torpedo and bombing attack plus scouting and antisubmarine patrol.

The Pacific Fleet's spearheading fighter, the Grumman F6F, reported aboard in 1943, here landing aboard the light carrier *Cowpens*. Hellcats largely destroyed Japanese airpower in the last two years of the war. *Courtesy author's collection.*

In the summer of 1943 the long-serving F4F Wildcat was replaced by Grumman's bigger, faster, longer-ranged F6F Hellcat. Combined with radio and shipboard radar, Hellcats would make fast carriers nearly invulnerable to conventional air attack. F6Fs largely destroyed Japanese airpower, credited with nearly as many enemy aircraft as Army fighters in the Pacific and China theaters combined. From early 1944 onward, Hellcats also became the finest naval night fighter of the war.

Beginning in late 1943 the Douglas Dauntless slowly was replaced by the Curtiss SB2C Helldiver. Though faster than the SBD, the '2C was no better as a bomber and suffered a painfully lengthy gestation. It entered combat during two carrier strikes on Rabaul, New Britain, in November but would not fully replace the Dauntless until July the following year.

Vought's distinctive F4U Corsair was America's first 400-mph single-engine production aircraft but poor carrier suitability limited its fleet service until 1944. *Courtesy author's collection.*

Almost lost in the shuffle was Vought's promising F4U Corsair. The cutting-edge design with its inverted gull wings first flew in 1940 but encountered serious problems in carrier suitability. The first two squadrons never deployed with the world-class fighter, VF-12 transitioning to F6Fs for a *Saratoga* cruise in 1943, and VF-17 riding *Bunker Hill* to Hawaii where Hellcats came aboard. Lieutenant Commander Tom Blackburn's Corsair pilots groused at their banishment to the Solomons where they rang up a stellar record operating from land bases. However, they did cycle through *Bunker Hill* during one of two Rabaul strikes in November.

Meanwhile, two Navy Corsair night fighter units were deployed: VF(N)-75 flying in the Solomons, while VF(N)-101 defied conventional wisdom by operating four-plane detachments from *Enterprise* and *Intrepid* (CV-11) in early 1944. Marine F4U squadrons would retrieve the Corsair's reputation by flying from carriers at year's end.

But aircraft and aviators were not enough. Linked by radio and radar, they needed fighter direction officers (FDOs), men specially selected for their vital task during a period when radar ranked second in priority only to the U.S. Navy's contribution to the Manhattan project. Former teachers and stockbrokers were preferred as prospective FDOs: men who could communicate clearly, assess priorities, and think on their feet. Their esoteric skills were increasingly called upon as the war progressed.

CENTPAC OFFENSIVE

The new carriers launched the Central Pacific offensive when *Essex*, *Yorktown*, and *Independence* sent strikes against Marcus Island on August 31, 1943. With more new-generation flattops becoming available, the standard task group organization became two Essexes and two Independence light carriers, with as many as five groups comprising the Fast Carrier Task Force (FCTF). Each task group included escorting cruisers and destroyers, often with battleships attached for additional antiaircraft firepower.

Every strike mission began with ordnance men who "built bombs," as these "ordies" who rolled inert weapons onto the hangar deck for loading onto aircraft. *Courtesy Tailhook Association.*

In November the Pacific Fleet flexed its muscles during two attacks against the Japanese naval-air bastion on Rabaul, New Britain. Covering the Bougainville amphibious landing, on November 5 Rear Admiral Frederick Sherman's bobtailed force launched ninety-seven sorties, targeting the ten Japanese cruisers in the large harbor. Old timer *Saratoga* and the new CVL *Princeton* put up every plane available, following an attack by Fifth Air Force bombers. While the tailhookers were engaged, their ships were capped by land-based fighters. The plan worked: eight of the ten enemy cruisers were hit, four seriously, against ten U.S. planes lost.

Six days later Rear Admiral Alfred E. Montgomery's new task group augmented Sherman's two decks, observing the twenty-fifth anniversary of Armistice Day. Three new-generation carriers contributed most of the weight to the attack: *Essex*, her sister *Bunker Hill*, and *Independence*, the first light carrier. The two-pronged American attack inflicted further damage on the seven thousand-ton cruiser *Agano*, but weather and defenses diluted the effects.

Rabaul offered a violent response, launching about 120 sorties opposed by a heavy CAP. The carrier fighters—including land-based Hellcats and Corsairs—eagerly claimed over 130 shootdowns, but splashed about thirty-five. Total U.S. losses were twenty-five planes, including four of *Bunker Hill*'s new SB2C Helldivers, led by Midway and Guadalcanal veteran James "Moe" Vose. But none of the Japanese got through—further proof of carrier aviation's ability to challenge land-based airpower. The combination of well-flown fighters, new-generation radar, and dedicated fighter directors had made a sterling debut.

That month escort carriers continued supporting amphibious operations in the Gilberts and Marshalls. Off Makin on November 24, *Liscome Bay*'s (CVE-56) early-morning lookouts sighted wakes inbound. The submarine *I-175* had closed to firing distance and put a torpedo in the sweet spot. It detonated bombs awaiting uploading for the day's missions and tore the ship in half. She sank with 644 of her 916 men, a stunning 70 percent. But she remained the only American carrier loss of 1943.

1944: YEAR OF DECISION

The FCTF alternately served under Admiral William F. Halsey's Third Fleet as Task Force Thirty-Eight and Admiral Raymond Spruance's Fifth Fleet as Task Force Fifty-Eight, shifting between each command for major operations. The fact that the two fleets used the same ships was only announced to the public at war's end.

Meanwhile, the growing number of escort carriers permitted more CVE groups. Four to six "jeeps" with destroyer screens steamed in each group, flying Avengers and the updated FM-2 "Wilder Wildcat" that replaced F4Fs from late 1943. Usually the escort carriers operated under Seventh Fleet control, covering amphibious landings, but as in the Atlantic they also served in anti-submarine units. Additionally, CVEs provided valuable service delivering replacement aircraft to forward-deployed fleet units.

Throughout the first half of 1944 the fast carriers struck a widening ring of targets from Kwajalein Atoll in the Marshalls to the Marianas. Notable were two raids against the Japanese fleet bastion at Truk ("Trook") in the Caroline Islands. The first in mid-February pitted eight carriers with some six hundred aircraft against 350 Japanese planes. It resulted in a spectacular early-morning combat that a Hellcat squadron commander termed "a Hollywood war," giving the U.S. air superiority over the "Gibraltar of the Pacific." With control of enemy airspace, dive bombers and torpedo planes had their pick of targets, sinking more than twenty combatant and merchant ships.

The first Truk strike featured a landmark event in U.S. carrier aviation: the first nocturnal air strike. *Enterprise* TBFs conducted a successful attack on anchored ships, locating them by radar and bombing from low level. The motivating influence was VT-10's skipper, Lieutenant Commander William I. Martin, whose aircrews hit a dozen ships while losing one aircraft.

A follow-up strike in April sealed Truk's fate—it was bypassed to wither with so many other Japanese garrisons.

Advanced fleet bases supported the fast carriers and other organizations. In the spring of 1944 Manus in the Admiralties, north of New Britain and New Guinea, was open for business. Journalist Dale P. Harper described the project as "one of the greatest and most speedy jobs of construction and base organization in world naval history."

In the Carolines was Ulithi Atoll with one of the finest anchorages in the Pacific. Operational from October, it could accommodate more than six hundred ships at a time.

It takes teamwork. Lt. Cdr. Jig Dog Ramage, gunner William Cawley, and Dauntless plane captain after a mission from *Enterprise*. *Courtesy author's collection.*

CLASH OF THE CARRIERS

The Central Pacific Offensive had an obvious destination: the Marianas. Located in mid-ocean, the Japanese-held islands boasted several airfields on Guam, Saipan, and Tinian. In American hands the bases would put B-29 bombers within range of Japan itself. There was no question of how Tokyo would react to Operation Forager.

American assault troops invaded Saipan on June 15, evoking a predictably heavy response from the Imperial Navy. There had been no fleet engagements in the twenty months since Santa Cruz, but the mandatory defense of Saipan ensured the largest carrier clash of all time. It pitted fifteen Task Force Fifty-Eight flattops against nine of the Japanese Mobile Fleet.

Vice Admiral Jisaburo Ozawa's plan called for land-based aircraft to shuttle between Guam and the Mobile Fleet carriers, placing the

Americans in an aerial vise. But after nearly three years of war, the Imperial Navy's quality and quantity were diminished. On the other side, Vice Admiral Marc Mitscher's TF-58 aircrews were thoroughly trained, combat-tested, and confident. The Fifth Fleet commander, Admiral Raymond Spruance, was required to defend the beachhead but gave his carrier commander considerable latitude.

The battle opened shortly after dawn on June 19 when a sizable portion of TF-58's 400 Hellcats flew CAPs over the task force and the islands. Several fights broke out as Japanese scout planes and fighters took off, but the major engagement began mid-morning. Ozawa's carriers launched the first of four strikes at the American force, which lacked precise knowledge of the Mobile Fleet's location.

It mattered little. With ample F6Fs on hand and expert fighter direction, each raid was intercepted and repulsed with severe loss. American fighter pilots had never enjoyed such good hunting. Of sixty-four Japanese planes in Raid One, only twenty-two survived. So it went throughout the day. Sailors standing topside on many ships could watch the progress of the air battle, as wispy white contrails

One of the classic carrier photos of the war shows a jubilant *Lexington* ace, Lt(jg) Alexander Vraciu, describing the results of his interception of Japanese dive bombers on June 19. *Courtesy author's collection.*

circled in the bright Pacific sky, punctuated by greasy streaks of falling aircraft—nearly all bearing rising suns.

When it was over, nearly three hundred IJN aircraft had been shot down or wrecked. Seven Hellcat pilots had splashed five or more "bandits," including Lieutenant (jg) Alexander Vraciu of *Lexington*'s VF-16. In a sizzling eight minutes, he downed six Yokosuka "Judy" dive bombers to become the Navy's leading ace. The pilot who succeeded him in the top spot was Commander David McCampbell, leading *Essex*'s Air Group Fifteen. He shot down seven planes in two sorties.

A *Hornet* Hellcat pilot unexpectedly found himself presented with a gift. Circling a downed U.S. flier off Guam, Ensign Wilbur Webb— a Pearl Harbor survivor—awaited a rescue aircraft. Then he noted a large formation overland. Investigating, he discovered a flock of Aichi Val dive bombers, so he joined the traffic pattern. Keying his mike he broadcast, "This is Spider Webb to any American fighter pilot. I have about forty of 'em cornered over Orote Point and I could use a little help." In minutes he shot down six with two more probably destroyed. His riddled F6F never flew again, but Webb joined the ranks of the instant aces. Small wonder that the battle entered history and legend as "The Great Marianas Turkey Shoot."

Mitscher lost barely thirty planes, including seventeen Hellcats in combat. While a handful of attackers got through the CAP, they inflicted no significant damage. The Japanese were not so fortunate, as aggressive American submarines found the enemy force, sinking Pearl Harbor veteran *Shokaku* and Ozawa's new flagship *Taiho*.

An Imperial Navy staff officer, Commander Masatake Okumiya, summarized his aircrews' dilemma: "They never stood a chance against the determined defense of the Hellcat fighters and the unbelievable accuracy and volume of the ships' antiaircraft fire."

Task Force Fifty-Eight scouts sought Ozawa's retreating force through most of the day June 20. *Enterprise* TBFs located him well to the west in mid-afternoon, over three hundred miles distant. Mitscher calculated the odds of retrieving some 220 planes in darkness, but he could not pass up the first shot at Japanese flattops in nearly two years. Turning to his staff on *Lexington*'s bridge, he merely said, "Launch 'em."

It was a long flight into the westering sun that evening, and darkness was approaching as the strike groups selected their targets. The priority had been chalked on ready room blackboards: "Get the carriers!" Though *Wasp*'s (CV-18) air group went for Japanese oilers, the others chose among Ozawa's three carrier divisions.

The results were disappointing. Intense enemy flak and aggressive fighters reduced the effectiveness of the strike, which sank just one carrier. *Belleau Wood* (CVL-24) Avengers launched torpedoes against the twenty-four thousand-ton *Hiyo*. The division leader, Lieutenant (jg) George Brown, had promised a hit, and he delivered. One pilot, probably Lieutenant (jg) Warren Omark, put his torpedo into *Hiyo*'s stern, causing unmanageable damage. Brown did not return, but the "Flying Hawk" sank that night.

Having sunk one flattop and damaged another, the Americans turned for home. About twenty planes were lost in the attack, but nearly two hundred others faced a daunting challenge: finding their way back on a moonless night.

Upon return to the task force, pilots found nearly every ship lit up. Mitscher, in a well-intentioned but counterproductive move, gave his famous order: "Turn on the lights." The beams helped guide gas-strapped aviators home, but many could not distinguish between the lights of carriers and cruisers or destroyers. Pilots landed in the water after wasting precious fuel in passes at escorts. Others crashed on deck, preventing squadron mates from getting aboard.

When it was over, nearly half of the 216 planes on the mission were lost. Fuel starvation was the main cause, with only five of the fifty Helldivers returning safely. In vivid contrast, just three of the twenty-seven Dauntlesses were lost. The Navy had already decided to stop buying SBDs, however, and the Douglas production line shut down. After two and a half years the Dauntless's contribution to America's war effort in the Pacific could hardly be exaggerated.

Task Force Fifty-Eight ships and aircraft spent most of the next few days seeking downed fliers, with surprising success. More than three-quarters of the missing airmen were rescued.

The First Battle of the Philippine Sea produced strategic results. The Imperial Navy was finished as an offensive force, and before year end B-29s were flying missions against Japan from Marianas bases.

Escort carriers delivered Army fighters to shore bases, from Morocco to Guam and beyond. Here Republic P-47s are catapulted off USS *Manbila* Bay in June 1944. *Courtesy Tailhook Association.*

Meanwhile, the British Eastern Fleet grew in strength and purpose as its carriers struck Japanese oil targets in Sumatra (now Indonesia). Between July 1944 and January 1945 HMS *Illustrious*, *Indomitable*, and *Victorious* launched five operations, flying Corsairs, Avengers, and British "home grown" Barracuda dive bombers and Seafire fighters. In keeping with broader Allied strategy, an

Admiral Jisaburo Ozawa led Japan's Mobile Fleet through defeats off the Marianas and the Philippines between June and October 1944. But given the disparity of forces, he could hardly have done better. *Courtesy author's collection.*

October strike against the Nicobar Islands ninety miles north of Sumatra helped draw Japanese attention away from the Philippines.

LEYTE GULF

The pace of the Pacific War accelerated after the Marianas, with the fast carriers at the tip of the spear. In a controversial move, the joint chiefs ordered the Marines to seize Peleliu in the Palau Islands to guard the eastern flank of the upcoming return to the Philippines. The First Division went ashore in mid-September, expecting to wrap up the craggy island in a matter of days. Instead, the operation lasted two and a half months, with critics arguing that it turned into an unnecessary, sanguinary meat grinder. Fast carriers supported the landings but had more urgent business six hundred miles westward in late October.

Army General Douglas MacArthur's 1942 pledge to return to the Philippines prompted high-level discussion regarding the advisability of seizing the Philippines or Formosa. For a variety of reasons—including a national debt to the long-suffering Filipino people—a huge amphibious force set its sights on Leyte Gulf that fall.

Third Fleet sought to weaken Japan at the periphery before striking the Philippines. Therefore, carriers hit Okinawa on October 10 and Formosa on October 12. Carrier aircrews estimated they destroyed 650 planes at Formosa, while Japan admitted half as many—still a heavy blow. Yet Tokyo, still slurping its homemade brew, gleefully announced sinking three dozen American ships, including battleships and carriers. Even the normally level-headed Kamikaze master, Vice Admiral Matome Ugaki, thought his airmen had destroyed three carriers and three other ships. In truth, two U.S. cruisers were badly damaged but survived.

"Scoreboards" appeared on nearly every combat carrier's superstructure. Here the senior aviators of Air Group Two aboard *Hornet* (CV-12) pose with claims for Japanese ships sunk and planes destroyed 1943–44. *Courtesy Tailhook Association.*

"Bull" Halsey's Third Fleet arrived off the Philippines with Task Force Thirty-Eight's four groups deploying sixteen fast carriers. From bases in Japan and the East Indies the Imperial Navy launched a three-pronged response with carriers, battleships, and scores of escorts. The sprawling, four-day slugfest began on October 24.

Halsey had released two groups to head eastward for replenishment when the crisis broke. He recalled Rear Admiral Gerald Bogan's Task Group 38.4, while allowing Vice Admiral John McCain's 38.1 to proceed to Ulithi, taking five flight decks out of action until late in the battle. Thankfully, Marc Mitscher's fast carriers were not the only flattops involved. Vice Admiral Thomas C. Kinkaid, who had commanded at Santa Cruz, led Seventh Fleet including eighteen CVEs for close air support and antisubmarine patrol.

Even during battles such as Leyte Gulf, aircrews endured periods of waiting. These pilots aboard the escort carrier *Saginaw Bay* belonged to "Taffy One" supporting the hard-pressed Taffy Three off Samar on October 25. *Courtesy Tailhook Association.*

n Sea, on the western side of the Philippines, carrier
.royed one of the largest battleships afloat. Three fast
..r groups launched multiple strikes against Vice Admiral Takeo
Kurita's five battleships, twelve cruisers, and fifteen destroyers. Some
260 blue aircraft swarmed the sixty-four thousand-ton *Musashi* for
more than five hours, hammering her with seventeen bombs and
nineteen torpedoes, heavily represented by *Enterprise* and *Franklin*'s
air groups. Ten aircraft fell to Japanese AA, but it was the first time
carrier planes sank a battleship underway, unassisted by surface
combatants. It would not be the last.

Kurita had already lost two cruisers to submarines and another
turned back with bomb damage, but after regrouping he continued
his mission to enter Leyte Gulf, unknown to Halsey.

Meanwhile, Japanese land-based aircraft posed a serious threat to
the fast carriers. Winging seaward in three large formations, they were
intercepted by relays of F6Fs well managed by fighter-direction officers.
But fighters were spread thin. In Task Group 38.3 *Essex*'s last two
available Hellcats were launched with hostiles inbound, putting Commander David McCampbell and Lieutenant (jg) Roy Rushing onto a
gaggle of Zekes. In the next ninety minutes McCampbell claimed nine
kills—the all-time U.S. one-day record—and Rushing six. In all, *Essex*'s
Fighting Fifteen was credited with forty-three kills that day.

In the same group *Princeton*'s shark-mouthed VF-27 fought hard
for its ship, splashing thirty-six raiders. But a single Yokosuka Judy
put a 550-pound bomb through "Sweet P's" flight deck, igniting
ordnance on the hangar deck. The light cruiser *Birmingham* (CL-62)
came alongside to take off survivors when a huge secondary explosion
swept the would-be rescuer, inflicting nearly seven hundred casualties.
Princeton was scuttled after an eight-hour ordeal, losing 108 men.
She was the first American fast carrier sunk since Santa Cruz and
remained the last. Carrier aviators claimed 270 kills on October 24,
the second highest count of the war.

But the Imperial Navy was not finished.

Under cover of darkness October 24–25, Kurita transited San Bernardino Strait between Luzon and Samar, eastbound, intending to fall upon MacArthur's vulnerable transports in the gulf. The Navy's first full-time night flying unit, Air Group 41 in light carrier *Independence*, had Avengers airborne that night, tracking the large enemy force. Mitscher assumed that Third Fleet had the information, but for reasons still unclear, Halsey ignored it.

Additionally, that afternoon Task Force Thirty-Eight search teams had found Ozawa's four carriers off Luzon's northeast coast. That information, later combined with *Independence*'s report of Kurita's eastward course, bothered some senior officers, who correctly deduced Ozawa's purpose: to draw the fast carriers north, clearing the way for Kurita's center force. Mitscher, informed of the developing situation, declined to intervene with Halsey.

Well to the south, the third prong of Tokyo's offensive met Seventh Fleet units in Surigao Strait separating Leyte and Mindanao—everything from PT boats to battleships. In the world's last major surface engagement, the annihilation was nearly complete, leaving the dogged Kurita pressing eastward while Jisabuo Ozawa—survivor of the Marianas—lurked well to the north with four partly equipped carriers.

LEYTE DAY TWO

Shortly past dawn on October 25, Vice Admiral Kinkaid's three escort carrier groups had patrols airborne. An Avenger sighted large ships with pagoda masts emerging from San Bernardino strait and radioed the alarming news.

All that stood in Kurita's path was Rear Admiral Clifton Sprague's Task Group 77.4.3, with six CVEs and seven escorts, off Samar's east coast. "Taffy Three" turned away, making smoke, launching aircraft, and hollering for help. Sprague faced four battleships, eight cruisers, and eleven destroyers. But support from Taffy Two added more Avengers and Wildcats to Sprague's numbers.

As the "smallboys" attacked with torpedoes and five-inch gunfire, aviators made repeated runs with bombs, torpedoes, and strafing passes. One Wildcat pilot made twenty-six runs, most of them without ammunition.

Unable to outrun the enemy, the 19-knot CVEs were chased down. *Gambier Bay* (CVE-73) succumbed to cruiser guns, as did three of the escorts. After HMS *Glorious* in 1940, she was only the second aircraft carrier sunk by surface ships. But Kurita, impressed with the ferocity of the "jeep" carriers' response, and mindful of the pummeling he had taken the day before, called off the chase. Just as an historic victory lay on the horizon, he disengaged. Kinkaid's transports—and MacArthur's source of supply—were safe.

Still, Taffy Three remained in peril. That afternoon *St. Lo* (CVE-63), originally named *Midway*, was attacked by a single Zero that made no effort to pull out of its dive. Wracked by fire, the little flattop went down, first victim of the Special Attack Corps: the Kamikaze had arrived. Six more CVEs were tagged that day.

While the drama played out near Samar, the Japanese waved an irresistible target under Halsey's nose. Ozawa's four carriers steamed off the northeast Philippines, seemingly representing the third major threat after the surface forces in San Bernardino and Surigao straits. Once ComThirdFleet got the news, Halsey reacted predictably: he rushed to destroy Tokyo's remaining flattops. In his haste, he committed a severe blunder, leaving San Bernardino unguarded. He assumed that battleships of Vice Admiral Willis Lee's powerful Task Force Thirty-Four would prevent an enemy force from entering the gulf. He did not realize as he pounded north that all seven battleships and their screens in Lee's contingency force remained integrated into the fast carrier task groups.

Bull Halsey was more a fighter than a thinker. An instinctive warrior, he rode to where he imagined the guns were sounding. Only when the stunning news arrived of Japanese battleships pounding

Taffy Three did he realize that he had been snookered. Worse, he wasted an hour or more ranting and sulking before deciding on a course of action.

Ozawa lay more than four hundred miles from the Taffies, and Halsey was in between. The Bull finally ordered Lee's battlewagons—racing ahead of the carriers—to reverse helm and move southward, although everyone knew it was far too late.

The four carriers in Ozawa's Mobile Fleet had deployed with just 116 aircraft, but by the morning of October 25 they retained only twenty-nine. The ensuing clash could only go one way.

Starting at 8:00 a.m. Mitscher launched 180 aircraft, the first of six strikes totaling more than five hundred sorties. The on-scene coordinators were air group commanders from TG-38.3: first from *Essex*, then from *Lexington*. The F6Fs brushed aside the dozen or so Zeros trying to defend their flight decks as "99 Rebel" and "99 Mohawk" assigned targets. *Lexington* and *Langley*'s aircrews wrote the final log entry for *Zuikaku*, survivor of Coral Sea, Eastern Solomons, and Santa Cruz. Other air groups sank CVLs *Chitose* and *Zuiho* as well as a destroyer.

Ozawa shifted his flag to cruiser *Oyodo*.

SINKING OZAWA

That morning *Essex*'s air group commander David McCampbell directed strikes that sank the light carrier *Chitose*. Relieving him as target coordinator was *Lexington*'s Commander Hugh Winters, controlling some two hundred aircraft. He recalled, "There was no chance for surprise, as the Japs were already bleeding some, so we didn't have to shoot on sight, so to speak. We wanted *all* the carriers, with maybe a BB or CA for the cherry on top."

Winters directed his squadrons against *Zuikaku*, *Zuiho*, and the larger escorts. He noted:

The heavy haze of AA smoke trailing off the quarter gave good windage for our dive bombers as we pushed over.... The ships were using new anti-aircraft stuff with wires and burning phosphorous shells which put up all different-colored fire and smoke around our planes. But we had faced so much deadly AA for so many lousy targets that it didn't bother us too much, hunting this big game. The boys were as cool as any professionals working in a hospital or law office.

The *Zuiho* limped on, burning, but the *Zuikaku* stopped and started to die on one side. She needed no more, but hung in there for awhile, and her AA battery was nasty. In the excitement, I stayed down too low (not very professional), and got some holes in my left wing. I knew it would be a long afternoon, so I throttled back to almost stalling speed and leaned out the fuel to practically a back-firing mixture.

Winters assigned subsequent air groups according to his target priority, and watched *Zuiho* sink, then *Zuikaku* capsize. "No big explosions, no steam from flooded firerooms, no fire and smoke—just a few huge bubbles. Quietly, and it seemed to me, with dignity."

Thus perished the last survivor of the Pearl Harbor attackers. The light carrier *Chiyoda* lingered a bit longer. Hugh Winters and wingman Ensign Barney Garbow had witnessed something unprecedented—they saw three aircraft carriers sink during one mission.

Halsey dispatched four cruisers and nine destroyers as a pickup team to complete the execution. They sank *Chiyoda* late that afternoon and pummeled a remaining destroyer. Carrier planes continued scouring Philippine waters during October 26 and 27, picking off a light cruiser and four more destroyers. It brought Japanese losses in the four-day battle to twenty-six combatants, totaling three hundred thousand tons.

Leyte Gulf officially entered the books as the Second Battle of the Philippine Sea, though most of the action occurred nearly one thousand miles from the June turkey shoot. Whatever the battle's official name, after October 1944 the Imperial Navy was finished.

Despite an unprecedented level of destruction inflicted upon the Japanese Navy, Leyte left a sour taste in many American mouths. Halsey's bungled arrangement for covering San Bernardino Strait resulted in the unnecessary loss of four Taffy Three ships and nearly six hundred lives. (*St. Lo* and *Princeton* could not be laid to Halsey's account.) The fault was shared, however, with MacArthur's unnecessarily complex communications structure and Kinkaid's acquiescence to it. Halsey stayed, and as events would show, he remained beyond all accountability.

Historians still debate whether Leyte represented the sixth flattop battle. Purists insist that it did not, because the carrier versus carrier phase was totally one-sided. By the time Halsey's air groups got at Ozawa on October 25, the four Japanese carriers were nearly empty. Even upon deployment, many Imperial Navy pilots could only launch from their flight decks, being untrained in shipboard landings. In any case, Leyte was the last time that carrier-based aircraft—or any others—sank opposing carriers at sea.

From the period after Leyte Gulf through December, eight more carriers were hit by Kamikazes. The attackers sent *Intrepid*, *Franklin*, and *Belleau Wood* stateside for repairs that would take between two and four months. It was becoming increasingly obvious: the only way to defeat the Kamikaze was to kill him, as he could not be deterred.

Toward that end, the Navy asked for help from the Marines. With a shortage of carrier fighters to combat Kamikazes, the Pacific Fleet began training leatherneck Corsair squadrons in carrier operations. The first two squadrons, VMF-124 and 213, were experienced Solomons units that reported aboard *Essex* at Ulithi in December. They had a rough initiation to Western Pacific weather, suffering heavy losses, but they paid their way. Eight more Marine squadrons joined them in the new year.

Meanwhile, nature reminded the U.S. Navy that Imperial Japan could be the lesser enemy. While refueling in mid-December, Halsey wanted to remain in position to support MacArthur's forces on Luzon, but a major tropic storm called Typhoon Cobra spun up in the Philippine Sea, tracking north-northwest. Ignoring warnings from meteorologists—complicated by some inaccurate forecasts—Halsey continued refueling. Consequently, he took Third Fleet into the mouth of the storm, prompting comparisons to the original Divine Wind that saved Japan from Mongol invasions in the thirteenth century. The result was a disaster. Battling one hundred mph winds, three destroyers capsized and nearly eight hundred men drowned.

Light and escort carriers were especially vulnerable, rolling eighteen to twenty degrees, whipped by violent winds. Avengers and Hellcats snapped their flight deck tie-downs and tumbled into catwalks or careened overboard. One loose fighter or bomber could cause havoc, colliding with other planes, smashing into fuel lines, and starting blazing fires.

Five fast carriers and four CVEs suffered damage, with *Monterey* (CVL-26) forced to Bremerton, Washington, for repairs after a serious fire on the hangar deck. Nine other ships incurred major damage; six suffered lesser damage. More than one hundred aircraft were destroyed or badly damaged at no expense to the enemy.

Summarizing the damage, Nimitz reflected that Typhoon Cobra "represented a more crippling blow to the Third Fleet than it might be expected to suffer in anything less than a major action."

Halsey might have been relieved of command after the storm, coming so soon after the Leyte fiasco. But perceived needs of the service prevailed: a board of inquiry faulted him for poor judgment while declining to recommend sanction. Many officers and sailors grumbled about *politics uber alles*.

However, there had been more action at the expense of Japan. The last carrier sunk in 1944 was *Shinano*, third of the Yamato-class battleships, converted to a carrier, and slated for sea trials in November. On the night of October 29, en route to Kure, she fell afoul of USS *Archerfish* (SS-311), which put four torpedoes into her starboard side, sinking the seventy-one thousand-ton behemoth in about six hours.

1945: CARRIERS TRIUMPHANT

American carriers, big and small, ranged widely in the first month of the last year of the war. On January 6 the U.S. Sixth Army landed at Lingayan Gulf on Luzon's west coast. The operation drew an immediate and violent response: in nine days suicide aircraft sank two dozen vessels and hit nearly seventy more. Again Seventh Fleet escort carriers supported the Army, but Kamikazes plagued the "jeeps" in the Sulu Sea. A Yokosuka P1Y Frances had narrowly missed *Ommaney Bay* (CVE-79) on December 15, but the twin-engine bombers were persistent. Another Fran got through the CAP on January 4, scraping the "Big O" and loosing two bombs. They exploded with catastrophic results inside the hull. Wracked by fires and exploding ordnance, the eleven-month-old carrier was abandoned in less than forty minutes and scuttled by destroyer torpedo.

In that same period five CVEs took suiciders aboard, requiring stateside attention to four. *Savo Island* (CVE-78) was repaired at Ulithi, where repair crews worked round the clock to return wounded ships to combat.

While Seventh Fleet supported the Army ashore, the fast carriers stretched their wakes to westward across the South China Sea. Faulty intelligence placed the thirty-nine thousand-ton battleships *Ise* and *Hyuga* at Cam Ranh Bay, French Indochina. Halsey coveted them. On January 12 Task Force Thirty-Eight launched nearly one thousand offensive sorties up and down the Tonkin coast, sinking more than forty ships, including a disarmed French cruiser—much to

En route to the South China Sea in January 1945, *Lexington* (CV-16) refuels from a tanker. The ability to keep task forces at sea for weeks was a crucial factor in the Pacific. *Courtesy Tailhook Association.*

Vichy's displeasure. The two Japanese battleships, with flight decks fitted aft, lay well out of reach at Singapore.

Very few airborne bandits were encountered, though *Essex*'s Marine Corsairs encountered a China-based B-24 Liberator that unaccountably fired on them and suffered the consequences. McCain lost twenty-three planes to all causes, but many fliers were rescued. One hardy group, aided by the French Foreign Legion, marched overland to evacuation at an obscure place called Dien Bien Phu.

Whether off Formosa, the Philippines, or Indochina, in early 1945 flattops continued operating within range of Japanese land-based airpower, requiring intelligent, capable officers to wield radar, radios, and fighter patrols.

COACHING THE FIGHTERS

One such was Lieutenant John Monsarrat, who served aboard USS *Langley* (CVL-27). Off Formosa on January 21, 1945, Monsarrat coped with the fast, dynamic world of radar combat.

> We were taking a new plot on the raid every minute, and the radar operator and I double checked to confirm that these bogeys were not showing IFF. By 1151 they had closed to fifty-five miles, and we had already lost two minutes of precious intercept time. Suspecting that the *Washington* (BB-56) had confused the bogeys with our own returning strike planes a few miles away, I urgently reported the new bogey position to the flagship.
>
> At 1205 we got our first "merged plot" indicating that our fighters and the raiding planes were at the identical range and bearing, but not necessarily at the same altitude.

By the time the Hellcats came to grips with four Kamikaze Zeros, it was too late. The first Mitsubishi splashed close aboard *Langley*, after dropping a bomb that blew a fourteen-foot hole in the flight deck. Monsarrat recalled:

> Just after the bomb hit, not more than thirty yards from one of the uprights in radar plot, I had my nose glued to the PPI (plan position indicator) scope...searching for the other planes. Looking up from the scope, I was appalled to see nearly everyone else down on the deck in a jumble of helmets and arms and legs. It is an instinctive reaction to hit the deck when confronted with an explosion, but it angered me to see our crew down there when we had work to do. With a roar I got them up in position, and none too soon. At 12:10, two minutes after we were hit, the second

Zero with its 550-pound bomb fused to impact deep inside a ship, plunged into the flight deck of the *Ticonderoga*. The carrier's planes, armed and gassed and spotted on the deck for takeoff…soon began to burn and explode.

Both *Langley* and "Tico" survived their damage, but the action off Formosa proved the conventional wisdom: Kamikaze defense had to be 100 percent effective.

February was a month full of events and history.

The Third/Fifth Fleet turnover was completed with Spruance again relieving Halsey. But Mitscher retained the conn of the carriers, which suited him completely.

On February 16 Mitscher returned to Japanese waters, having commanded the original *Hornet* that launched the Doolittle raid nearly three years before. Again flaunting the conventional wisdom that carriers could not compete with land-based airpower, sixteen fast carriers spent two days gaining temporary control of Japanese airspace.

Fighter sweeps lifted away from pitching, rolling decks barely sixty miles off the Honshu coast. Clad in unaccustomed winter clothes, pilots gawked at postcard scenery: snowcapped Mount Fuji and downtown Tokyo.

Strafing and rocketing enemy airfields, Hellcats and Corsairs hunted through the clouds for airborne hostiles. About one hundred Japanese planes rose to contest the first wave of blue raiders, initiating some of the fiercest dogfights to date. Throughout the day Navy fighters claimed 270 kills, matching the record at Leyte Gulf. (Marine Corsairs contributed twenty-one more.) The best of the shooting went to *Hancock*'s Hellcats with seventy-one victories and one loss, mainly in four large combats over the Chiba Peninsula and three airfields.

Avengers and Helldivers attacked industrial plants, but results were limited by low ceilings and visibility. One-third of the fifty-plus aircraft losses were due to weather or difficult operating conditions at sea.

A restored Fairey Swordfish of the Royal Navy Historic Flight during a 2012 demonstration in Britain. *Courtesy Ministry of Defence*

The first U.S. carrier monoplane was the Douglas TBD, later named Devastator, here sporting *Yorktown*'s (CV-5) red tail. *Courtesy Tailhook Association.*

A Grumman F3F-2 of Fighting Squadron Six off USS *Enterprise* (CV-6) during filming of the 1940 movie *Flight Command*. The pilot probably was future Captain Ed Pawka who finished his career flying Mach 2 RF-8 Crusaders. *Courtesy James H. Farmer collection via John Cassidy.*

Named for CV-5 sunk at Midway, *Yorktown* CV-10 entered combat in 1943 with the new generation of aircraft including Grumman TBF Avengers and F6F Hellcats. *Courtesy Tailhook Association.*

A Marine Corps TBM-3 Avenger ready for launch from USS *Cape Gloucester* (CVE-109) in the Western Pacific shortly after V-J Day, September 1945. *Courtesy Tailhook Association.*

An imperial carrier that never deployed, the 25,000-ton *Amagi* turned on her side from bomb hits in Kure Harbor in July 1945. *Courtesy Tailhook Association.*

The workhorse of post-WWII carrier aviation was the Douglas Skyraider attack aircraft, here in the AD-2 version demonstrating its exceptional ordnance capability: twelve rockets, two heavy bombs, and a torpedo. *Courtesy USN.*

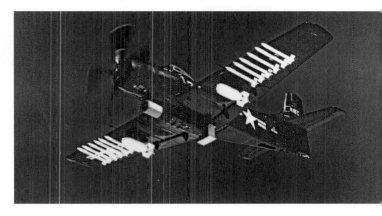

Grumman F9F Panthers of Air Task Group One aboard USS *Boxer* (CV-21) in 1953, the ship's fourth Korean War combat cruise. *Courtesy USN via Henk van dr Lugt.*

An F7U-3 Cutlass of Attack Squadron 86 takes a waveoff during USS *Forrestal's* (CVA-59) shakedown cruise in 1956. *Courtesy Tailhook Association.*

One of the classic Navy color schemes belonged to VFAW-3, flying Douglas F4D-1 Skyrays from San Diego in the late 1950s. *Courtesy USN.*

"Center ball" in the mirror landing system tells a USS *Yorktown* (CVS-10) aviator that he is on glide slope to landing c. 1960. *Courtesy Tailhook Association.*

"Cross-deck" evolutions between allies with a Royal Navy Sea Vixen interceptor launching from the antisubmarine carrier USS *Yorktown* (CVS-10) circa 1965. *Courtesy USN.*

Designed for nuclear attack, the Douglas A-3 Skywarrior, here aboard USS *Enterprise* (CVN-65) became the enormously versatile "Whale" which flew refueling and intelligence missions. *Courtesy Tailhook Association.*

Fairey Aviation produced a variety of British naval aircraft including the three thousand-hp turboprop Gannet operated by the Royal Navy from 1953 to 1978. Australia, West Germany, and Indonesia also flew the type. *Courtesy Tailhook Association.*

The Royal Navy operated F-4K Phantoms from HMS *Ark Royal* (R09) during the 1970s, visiting the United States during the bicentennial year. *Courtesy author's collection.*

Air Wing 19 made seven Vietnam deployments aboard USS *Oriskany* (CVA-34) from 1967 to 1976, adding to two 1950s cruises. This F-3J Crusader goes around after a missed approach to the "O-boat." *Courtesy USN via R. R. Powell.*

An RA-5C Vigilante escorted by an F-4J Phantom off USS *Constellation* (CVA-64) over the Tonkin Gulf in 1971. *Courtesy USN.*

A VF-111 F-14A Tomcat launches a Phoenix radar-guided missile during fleet evaluation tests. The Sundowners made fourteen deployments with Tomcats aboard USS *Kitty Hawk* (CV-63)and *Carl Vinson* (CVN-70) from 1979 to 1994. *Courtesy Tailhook Association.*

Among the world's most sophisticated electronic warfare aircraft was Grumman's EA-6B Prowler, operational from 1971. This VAQ-141 aircraft was snapped during a 1990 cross-country flight. *Courtesy Rick Morgan.*

During Operation Desert Storm some Navy aircraft received nonstandard desert color schemes, as this A-7E Corsair II aboard USS *John F. Kennedy* (CV-67). *Courtesy USN.*

A *John F. Kennedy* ordnance man prepares Sidewinder air-to-air missiles for loading in the Red Sea during Operation Desert Storm in 1991. *Courtesy USN.*

An F-14A Tomcat and A-6E Intruder from USS *John F. Kennedy* on a "sandblower" mission during Operation Desert Storm. *Courtesy Dave "Hey Joe" Parsons.*

A show of U.S. sea power during Operation Desert Storm in 1991 included Task Force 155 with the carriers *Saratoga* (CV-60), *America* (CV-66), and *John F. Kennedy* (CV-67), plus five guided-missile cruisers and two destroyers. *Courtesy USN.*

"Miss Piggy" was the generic name for Lockheed US-3As converted from S-3A Viking submarine hunters delivering supplies to carriers in the Persian Gulf during Desert Storm. *Courtesy Rick Morgan.*

Carrier aviators describe twilight landings as "pinkies," evident in this approach to *Kitty Hawk* (CV-63) in 1993. The lighting emphasizes the axial deck's 11-degree port offset. *Courtesy USN.*

A boatswain's mate nudges an FA-18 Hornet's nose-gear tow bar into the catapult shuttle aboard USS *George H. W. Bush* during 2004 operations. *Courtesy USN.*

Following 2015 operations against the Islamic State in Iraq, France's *Charles de Gaulle* launched Rafale M strike-fighters against targets in Syria during 2016. *Courtesy Marine Nationale.*

A colorful E-2C Hawkeye surveillance aircraft of VAW-115 lands aboard USS *Ronald Reagan* (CVN-76) during 2016 Seventh Fleet operations. *Courtesy USN.*

U.S. Navy FA-18 Hornets refueling in flight from an Air Force tanker over Afghanistan during "the long war" in 2010. *Courtesy USN.*

Two carriers with very different histories are India's Russian-built *Vikramaditya*, commissioned in 2013, and Russia's *Kuznetsov*, commissioned in 1990. *Wikimedia.*

China's first carrier, the 53,000-ton *Liaoning*, built in Russia 1985–88, was completed in China and commissioned in 2012. *Courtesy Tailhook Association.*

Liaoning's fighters are Chinese-built J-15s based on Russia's Sukhoi 33, with first shipboard landings in 2012. *Courtesy Tailhook Association.*

Northrop-Grumman's X-47B Unmanned Carrier-Launched Airborne Surveillance and Strike System landed aboard USS *George H. W. Bush* (CVN-77) in 2013. It led to the current Carrier-Based Aerial Refueling System. *Courtesy USN.*

The F-35C Lightning II is the U.S. Navy variant of the three-service Joint Strike Fighter program. After years of delays and cost over-runs it completed carrier-qualification tests aboard USS *Nimitz* (CVN-68) in November 2014. *Courtesy USN.*

Perhaps of greater significance, at Formosa, in the Philippines, and in Japan itself, carrier airpower had dominated powerful land-based aviation throughout the Western Pacific. No longer could pundits claim that carriers were inferior to large air forces ashore.

TOKYO FROM AN AVENGER

Lieutenant Commander Donald A. Pattie, a veteran of the North African operation, commanded Torpedo Squadron Twenty-Three in USS *Langley* (CVL-27). He led his Avengers over Tokyo on February 17, en route to the Tachikawa engine factory. In his memoir he recalled:

As we flew over the city...the imperial palace was easily distinguished, being a huge cream-colored structure.... In our approach we had an escort of fighters abeam and slightly above on each side. Glancing at the fighters on my left, I suddenly saw a Zero swoop down on the tail of our air group commander (J. J. Southerland). Before I could grab the radio and warn him, the Japanese pilot rolled over on his back and shot the commander down while inverted. It was not a show of flamboyance but a highly professional maneuver, executed with superb airmanship. Anyone suggesting the Japanese were poor pilots need only have seen it.

The sky was black with anti-aircraft bursts, and everywhere I looked, dogfights were taking place and planes going down. To grasp the intensity, one must realize that some 500 airplanes plus all the AA batteries within firing range were concentrated in one huge melee over the city.

Scanning the suburbs, I located our target and signaled my flight to space out. From that point on we were oblivious to all outside distractions. There were a number of factory buildings in the compound but I chose the main assembly building. Pushing over in the dive, we bore down with vengeance. To insure an effective attack, I held my release till the last moment, pulling out at the treetops. Looking back, I watched with satisfaction as all four bombs exploded inside the building. The others scored hits within the compound so I was satisfied the squadron had done a good job.

The Tokyo strikes also marked the debut of the first big-deck night air group, involving—predictably—Commander Bill Martin and *Enterprise*. Martin's Air Group Ninety included veterans of his old VT-10, which had bombed Truk shipping in the dark twelve months before. Flying Night Hellcats and specially modified Avengers, Martin's men approached nocturnal carrier aviation with an enthusiasm bordering on evangelism. Big E was joined by the bigger, older *Saratoga*, operating the combined day-night Air Group Fifty-Three in Rear Admiral Matthias Gardner's Task Group 58.5.

The second day, February 17, was cut short with worsening weather. Nonetheless, fighter pilots claimed almost one hundred more shootdowns and, more importantly, they kept every Japanese snooper away from the task force.

Immediately after the Tokyo strikes, attention diverted 750 miles southward to the Bonin Islands and the "burned out porkchop" called Iwo Jima. A dozen escort carriers supported the Marine assault troops which went ashore on February 19. The joint chiefs wanted Iwo because it put Army fighters in range of Tokyo, supporting B-29s operating from the Marianas.

Fast carrier aircraft, including Marine Corsairs, conducted successive air strikes against the black-sand beaches, sometimes strafing within two hundred yards of the infantry. Then Mitscher reversed helm northward to continue suppressing Homeland airpower with more attacks on Honshu airfields.

Japan's reaction was understandable—Iwo Jima belonged to the same prefecture as Tokyo. Anticipating round-the-clock opposition, *Saratoga* left TF-58 to provide night-time protection off Iwo. On the afternoon of D+2, February 21, the Kamikazes swarmed Sara.

Shipboard gunners opened massive antiaircraft fire against one suicide bomber after another. But in merely three minutes, *Saratoga* absorbed four of six attacking Kamikazes and at least three bombs. Badly wounded, she pulled off, barely forty miles from Iwo.

The Japanese were not finished. Funneling more planes down from the homeland, they bombed the burning carrier again, raising the death toll to 123. She survived, but her war ended that February evening.

Nor was that all. The "jeep" *Bismarck Sea* (CVE-95) was hit by two Kamikazes, sinking with nearly one-quarter of her crew. She was the last Allied carrier ever sunk.

Badly in need of night-fighter protection, the Iwo invasion fleet received *Enterprise*. She provided unprecedented coverage, flying nonstop for a week: 174 hours without respite. Nothing like it had ever been done, and years would pass before it was duplicated.

BACK TO HOME WATERS

In March the fast carriers resumed attacks on Japanese ports, inflicting heavy damage on *Ryuho* (hit in the Doolittle raid three years before) and lesser damage on CVE *Kaiyo*, both about fifteen thousand tons.

Other Imperial Navy carriers at the time were the near sisters *Katsuragi* and *Amagi*, each over twenty thousand tons, employed as overqualified transports before lying doggo under nets at Kure. Several late-war ships remained incomplete, including Unryu class vessels *Kasagi*, *Ikoma*, and *Aso*, plus *Ibuki*, partly converted from a cruiser. Taking a page from the American book, Japan began converting four tankers to carriers, but the two completed never became operational.

The Homeland operations were far from one-sided, however. Operating off Japan on March 19, *Franklin* (CV-13) was caught in an unpardonable state of unreadiness. Captain Leslie Gehres, a notoriously unpopular skipper, had driven two hundred sailors and a few officers to desert when he assumed command. That morning "Big Ben" was in a relaxed condition less than sixty miles from the enemy shore. A Japanese dive bomber dropped out of the overcast and scored a bullseye, igniting a horrific series of secondary explosions among armed and fueled planes on the flight deck and others below. In minutes unlucky CV-13 was a burning, blazing inferno, ripped by a series of explosions that seemed certain to kill her. But due to the leadership provided by Rear Admiral Gerald Bogan's task group staff, and also to raw courage and a dogged refusal to quit, the crew extinguished the fires and the ship limped away.

Franklin took a horrific 40 percent dead of 3,220 aboard. Gehres's action report listed 724 men killed, but in truth the blackened, battered carrier lost 807, as well as 487 wounded. It was America's third-worst for a single action of the war, behind battleship *Arizona* and cruiser *Indianapolis*. Later Gehres tried to prosecute those forced by fuel-fed fires to abandon ship, saying they had deserted their posts. The actual number of dead has never appeared in official U.S. Navy records.

Among the heroic members of Big Ben's crew was the Catholic chaplain, Lieutenant Commander Joseph O'Callahan, who received the Medal of Honor for his inspirational leadership and rescue efforts. Lieutenant (jg) Donald Gary also received "the Congressional" for repeatedly returning to an isolated compartment, leading three hundred men to safety. Twenty-one *Franklin* men earned the Navy Cross for actions that day, including Leslie Gehres, in a stunning triumph for the Navy old-boys' club.

Franklin survived but, though largely repaired, never returned to service.

BRITISH PACIFIC FLEET

The British Pacific Fleet (BPF) had been activated in November 1944, replacing the Eastern Fleet. Most significantly the BPF struck oil targets in Sumatra in January 1945. But as the war drew closer to Japan, the Royal Navy's carriers offered a capability that U.S. planners could not ignore. Consequently, four Royal Navy carriers joined Spruance's Fifth Fleet as Task Force Fifty-Seven. The British flew a mixture of aircraft—their own Supermarine Seafires, Fairey Firefly strike-fighters, and Fairey Barracuda dive bombers, plus Corsairs, Hellcats, and Avengers. Ten fast carriers rotated in and out of TF-57, while two afloat maintenance carriers—HMS *Pioneer* and *Unicorn*—were based in the admiralties and Philippines.

George Bernard Shaw famously noted that the British and Americans are two peoples separated by a common language. That certainly applied to the U.S. and Royal navies, which employed different

The British Pacific Fleet flew U.S. and British aircraft, including the high-performance Seafire version of the famous RAF Spitfire. Seafire Mk IIIs warm up for launch from HMS *Implacable* in 1945. *Courtesy Tailhook Association.*

terminologies. The British equivalent of an LSO was a DLCO (deck landing control officer or "batsman"); RN carriers had lifts (elevators) and boosters (catapults), while aircraft (aeroplanes) had airscrews (propellers) and alighting gear (landing gear). Nevertheless, with common codebooks and communication procedures most of the wrinkles were ironed out. Apparently the exception was LSO signals, for the rare occasions when "crossdeck" operations occurred with Americans landing on RN carriers and vice-versa. Most American LSO signals were advisory ("high" meant "You are too high") rather than instructive ("Go higher").

Combined Anglo-American fast carrier strength was fifteen fleet carriers, six light carriers, nine battleships, twenty-three cruisers, and scores of destroyers. Nothing remotely like it had ever trailed a wake in any sea.

Royal Navy escort carriers also contributed over a wide area throughout the year. From January through July, seven British-built CVEs kept pressure on Sumatra, the Nicobars, Malaya, and Singapore. As many as four ships at a time operated together, embarking one hundred aircraft that produced results. Some of the major oil facilities lost 30 to 50 percent of production capacity for weeks or months.

Finally, the biggest Royal Navy CVE operation was called "Zipper," with six carriers covering the re-occupation of Malaya and Singapore immediately after V-J Day.

OKINAWA

Operation Iceberg—occupation of the Ryukyu Islands—began on April 1, 1945. It was not only April Fool's Day, it was also Easter Sunday. The northern portion of Okinawa lay only four hundred statute miles from Kyushu, and Iceberg was certain to draw a furious response.

Okinawa shaped up as the penultimate battle of the Pacific War— the last step before Japan itself. Defended by about seventy thousand

Japanese troops plus thousands of conscripted Okinawans, the islands were assaulted by the U.S. Tenth Army comprised of seven Army and Marine Corps divisions totaling some 180,000 men, plus reserves and support units.

To support Iceberg, the carriers had to remain in a limited area, usually no more than one hundred miles offshore. That requirement solved the enemy's main problem—locating his target. For two months the fast carriers, ably assisted by the CVEs, fought a continuous battle against conventional and suicide air raids in addition to flying ground support missions for U.S. infantry.

The carrier airmen brought enormous power to Okinawa, with more than one thousand planes in Mitscher's force, plus two hundred more in four British ships. As before, the fast carriers operated round the clock. *Enterprise* remained the sole night owl at the time among fourteen other U.S. carriers deployed in four task groups, with more ships on the way.

Eighteen escort carriers under Rear Admiral Calvin Durgin, "Mr. CVE," embarked 450 planes providing close air support, antisubmarine patrol, and combat air patrol. Additionally, on D Plus Three, four jeep carriers delivered two Marine air groups of Corsairs and Night Hellcats to operate ashore as "plank owners" in the Tactical Air Force.

There had never been anything like it.

But there had also never been anything like Japan's Special Attack Corps. The Kamikaze hatcheries spawned an unrelenting stream of suiciders that winged southward from their Kyushu nests. However, Japanese response on the first two days was surprisingly light: carrier pilots only splashed ten hostiles each day. Activity jumped on April 3, with nearly fifty shootdowns. Far worse was yet to come.

The Kamikaze master, Admiral Matome Ugaki, launched Operation *Kikusui* on April 6. U.S. Navy fighters claimed 257 kills, fourth highest daily toll of the war. Most heavily engaged were *Essex*'s

VF-83 with fifty-six claims, and forty-seven by *Belleau Wood*'s VF-30. Three of Fighting Thirty's pilots became aces that day, executing a succession of Vals and fighters bent on suicide.

Between early April and June 21, the Special Attack Corps lofted more than 1,400 "Floating Chrysanthemums" in ten waves. By sheer numbers they broke through the Hellcat, Corsair, and Wildcat pickets to sink thirty ships and damage more than ten times that number, with some five thousand sailors killed. The U.S. Navy had never absorbed so many fatalities, but off Okinawa and Kyushu the fast carriers proved "the fleet that came to stay."

THE LAST BATTLESHIP

Though the Imperial Navy's offensive capability had ended nearly six months before at Leyte, one last effort remained. In response to the Okinawa landings, the huge battleship *Yamato* sortied southward with a light cruiser and eight destroyers. Her sixty-four thousand-ton sister, *Musashi*, had succumbed to carrier ordnance in the Philippines, but Tokyo hoped that *Yamato* could beach herself as an unsinkable heavy artillery battery. To that end, she lacked the fuel to return to Japan, while her escorts contained minimal fuel. They departed April 6 and were found the next day by Martin PBM Mariner flying boats, two hundred miles north of Okinawa.

Admiral Spruance's Fifth Fleet intended to destroy the Japanese force with overwhelming airpower but retained heavy surface units to shortstop an unexpected enemy thrust at the amphibious force.

In three waves Mitscher's TF-58 aviators hammered at the *Yamato* force from 12:30 onward, led by a strike from nine carriers. The attacks lasted about two hours with more than three hundred sorties pounding torpedoes, bombs, and rockets into the Japanese ships. Cruiser *Yahagi* proved astonishingly tough, taking twelve bombs and seven torpedoes. She capsized to port and exploded beneath a huge mushroom cloud that presaged a more impressive cloud four months later.

The extent of *Yamato's* damage was not definitely known, as fewer than three hundred of her 3,330 crew survived. A frequently cited figure was eleven torpedoes and six bombs.

Mitscher had launched 386 sorties against the *Yamato* force, more than Nagumo put over Pearl Harbor. Japanese gunners downed ten blue airplanes, but the aviators recorded nearly a clean sweep. Only four damaged destroyers survived.

By month's end carrier pilots were credited with 1,050 aerial kills (120 by Marine squadrons) on twenty-four days. But the suicide bombers learned as much as the defenders. Sometimes trading strength for stealth, individual aircraft and small formations sought the electronic seams of radar coverage between task groups, presenting fighter directors with multiple blips on diverse headings and altitudes. Then-Lieutenant Commander Henry Rowe, a task group FDO, recalled, "Our biggest concern was the loner who snuck through at dusk because sometimes we couldn't track him or, if we had him on radar, we couldn't vector fighters onto him soon enough. With his altitude he could see us better than we could see him."

MEMORABLE MAY

After the April siege, air action abated. Carrier squadrons claimed 270 kills in May (barely one quarter of the April figure) and merely twenty in June, all in the first eight days. The last Marine squadrons left the fast carriers when VMF-112 and 123 completed their *Bennington* (CV-20) deployment in June.

Meanwhile, Marine escort carrier groups (MCVEGs) had been formed, each containing a Corsair and Avenger squadron primarily to support leatherneck ground forces. Fourteen of the sixteen planned MCVEGs were established, but only four saw combat. The first two deployed to Okinawan waters in the second *Block Island* (CVE-106) and *Gilbert Islands* (CVE-107). *Vella Gulf* (CVE-111) briefly operated in the Marianas and arrived at Okinawa shortly before V-J Day, while *Cape Glocester* (CVE-109) patrolled off Okinawa, Borneo, and the China coast until August.

Clearly Tokyo was hoarding its air strength for the invasion anticipated late that year. But the Kamikazes remained active, and they were effective—chillingly so on two days in May.

On May 11 two Kamikazes arrived overhead Mitscher's flagship, *Bunker Hill*, in Task Group 58.3. Descending from the clouds, the first dropped a 550-pound bomb that punched through the flight deck and out the hull before it exploded. The aircraft then dove into the deck, igniting the all too familiar sequence of fuel and ordnance. Less than a minute later another suicider plunged through heavy AA fire, retaining its bomb to impact.

Bunker Hill reeled under the multiple blows, fighting massive fires for several hours. When the crisis passed, she was beyond mortal danger but unable to operate aircraft while suffering massive casualties: 389 dead and 264 wounded. There was no option but to send her stateside, and she remained in Bremerton, Washington, until after the war.

Mitscher was forced off his flagship and, with a reduced staff, transferred to *Enterprise*. But three days later the same Kamikaze squadron struck again. A persistent Zero pilot stalked *Enterprise* through low clouds, awaiting his moment. When he saw it, he dived. Under heavy gunfire, he saw he was going to overshoot and, in an elegant piece of flying, he half-rolled and dived inverted into the forward elevator.

Casualties were relatively few, including fourteen killed, but the Big E was out of action. Her long war, which began at Pearl Harbor,

The Big E's long war ended on May 11, 1945, when a well-flown Kamikaze dived into *Enterprise's* deck, blowing much of the elevator 400 feet in the air. With more battle stars than any other ship, she was under repair when the war ended. *Courtesy author's collection.*

was effectively over. Mitscher and his staff moved off *Enterprise*, taking refuge in *Randolph* (CV-15)—their third flagship in four days.

In his memoir, Halsey described his impression of Kamikazes:

> I would be a damn fool to pretend that individual Kami-
> kazes did not scare me; they scared me thoroughly and
> repeatedly. But the Kamikaze conception (*sic*) did not scare
> me for a moment. I was confident that we could devise
> tactics to counter it, if our men were rested, our comple-
> ment of planes was full, and our fleet was on the offensive.
> The early attacks, I reemphasize, caught us with tired men
> and few planes. We would have been crippled by the loss
> of our indispensable tanker force, but the Japs were too
> stupid to strike it.

Halsey's tribute to the tankers was well founded. Thanks to the superb fleet service force, under Vice Admiral William L. Calhoun for most of the war, at-sea replenishment kept the flattops supplied with fuel, ordnance, and replacement aircraft. The fast carriers seldom if ever experienced a plane shortage. Halsey was correct that the Kamikazes would have been far more effective had they located and attacked oilers and supply ships. It was the seagoing equivalent of Nagumo's failure to target Pearl Harbor's tank farms rather than U.S. battleships.

The task force received another night-flying carrier in early June when the new Essex class ship *Bon Homme Richard* (CV-31) arrived. Her Air Group Ninety-One remained active through the end of hostilities.

THE HOMELAND IN JULY

Operating from its advanced base at Leyte, Task Force Thirty-Eight sailed northbound on July 1. Halsey bore a target list including combatant and merchant shipping, transport and production facilities, and the aircraft industry and bases.

Weather helped screen the carriers' approach as they reached launch points less than two hundred miles offshore on July 10. It was the first time tailhook aircraft had overflown Tokyo since the initial February missions. Significantly, this time no defenders rose to contest the raiders. By now Japanese airpower was largely defeated or suppressed as Tokyo retained aircraft for the expected invasion. Carrier aviators claimed more than one hundred planes destroyed on the ground, but clearly the "imperial eagles" were ceding their own airspace.

On July 14–15 the task force attacked Hokkaido, the farthest north carrier planes had yet struck. Thirty merchantmen and four escorts were sunk, but the most important result was sinking six high-speed coal ferries. Combined with heavy attrition among Japanese coastal vessels, imports of coal to Honshu were slashed by about 50 percent. No Navy Crosses were awarded for sinking colliers, but the effect on Tokyo's war effort far exceeded any damage inflicted on immobile carriers or battleships.

At the same time, Halsey's battleships shelled Japanese facilities within range of sixteen-inch guns, causing some dissent among aviators. Members of McCain's staff grumbled about wasting fuel capping the "blackshoes" who turned furniture factories into matchsticks.

With eighteen Anglo-American fast carriers available, strikes were launched against Tokyo environs on July 17 and 18, with minimal results. Pilots fought the weather far more than the Japanese in order to bomb a battleship and assorted combatants at Yokosuka.

KURE: UNNECESSARY LOSSES

The month ended with three days of unnecessary strikes—and casualties—at Kure.

The Imperial Navy, largely immobilized with fuel starvation, crowded the harbor with combatants of all types including battleships and carriers—about 300,000 tons. None of the ships posed a threat. The harbors were choked with mines, while American submarines trolled the home waters, and U.S. aircraft owned Japanese airspace. But the fat pickings proved irresistible to Bull Halsey, who relished his orders from Nimitz and ultimately from Chief of Naval Operations Ernest King in Washington. He ordered a series of strikes against the perceived easy pickings that would look good on the postwar scoreboard when the Army Air Force inevitably clashed with naval aviation.

In truth, Kure was history's biggest flak trap. Aside from the antiaircraft guns on dozens of warships, the shore surrounding the harbor was packed with light, medium, and heavy caliber weapons. McCain expressed doubt about the proportional worth of the targets against the cost of destroying them. But having made his pitch, he did what careerists usually do—he followed orders. His aircrews paid the price for his compliance.

On July 24, 25, and 28, McCain launched as many as 1,700 sorties per day in an all-out effort to put major combatants in Kure's muddy bottom. Most visibly hit were the new carriers, sisters *Unryu* and *Amagi*, which absorbed several heavy bombs during the three-day blitz. *Unryu* capsized while *Amagi* ran her 37,400 tons aground, heeling at a severe angle to port.

Katsuragi sustained severe damage topside but remained afloat.

Three battleships were pounded repeatedly and settled onto the harbor floor. They were *Ise* and *Hyuga* (objects of Halsey's Tonkin Gulf foray in January) and *Haruna*, first reported sunk in 1941. Because Okinawa-based B-24 Liberators also attacked Kure, some inevitable disputes arose as to who deserved the most credit for the dreadnoughts.

Three modern cruisers and two obsolete cruisers also were sunk or put out of action with numerous escorts. Meanwhile, a late July surge sent more imperial aircraft against the fast carriers whose fliers splashed fifty-six in four days ending July 28.

In the end, Halsey's ego and the Navy's institutional ambition cost some eighty aircraft and about a hundred young lives to feed old men's personal and professional agendas.

AUGUST ENDGAME

In the first week of August, the fast carriers received a respite of sorts when the force stood clear of a storm, prompting some sailors and fliers to mutter snarky comments about Halsey's previous weather problems. A lesser typhoon than December's had battered the fleet in June, with 145 carrier aircraft written off or damaged. But by then Halsey was bulletproof; his failure to avoid the storm had gone almost unnoticed by Nimitz and King.

Meanwhile, Third Fleet was advised against overflying some Japanese cities in the period. The reason became clear when Hiroshima was largely destroyed by atomic attack on August 6. Three days later, with no sign of capitulation from Tokyo, another B-29 dropped one bomb on Nagasaki. Still, Japan's war cabinet declined to surrender.

That same day, August 9, during attacks on ports far north on the Honshu coast, a dramatic event played out with the British Pacific Fleet. HMS *Formidable* launched fighter strikes against Onagawa Bay on Honshu's north coast where Lieutenant Robert Hampton Gray led his Corsairs in a low-level attack. The veteran Canadian took flak damage to his plane during the ingress but pressed his attack, placing a bomb on a frigate before dying in the ensuing crash. The escort sank with all hands, and Gray received the last Victoria Cross of the war.

V-J DAY

The fast carriers flew their final missions over Japan on August 15, Tokyo time. That morning, with strikes in progress, Washington confirmed that the emperor had overridden his doom-laden cabinet and agreed to unconditional surrender. The strike groups were recalled, but it was too late for some. Six of *Yorktown*'s Hellcats were embroiled in a lopsided dogfight, claiming nine kills while losing four planes and pilots.

Indefatigable Seafires also fought a last-minute combat, losing one against claims for seven Zekes. The missing pilot was murdered by vengeful captors after the surrender announcement.

One of the *Hancock* pilots who heard the recall was Lieutenant (jg) Richard Newhafer, later a novelist and screenwriter. He said the order brought "all the hope and unreasoning happiness that salvation can bring." Suddenly granted a future, exuberant young men broke formation and flew joyful aerobatics. On many ships, sailors took turns sounding long whistle blasts.

The rest of the day was spent reinforcing the CAP against enemy pilots who may not have received the word—or who ignored it. In all, U.S. carrier squadrons shot down thirty-four Japanese planes, "in a friendly sort of way" according to Halsey's directive.

The last credited victory of the war went to Ensign Clarence Moore of *Belleau Wood*'s VF-31, raising the official tally by Navy fighters, dive bombers, and torpedo planes to 6,826 since that long-ago Sunday morning at Oahu. It had been a long, sanguinary road back, but carrier aviators had led the way.

America's most beloved war correspondent was Ernie Pyle, the bard of the Italian campaign before moving to the Pacific. In his column of March 19, 1945, he wrote:

"Operation Airshow" involved hundreds of U.S. aircraft overflying Tokyo Bay after Japan formally surrendered aboard the battleship *Missouri* on September 2, 1945. *Courtesy USN.*

An aircraft carrier is a noble thing. It lacks almost everything that seems to denote nobility, yet deep nobility is there.

A carrier has no poise. It has no grace. It is top-heavy and lopsided. It has the lines of a well-fed cow.

It doesn't cut through the water like a cruiser, knifing romantically along. It doesn't dance and cavort like a destroyer. It just plows. You feel it should be carrying a hod (for bricks), rather than wearing a red sash.

Yet a carrier is a ferocious thing, and out of its heritage of action has grown its nobility. I believe that today every navy in the world has as its No. 1 priority the destruction of enemy carriers. That's a precarious honor, but it's a proud one.

Pyle was killed on Okinawa thirty days later.

AIRCRAFT CARRIERS COMMISSIONED IN WORLD WAR II (SEPTEMBER 1939–SEPTEMBER 1945)
(DEFINITIONS VARY WITH NATIONALITY).

NATION	FLEET	LIGHT	ESCORT	TOTAL
UNITED STATES	29	9	78	116
GREAT BRITAIN	6	7	54*	67
JAPAN	12	4	5	21
TOTALS	47	20	137	204

*Includes thirty-eight U.S.-built ships.

World War II yielded the greatest shipbuilding period in history; nothing remotely like it existed before or since. The three carrier navies had acquired 204 flattops, which seven decades later still represents 80 percent of all conventional carriers ever produced.

Including prewar ships, the world's navies lost forty carriers, including twenty-one Japanese. America lost eleven. Britain lost eight including *Dasher* to an internal explosion. Seventeen were sunk by air attack, mostly from other carriers, while submarines accounted for nineteen.

Despite attrition, at war's end the world carrier population stood at a level never to be matched. The U.S. Navy had ninety-nine flattops in commission, including seventy-three escort carriers. Meanwhile, Britain's Fleet Air Arm counted fifty-nine carriers, 3,700 aircraft, seventy-two thousand personnel, and fifty-six stations.

Those levels were about to plummet, never to return. But the carrier's position atop the naval pyramid was secure.

FIVE

WARS HOT AND COLD

1946–1991

Carrier Air Wing Six off USS *Franklin D. Roosevelt* inbound to a weapons range in Puerto Rico during 1969 pre-deployment training. *Courtesy R. L. Lawson collection, National Museum of Naval Aviation.*

KING'S VIEW
ALMOST BEFORE THE SMOKE OF WORLD WAR II CLEARED, THE

U.S. Navy anticipated a reduction of forces, despite the aircraft carrier's inarguable wartime dominance.

In 1945 Fleet Admiral Ernest J. King wrote,

It is necessary to keep in mind that the present tentative active fleet is what it is proposed to have ready for instant action upon completion of demobilization next fall.... The assumption[s] upon which the Basic Post War Plan is based (until the end of 1947) are as follows:

(a) There is no prospective enemy in possession of a large fleet.

(b) There is no prospective enemy that is largely dependent upon imports, as was the case with Japan. Consequently, the field for submarine action will be more limited than it was in the last war.

(c) Enemy action on the sea (if war comes before the end of 1947) will consist largely of operations by submarines, land based aviation, and possibly cruiser raids.

(d) Possible action, if necessary, would consist of air attacks upon enemy production centers and lines of communication; [and] conduct and support of amphibious operations.

Though King supported two new carriers at the expense of cruisers, clearly the chief of naval operations (CNO) envisioned a changed naval world.

In the fall of 1945 America had an embarrassment of riches. With ninety-nine carriers in commission, six Essexes and four CVEs on order were cancelled, while two incomplete Essexes were scrapped. *Oriskany* (CV-34) was set aside for a major rebuild, and would not be commissioned until 1950.

Eight of the nine Independence CVLs survived the war, and the lead ship was expended in the 1946 Bikini Atoll atomic bomb test. In the early 1950s *Belleau Wood* (CVL-24) and *Langley* (CVL-27) went to France as *Bois Belleau* and *La Fayette*, respectively, while *Cabot*

(CVL-28) was transferred to Spain as *Dédalo* in 1967. As Spain's flagship, she was modified in the mid-1970s to operate AV-8 Harrier "jump jets"—a significant advancement for the *Armada Española*. She returned to the United States in 1989, where a group of sponsors hoped to preserve her, but the cost was prohibitive.

Escort carriers suddenly became a glut on the world market. The last of nineteen Commencement Bay ships, *Tinian* (CVE-123), was completed but never commissioned as an aircraft carrier. She became a Reserve Fleet helicopter carrier that never deployed.

Thetis Bay (CVE-90, redesignated LPH-6) became the first dedicated helicopter carrier, providing a test platform for the Marine Corps concept of seaborne vertical envelopment. She was modified for that purpose in 1955, redesignated CVHA-1, and eventually became an amphibious assault ship, LHP-6. Her career ended in 1964. Other CVEs became communications ships as their decks sprouted antennae.

MIDWAY CLASS

During the war the Navy evolved the concept of the "battle carrier," bigger and more capable than the Essex class. Of six CVBs planned, three were ordered, with *Midway* (CV-41) and *Franklin D. Roosevelt* (CV-42) commissioned immediately after V-J Day, followed by *Coral Sea* (CVB-43) two years later.

The Midways were transitional ships. Originally displacing forty-five thousand tons, they were envisioned as embarking more than 120 aircraft. The concept proved unworkable, however, and in fact undesirable. Early experience demonstrated the difficulty of operating so many planes with four squadrons of Corsairs (sixty-three F4Us) and Helldivers (fifty-three SB2Cs). Because of their size, the CVBs were better equipped for operating jets and larger piston

The new generation arrived after V-J Day with three Midway class carriers. Here, in 1946, USS *Franklin D. Roosevelt* (CVB-42) provides a size comparison with USS *Essex* (CV-9). *Courtesy Tailhook Association.*

aircraft simultaneously. *Midway*, for instance, briefly flew twin-jet McDonnell FH-1s in 1949 but retained piston-engine fighters until 1950.

The three ships were assigned to the Atlantic Fleet for much of their careers, tentatively opposing the Soviet threat. *Midway* and *Coral Sea* served into the 1990s, with *Midway* becoming a museum ship in San Diego. The hard-used *FDR* (uncharitably called "Filthy Dirty Rusty" late in her career) was sold in 1977.

THE NUCLEAR MISSION

The Army Air Force brought the world's greatest war to an end when it dropped two atomic bombs on Japan in August 1945. But with World War II concluded, another battle commenced, fought with great fervor on both sides of the Potomac. In the postwar world, partisans urgently pushed their clashing agendas regarding how best to foil Soviet aggression.

In October 1947, the War Department and Navy Department were merged into a unified Defense Department, including a separate United States Air Force. American airmen at last received what they had long coveted: full status as an independent branch.

The change led to tensions between the military branches. Naval aviation especially became anxious to build up its nuclear capability. Because the Air Force owned a monopoly on nuclear weapons delivery, flying admirals believed—with good reason—that unless carriers could operate nuclear-capable aircraft, their branch likely was doomed.

They were not overreacting.

The defense establishment was dominated by Army and Air Force partisans. President Harry Truman, like so many Army officers of the Great War, cordially detested the Marine Corps for its splashy headlines in 1918. When the few Marines in France had dominated press coverage despite the far larger Army force, institutional memories lingered. Truman's secretary of defense, Democrat machine politician Louis Johnson, was sardonically dubbed "Rowboat" for his openly anti-naval bias.

The flying admirals and the Navy waged a heartfelt political battle for survival. They perceived naval aviation being reduced to maritime patrol and sea-based antisubmarine forces, leaving the offensive missions to the "blue suits."

The "revolt of the admirals" peaked in 1949 under Chief of Naval Operations Admiral Louis Denfeld, a battleship sailor from the Annapolis class of 1912. Technologically, the competing services were represented by the Air Force's Convair B-36 intercontinental bomber, and the Navy's nascent USS *United States* (CV-58), the

first "super carrier." Intended to operate large nuclear-armed bombers, the sixty-eight thousand-ton flattop was authorized in 1948 but
immediately fell afoul of service politics. Under intense criticism,
her keel was laid at Newport News, Virginia, in April 1949, but she
was cancelled five days later.

The Truman administration sided with the Air Force, prompting
Denfeld to publicly protest the decision. Truman demanded his resigna-
tion, thereby worsening what Denfeld already described as the Navy's
lowest morale in three decades. It was the last time a CNO resigned
over anything, while the secretary of the Navy also left in protest.

Meanwhile, naval aviation sought a means of launching atomic
bombers in order to gain a seat at the nuclear table. The effort took
two very different approaches.

The first was decidedly a non-carrier aircraft. Lockheed's P2V
Neptune was a twin-engine patrol bomber that had first flown shortly
before the war ended. Large enough to carry an early A-bomb, the
Neptune was dragooned into service as a one-way bomber. In 1948,
fitted with jet packs, a P2V got off *Coral Sea*, proving the basic concept. Further tests showed that a P2V-3C model could launch with a
useful load and enough fuel to fly 2,500 statute miles. After bombing
its target, the crew was expected to reach a friendly landing area or
ditch for pickup at sea.

That same year North American began testing a nuclear bomber
capable of launching from and landing on carriers. The AJ-1 Savage
was powered by two Pratt & Whitney R2800 radial engines—the
same power plant in the wartime Hellcat and Corsair—plus an Alli-
son J33 jet in the fuselage. It possessed comparable range to the P2V
and was substantially faster. The Savage's bomb was the Mark 4, a
10,800-pound weapon yielding up to 30 kilotons.

In all, 140 production AJ-1s and -2s were delivered beginning in
1950, but the Navy's rush to obtain nuclear capability forced shortcuts
that affected reliability. Nonetheless, five fleet squadrons flew

Savages, which could be accommodated with considerable effort aboard Essex class carriers as well as the three Midways. The "special attack" mission soon passed to newer aircraft, however, leaving AJs to photo and aerial tanking missions.

The postwar force reduction was inevitable, and depleted funding was made obvious by scanty carrier usage. In 1946 only seven carriers deployed, two without air groups. The figures were little better during the next two years, resulting in some bizarre situations. Carrier pilots and aircrews cadged rides in transport and patrol aircraft, "boring holes in the sky" to earn their four hours per month for flight pay. During *Tarawa*'s (CV-40) 1948 world cruise, the air group commander saved authorized flight hours for the last day of one month and the first of the next month to provide minimal continuity for cockpit proficiency.

The Truman administration was voted out of office in 1952, following the bitter, hard-fought revolt of the admirals, which left career lifeblood all over Washington's marble hallways and ornate carpets. Ironically, Truman was succeeded by the foremost U.S. Army general of the Second World War, Republican Dwight D. Eisenhower. Perhaps because he never fought in the Great War, Eisenhower had no visible anti-Navy bias. In fact, he used the threat of carrier airpower to bring the Chinese and North Koreans to the bargaining table, concluded the uneasy 1953 armistice, and proceeded to build much of the Cold War Navy.

ARRIVAL OF THE JETS

While navalists pondered and argued, aviation progress began a headlong rush into the future, propelled by an exciting concept.

Ever the innovators, the British led the world in proving jets aboard carriers. Lieutenant Eric Brown—already the world's leading tailhooker—admitted he was "desperately keen to beat the Americans at being the first to operate jets from carriers." On December 2, 1945, he made a ten-minute refresher flight in a prototype De Havilland Sea Vampire. The next day he logged four landings aboard the light carrier HMS *Ocean*. (In an ironic development, *Ocean* also recorded the last biplane "traps" when Fairey Swordfish flew aboard during Britain's evacuation of Palestine in 1948.)

The Americans were seven months behind. Off the Virginia coast on July 21, 1946, Lieutenant Commander James J. Davidson launched from *Franklin D. Roosevelt* in McDonnell's experimental XFD-1 Phantom. He made several landings, proving the validity of all-jet carrier aircraft as opposed to Ryan's FR-1 Fireball, a composite prop and jet fighter.

As a contingency the Navy modified an Army jet, Lockheed's P-80A Shooting Star, for carrier use. That November Marine Lieutenant Colonel Marion Carl, arguably the finest naval aviator of his generation, completed catapult launches and arrested landings aboard *FDR*.

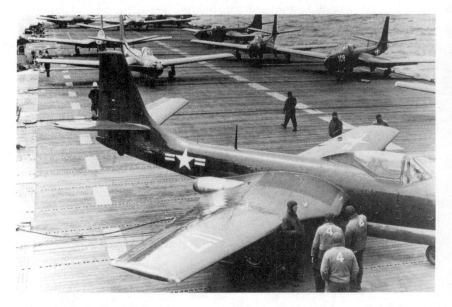

The U.S. Navy's first carrier-based jet was McDonnell's FH-1 Phantom, deployed by VF-17A aboard the light carrier USS *Saipan* in 1948. *Courtesy Tailhook Association.*

However, demonstrations were one thing—routine operations were another. The Navy's first all-jet squadron, Lieutenant Commander William N. Leonard's VF-17A, began receiving McDonnell FH-1 Phantoms in July 1947. Postwar construction included two 14,500-ton light carriers, *Saipan* (CVL-48) and *Wright* (CVL-49), both featuring in jet development. *Saipan* gained the distinction of operating the first all-jet squadron when VF-17A qualified in its Phantoms in May 1948.

Some of the early problems of operating jets from carriers were short range and endurance. In the era before in-flight refueling, those concerns posed both a technical and operational concern. Two exceptions were Douglas's F3D Skyknight, the Navy's first jet night fighter, and McDonnell's F2H Banshee. Both were powered by twin axial-flow Westinghouse J34 engines that provided better fuel consumption and performance than centrifugal-flow jets. One demonstration came in October 1954, when Ensign Duane Varner flew an F2H-2 nonstop coast to coast, some 1,900 miles from NAS Los Alamitos, California, to NAS Cecil Field, Florida. The four-hour flight was accomplished without aerial refueling.

Three years later came an even more impressive feat: the first "Pac to Lant" transcontinental flight from one carrier to another. On June 6, 1957, Commander Robert G. Dosé of developmental squadron VX-3, who two years before had logged the first American mirror landing, launched from *Bon Homme Richard* with Lieutenant Commander Paul Miller, his operations officer. The two F8U-1s cruised at forty-five thousand feet to the Dallas area, descending to twenty-five thousand where two AJ-2 Savage tankers awaited. With tanks topped off, the Crusaders rocketed back to forty-five thousand and cruised at .96 Mach eastbound.

Saratoga was fifty miles off Jacksonville when the Crusaders screamed into the break for a high-speed pass. They trapped after nearly three and a half hours in the air, setting an unofficial cross-country record. Furthermore, they were greeted by President Eisenhower, who was aboard for a look at naval aviation. His administration was good to the Navy, laying down almost one carrier a year during his tenure.

RETURN OF THE FRENCH

With the homegrown *Béarn* inactive most of her career, and by now completely obsolete, the French Navy looked abroad for new flight decks. The process began in early 1945 when the former HMS *Biter* passed to the *Marine*. Operational since 1942, the 8,300-ton CVE had sustained damage requiring repair in Britain, where she returned to American control and thence to France. She was commissioned as *Dixmude*, named for the 1914 battle along the Belgian border. First employed as an aircraft ferry, she then deployed to Indochina waters where events awaited. Her usual complement was SBD-5s, the last Dauntlesses flown from a carrier.

In the mid-1950s, after nearly thirty years, France resumed carrier construction by laying down two twenty-two thousand-ton, angled-deck ships: *Clemenceau* in 1955 and *Foch* in 1957. They entered service in 1961 and 1963, respectively, accommodating new jet aircraft, notably the Etendard series of strike fighters. In later service they operated F-8 Crusaders and Super Etendards.

Foch was decommissioned in 2000 and went to Brazil as *São Paulo*. As flagship of the *Marinha do Brasil*, in 2015 she operated Douglas A-4 Skyhawks, turbine-powered Grumman S-2 Trackers, and helicopters. *Clemenceau* was scrapped in 2009, replaced by a new generation carrier.

KOREA: JUNE 25, 1950–JULY 27, 1953

When communist North Korea's forces smashed southward across the thirty-eighth parallel on June 25, 1950, U.S. naval aviation was caught in a period of decline. What five years previously had been the most powerful Navy ever to sail earth's oceans had now been reduced to a fraction of its former glory.

That month the Navy possessed fifteen active carriers: the three Midways with four Essexes, four light carriers, and four escort carriers. The Midways were assigned to the Atlantic Fleet, anticipating that their heavy airpower might be needed against the Soviet bloc. Overall, the Navy counted 10,400 pilots for its 9,422 combat aircraft. Relying heavily upon the Reserves, by 1953 the aviator pool had increased to 18,200 while thirty-four carriers of all types were in commission. However, aircraft attrition was a constant concern.

When the armistice took effect in July 1953, naval aviation was six hundred combat planes short of the prewar number. Meanwhile, nine Essex-class carriers were returned to fleet service during the war. Thirteen escort carriers were recommissioned from 1950 to 1952, including five employed in Sealift Command. Four deployed to Korean waters, providing close air support (CAS) and antisubmarine warfare (ASW) capabilities.

In all, eleven CVs (redesignated attack carriers or CVAs in October 1952), five CVEs, and one CVL made a total of thirty-eight combat deployments. Those seventeen ships operated thirteen air groups, six antisubmarine, and five Marine Corps squadrons from the Pacific and Atlantic commands, including some "creative organization" of air task groups. Comprised of Regular and Reserve squadrons, ATG-1 and -2 circumvented congressional limits on carrier unit organization when the need was greatest.

It is not possible to overstate the importance of the Naval Air Reserve to Korean War carrier aviation. No fewer than eighteen Reserve squadrons logged twenty-nine deployments, including five Reserve air group cruises. By November 1951 nearly three-quarters of all Navy air strikes were flown by Reservists, including those in Regular squadrons.

If the Reserves were crucial to naval aviation, so too were World War II aircraft. The versatile Vought F4U Corsair was a mainstay of Task Force Seventy-Seven throughout the war, as was the Douglas AD Skyraider. Between them, the "recips" logged nearly 75 percent of all offensive sorties by U.S. carrier aircraft and sustained about six times the losses of jets. To meet that requirement, the sub-arctic operating environment forced the Navy to modify Corsairs and Skyraiders for extreme winter conditions.

Grumman's long-lived F9F series entered service in 1949, from the straight-wing Panther to the swept-wing Cougar. These F9F-2s off USS *Boxer* patrolled the Korean coast in 1951. *Courtesy USN.*

In fairness to the jets, Grumman's F9F Panther series recorded more carrier sorties than any aircraft (51,067), but only half were offensive missions. Additionally, four squadrons deployed with McDonnell F2H Banshee jets.

CARRIERS IN THE BALANCE

Naval aviation's success in Korea was felt from start to finish, but never more than in the beginning when USS *Valley Forge* (CV-45) with Air Group Five was the only U.S. carrier in "WestPac." Launching her first air strikes on July 3, 1950 she was quickly joined by *Philippine Sea* (CV-47) and a growing number of PacFleet ships. The "Happy Valley" provided critically needed air support of beleaguered South Korean and American troops.

Allied fortunes alternately waxed and waned before Asia's massive manpower, and in-country airpower was not always available. The carriers were badly needed throughout the war, especially in the early months when allied aircraft offered the primary counter to communist manpower.

When General Douglas MacArthur pulled off the masterful Inchon landing that September, reversing the course of the war, carrier planes were overhead. Seldom was the traditional mobility and territorial independence of carrier aviation so well demonstrated.

The British also contributed. HMS *Triumph* was approaching Hong Kong when the crisis broke. She diverted to Japan and Okinawa for provisions. On July 3, *Triumph* and "Happy Valley" conducted the first carrier missions of the war. Prop-driven Supermarine Seafires and Fairey Fireflys coordinated with U.S. Panthers, Corsairs, and Skyraiders.

The Royal Navy kept its commitment: *Triumph* was followed by *Theseus* in 1950–51, then *Glory* in September 1951, relieved by the Australian light carrier *Sydney*. *Glory* and *Ocean* deployed in 1952, returning again near the end of hostilities.

Bataan (CVL-29) was the only light carrier deployed to Korean waters, making three cruises with Marine Corsair squadrons. Five escort carriers operated off Korea, however, with *Bairoko* (CVE-115), *Badoeng Strait* (CVE-116), and *Sicily* (CVE-118) logging three cruises each. They embarked Marine F4Us and Grumman AF-1 and -2 Guardian ASW planes, though the AFs had little to do. The Yellow

Sea off Korea's west coast, with an average depth of only 145 feet, is much too shallow for submarines. The Sea of Japan, off Korea's east coast, is far more conducive to submarine operations, averaging 5,700 feet, but the strait leading from Japan is less than five hundred feet deep—a nearly impassable choke point for submarines.

CAS: JOB ONE

The value of carrier aviation was proven repeatedly, to the benefit of hard-pressed ground troops who needed close air support (CAS). From early August 1950, allied forces were compressed into the shrinking perimeter around Pusan, occupying barely 10 percent of South Korea's land area. Of the U.S. Air Force's nine fighter and medium bomber air wings available during 1950, only one remained in Korea through year-end, with another rotating in and out. Just to reach the Korean coast, Japan-based squadrons flew at least 250 miles round trip. Thus, sea-based airpower had to take up the slack—and it did.

Close air support was the primary role of Marine Corps F4U-4s, WWII fighters that soldiered on in Korea. This Corsair is fully armed for a predawn launch off the escort carrier USS *Sicily* in the winter of 1950–51. *Courtesy Tailhook Association.*

Another intrinsic benefit of naval aviation was its institutional experience with close air support. From start to finish, 46 percent of all Navy-Marine sorties were CAS, and though slightly less than the Air Force figure, naval aviators had long experience in the doctrine and technique of close support. It was not always true of the Air Force and other allied fliers. In fact, one of the lessons learned from Korea was the importance of integrated training between air and ground forces. Sometimes Air Force pilots lacked the ability to communicate with Army infantry, and while naval aviators usually could talk to Marines, occasionally nobody could talk to the Army. USS *Sicily*'s (CVE-118) Captain John Thach recalled, "The pilots would come back and say, 'We couldn't help. We wanted to. We were there and we couldn't get in communication with people.'"

In happy contrast, the close-knit Marine air-ground team was especially effective owing to prewar doctrine and commitment to CAS integration into infantry training.

Allied forces captured large numbers of North Korean soldiers in the 1950 battles, producing valuable intelligence. Interrogations revealed that aircraft, or fear of them, was the second greatest factor affecting enemy morale, after food shortages. The next largest factors were poor training and equipment. More directly, by September combined allied air interdiction reduced communist supplies to barely 10 percent of the June level.

The seesaw war up and down the Korean peninsula appeared headed for a conclusion toward year's end, with vainglorious theater commander Douglas MacArthur predicting early victory. He ignored Peking's warnings to stop well south of the Yalu and downplayed information of Chinese involvement starting in October.

Subsequently, Navy and Marine fighter bombers helped keep the massive Chinese floodtide from drowning all before it—especially during the withdrawal from Chosin Reservoir at year end. Following

186   ON WAVE AND WING

the Christmas evacuation from Hungnam, which ceded all of North Korea to the communists, the war settled into a stalemate.

Despite persistent, and sometimes heavy losses, there were results. Allied airpower was essential against Asia's quilted troops streaming south from Manchuria. The Marines could not speak too highly of the CAS provided by carrier aviators during the long, frozen trek to the coast from the Chosin Reservoir in December 1950. Even Army infantrymen spoke admiringly of the short response and precision accuracy of the dark-blue Navy and Marine aircraft.

One of the war's most remarkable events began as a CAS mission on December 4, when *Leyte* launched Corsairs to support Marines near Chosin Reservoir. The section leader, Lieutenant (jg) Jesse Brown, made a crash landing with flak damage to his F4U-4, but he got caught in the cockpit, unable to leave the plane. With darkness approaching, he needed immediate help.

Brown's wingman was Lieutenant (jg) Thomas J. Hudner, who only knew that a shipmate was in trouble. Hudner dropped his flaps, kept his wheels up, and executed a belly landing on the snowy slope. Upon reaching his friend, Hudner found that Brown was injured, trapped by the buckled fuselage. Another Corsair radioed for help, and while a Marine helicopter motored inbound, Hudner continued tending to his friend.

Hudner and the helo pilot tried to chop Brown from the fuselage, to no avail. With darkness imminent, Jesse Brown lapsed into unconsciousness, and the rescuing pair had no choice but to depart. Tom Hudner received carrier aviation's only Medal of Honor for the Korean War.

Aircrew morale and mission effectiveness were affected by rules of engagement. Truman allowed allied forces to bomb only the southern half of bridges across the Yalu River, which separates North Korea and China. Naval aviators and other allied airmen were stymied by the administration's fear of a Chinese response, when at least 100,000 Chinese already were committed to combat.

Although carrier aviators concentrated on interdiction and close air support, they made significant contributions on a larger scale. On May 1, 1951, Skyraiders from USS *Princeton* (CVA-37) were tasked with holing the strategic Hwachon Dam, controlling a reservoir in the path of allied forces along the Thirty-Eighth Parallel. Bombing was ineffective so planners wanted the dam breached with aerial torpedoes to prevent the communists from releasing a deluge that could sweep all before it. Eight pilots from two of "Sweet P's" AD-4 squadrons were selected to attack the dam. Only three had ever dropped a torpedo, but the procedure was straightforward.

The most unusual air mission of the Korean War was flown by USS *Princeton's* Douglas Skyraiders, launching torpedoes against the Hwachon Dam in May 1951. Holing the dam prevented the communists from flooding the approaches. *Courtesy USN.*

Led by pipe-puffing Commander Robert Merrick, the Skyraiders were escorted by Corsairs as flak suppressors. Merrick led his torpedo men through four thousand-foot mountains, arriving over the reservoir in the required profile: 160 mph at one hundred feet off the water. The pilots' aim was excellent, as six "fish" struck the targeted floodgates or near enough to inflict damage. With holes in both sides, the dam was rendered largely ineffective as a flood-generating source.

Subsequent air attacks were made on Korean power generating facilities, including a campaign in the summer of 1952. Four Task Force Seventy-Seven carriers—*Bon Homme Richard*, *Philippine Sea*, *Princeton*, and *Boxer*, (CV-21)—cooperated with Air Force and Marine land-based units to strike six facilities of the Sui-ho dam complex on the Yalu River. In the first strike, on June 23, tailhookers demonstrated their proficiency by putting thirty-five Skyraiders on and off the target in about two minutes. A Corsair was shot down by flak with the pilot saved.

The two-day bombing total was 730 Air Force and Marine sorties plus 536 from carriers. The attacks reduced 90 percent of the facilities' hydro-electric output for two weeks and reportedly deprived China of one-quarter of its electricity.

Probably the most significant of aviation's setbacks were doctrinal. Far East Air Forces, notably Fifth Air Force, established Operation Strangle in an effort to interdict enemy supplies and communications to the battle area. "Strangle" sought to duplicate the results of the original operation in Sicily in 1943. But success eluded Allied airmen over Korea due to two factors: immunity of Chinese bases in Manchuria, and the relative simplicity of the enemy supply system. Even Task Force Seventy- Seven's "Cherokee" strikes dividing North Korea into what a later generation would call "route packages" failed to achieve desired results. Clearly, tactical aviation could be better employed—and it was.

THE BRAVEST MAN IN THE NAVY

In February 1952 novelist James Michener visited USS *Essex* off Korea. The material he gathered was integrated into his novel *The Bridges of Toko-Ri*, and part of a report he wrote is cited here:

Salty Rear Admiral John Perry, commanding the U.S. Navy's Task Force 77 off the east coast of Korea, decided that the Bald Eagle of the *Essex* had done enough.

"No man in this task force is required to risk his life more than four times in a row," Perry growled yesterday afternoon.

He laid plans forthwith to stop the bravest man in the Navy from flying any more low-level missions against the Chinese communists.

"This fellow has been shot down into the ocean twice," said Perry. "He has floated in the icy waters where other men have frozen to death. He has brought an almost shattered plane into an emergency landing field. And he has limped back to this carrier on a plane containing 59 holes through the wings and body. From now on he's to do paper work."

The man Perry referred to is 35-year-old Comdr. Paul N. Gray of St. John, Kansas, leader of Fighter Squadron 54, and if there is a braver American fighting in Korea nobody has told the navy about it.

Gray is completely bald, very handsome and apparently without fear. He flies the heavy AD fighter-bomber and when he takes it off the carrier deck, it is as heavily loaded as a B-17. Gray's specialty is going in low for some North Korean bridge or railroad train, flying through heavy flak and getting whatever he goes after. In the past months he has flown nearly a hundred missions against some of the toughest flak concentrations in the world.

But this morning, before the word got to Gray, he was off again. In the bitter cold morning light, with a 45-mile wind shipping icy spray across the deck, Gray hurried out to his fifth plane, revved it up, and roared out toward the railroad bridges and trains in North Korea.

I watched this gallant man go and I was in the wardroom when the sickening news was broadcast. "Commander Gray has been shot down. He landed in the ocean off Wonsan but has not yet been recovered."

An anguished hush fell over the Essex.... A young kid next to me started to pray.

Then came the astonishing news. "The destroyer Twining has succeeded in picking up Commander Gray off Wonsan."

The card games resumed, and a comedian posted a sign: "Use caution when ditching in Wonsan Harbor. Don't hit Commander Gray."

Gray retired as a captain and died in 2002.

FIGHTING YAKS AND MiGS

Korea introduced the Navy to jet combat. Initially two *Valley Forge* VF-51 Panthers gunned a pair of North Korean Yak piston

The first verified jet versus jet kill was scored by VF-111's Lt. Cdr. William T. Amen of USS *Philippine Sea* in November 1950. Flying an F9F-2 Panther, he downed a Soviet-flown MiG-15. *Courtesy author's collection.*

fighters in July 1950. Then in November Lieutenant Commander Robert Amen of *Philippine Sea*'s VF-111 scored the world's first jet versus jet victory, downing a Soviet MiG-15.

Despite the technical inferiority of F4Us and F9Fs against MiG-15s, U.S. carrier aviators officially downed thirteen communist aircraft while losing four in aerial combat from 1950 to 1953. The 3-to-1 exchange ratio exceeded that of naval aviation during the first half of the Vietnam War, despite far more sophisticated fighters such as the F-4B Phantom II.

The finest performance of a naval fighter pilot was logged by Lieutenant E. Royce Williams of VF-781, flying from *Oriskany* on November 18, 1952. With his F9F flight vectored to intercept bogies from Vladivostok, the flight dispersed and Williams found himself alone among seven Soviets. In a mind-blurring contest he expertly used his four 20mm cannon to down at least three MiGs—possibly all four lost. Upon return to the ship his shot-up Panther was junked, but the communist losses were confirmed after the collapse of the Soviet Union five decades later.

THE VEILED FIST

Carrier aviation played a still unappreciated role in ending the Korean War. In early 1953 the new Eisenhower administration used back-channel Indian diplomatic routes to alert Pyongyang and Beijing that Washington was considering the nuclear option in the absence of substantive truce talks. Tokyo's official neutrality prohibited the Americans from operating B-29s from Japanese soil, and security concerns prevented basing Superfortresses in Korea, so, naval aviation offered the only option for pressuring the communists into meaningful negotiations. Deploying in April, the Atlantic Fleet carrier *Lake Champlain* (CVA-39) embarked a detachment of F2H Banshees capable of delivering nuclear weapons. The Mk 7 bombs, weighing

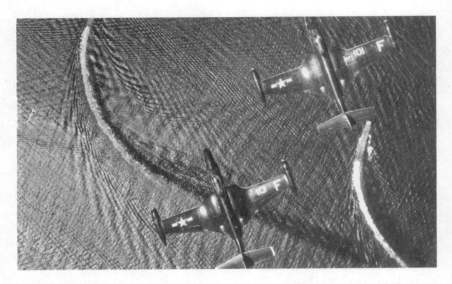

McDonnell F2H-3 Banshees overhead USS *Lake Champlain* and the battleship USS *New Jersey* in 1953. *Courtesy USN via Ray Bean.*

less than a ton, were optimized for tactical aircraft but produced far greater yield than the World War II weapons.

The armistice was signed in July.

KOREAN SUMMARY

For most of the war, two Essex-class carriers and one or more CVL/CVEs were on station off Korea, in the Yellow Sea and the Sea of Japan. In all, attack carriers logged 1,727 days of offensive operations, providing an ever-increasing number of combat and support aircraft. Five British Commonwealth carriers with thirteen squadrons cycled in and out of the war from the beginning, but U.S. Navy monthly figures alone were impressive. From an initial complement of Air Group Five's seventy-five aircraft, the figure reached 287 carrier planes on station by the end of 1950. That number reached 290 in 1951, and peaked at 309 in April 1952. By June 1953, the number was nearly 290.

The pace of operations weighed heavily on ships and air groups. The most extreme example occurred when *Valley Forge* returned to San Diego on December 1, 1950, after deploying May 1. The Chinese communist intervention required her immediate return, so she hastily unloaded Air Group Five, embarked Air Group Two, and was westbound again by December 6. By war's end "Happy Valley" had made three combat cruises—a figure matched by *Princeton* and "Phil Sea." *Boxer* exceeded that number with four deployments.

It was much the same with flying units. Of the thirteen air groups or air task groups deployed, seven made two combat cruises, while Air Group Five made three. Nor were the Marines exempt—the Checkerboard Squadron, VMF-312, was embarked in four carriers for six periods between November 1950 and May 1953.

The unrelenting exposure to combat and the ordinary rigors of carrier operations meant steady attrition. Start to finish, a carrier air group could expect to lose 10 percent of its aircrew during a combat deployment. In all, the carriers lost 722 aircraft to all causes (over half were F4Us), with 358 losses attributed to enemy action. Another 532 Navy and Marine aircraft were lost among land-based and seaplane units.

Some cruises were worse than others. *Princeton*'s back-to-back turnaround with Air Group Nineteen and 19 X-Ray lasted November 1950–May 1951 and May–August 1951, respectively. In that time Air Group Nineteen lost its air group commander and a fighter skipper, while 19X also lost its CAG. Other leadership was hard hit during *Kearsarge*'s (CVA-33) 1952–53 deployment, when three Air Group 101 squadron commanders were killed.

In less than thirty days in 1951, *Essex* lost eighteen planes (one-fifth of its total) plus eight aircrew and seven sailors. Most were noncombat casualties.

At the end of *The Bridges at Toko-Ri*, Michener's Rear Admiral George Tarrant muses, "Why is America lucky enough to have such men? They leave this tiny ship and fly against the enemy. Then they must seek the ship, lost somewhere on the sea. And when they find it, they have to land on its pitching deck. Where did we *get* such men?"

Michener's Toko-Ri legend is close enough to reality to pay homage to those aircrews who flew props and jets from axial-deck carriers, by day and night, for three long years. They lost 253 personnel (twenty-five Marines) for 35 percent of all U.S. Navy deaths in the Korean War.

Their sacrifice helped ensure the existence of an independent Republic of Korea.

PARLEZ-VOUS CARRIER?

In 1953 Lieutenant William F. Tobin had a nine-month exchange tour with the French Navy. His expertise as a landing signal officer

Lieutenant William F. "Toby" Tobin logged an exchange tour as a landing signal officer with the French Navy in 1953. "Le Tobe" was a popular figure in both navies. *Courtesy Tailhook Association.*

commended him to the *Marine Nationale*, where he made a lasting impression. He recalled:

> When I was picked for the exchange tour there was just one problem—I didn't speak French. But I decided it didn't matter—after all, the airplanes never knew *le difference*. Besides, the French aviators were so anxious to practice English on me that I didn't have to learn French!
>
> We had one problem, though. Most of the French Navy pilots had been indoctrinated by the British, whose LSO signals mostly were the reverse of ours. We all adjusted without difficulty and I settled into shipboard life aboard *La Fayette* (formerly USS *Langley*) for NATO exercises.
>
> There were differences, of course. For one thing, wine was served with every meal and the bar was open twenty-four hours. It was on the honor system—pour your own and pay up at month's end. I never even saw a Frenchman get tipsy.
>
> At NAS Hyeres, France, I waved day-night field carrier landing practice (FCLP) for F6Fs, SB2Cs, and TBMs. After qualifications on *La Fayette* I was transferred to Karouba, Tunisia, to conduct FCLP for F4U-7 Corsairs. All of *Flotille* 14-F's aviators were outstanding, and qualified aboard ship without incident. Those who have landed Corsairs aboard CVLs will appreciate that the combination of the narrow deck and F4Us—especially the dash seven—was not usually a happy marriage.
>
> Although my pilot buddies talked to me in English, the Karouba control tower did not. I tried my best French to request takeoff but got no reply. Overhead was a lonely TBM pilot doing an engine run-in who called, "Hey, Tobin, are you ready to go?" I said that I was. He called

the tower, which replied immediately and the friendly TBM pilot said, "Okay, you can go now." So I spent the whole flight practicing landing instructions in French.

Time for landing, I let fly in my best French (again) and quick as a flash the tower answered in English. A supervisor had latched onto a controller who spoke English and told him to get that Yank out of the air before he wrecked the place.

Among *La Fayette*'s squadron COs was Lieutenant Philippe de Gaulle, son of the general and future president. Philippe is a fine gent and an outstanding naval aviator. I asked him why he chose the Navy instead of the Army, and he said in the Navy he was on his own. In the Army he might be suspected of favoritism every time he was promoted.

My experience with the French Navy was one of the finest of my career.

La Fayette flew Hellcats, which were familiar to Tobin. During operations off Indochina, he convinced his hosts to let him "snivel" a couple of missions in F6Fs. Thus "Le Tobe" became the only two-war Hellcat pilot. He retired as a commander and died in 2001, age eighty.

DECADE OF PROGRESS

During the 1950s carrier aviation experienced a growth in technology and operational capability unlike anything before. Supersonic tailhook aircraft represented a quantum leap, but ship design, operating systems, organization, and training achieved unparalleled levels of innovation and sophistication, with effects still evident sixty years later.

ANGLED DECK

Early in the jet era, higher speeds presented a challenge in carrier landings. It was bad enough with straight-wing jets such as Grumman F9F-2 Panthers and F2H Banshees, but when swept-wing fighters entered service with the F9F-6 Cougar and FJ-2 Fury, the situation only worsened. In some quarters, the Navy faced the potential end of high-performance aircraft at sea. Carriers might become little more than antisubmarine platforms.

Occupational hazard: an F2H-3 Banshee strikes USS *Oriskany's* ramp in a 1954 landing attempt. Like most Essex class carriers, *Oriskany* later received an angled deck that drastically reduced accidents. *Courtesy Tailhook Association.*

The problem was multi-layered. The new jets' faster speeds meant less time to line up for a proper carrier approach, hampering landing signal officers' ability to pass corrections to pilots. Moreover, jets usually weighed more than piston aircraft, imposing greater strain on airframes and arresting gear.

In early 1949 the Naval Air Test Center at Patuxent River, Maryland, identified three possible solutions: developing a power-on landing technique; replacing the LSO with a glideslope indicator (much like the Japanese Navy's wartime equipment); or using an angled flight deck. The latter pair in concert proved the solution.

An angled deck solved two problems at once. First, it freed the carrier from having to accommodate high-performance aircraft on a straight deck, with all that entailed. On axial decks, aircraft either "trapped" safely or smashed into the barriers (and possibly into planes parked forward). Captain Wally Schirra, later a three-flight astronaut, described the situation: "In those days you either had an arrested landing or a major accident."

Secondly, on an angled deck, in the event of a waveoff or a "bolter" (failure of the tailhook to snag a wire) the pilot added power and went around for another approach. Flight deck operations could continue without interruption.

The Royal Navy attributed the angled deck concept to Captain Dennis R. F. Campbell and Mr. Lewis Boddington of the Royal Aircraft Establishment. The test platform was HMS *Triumph*, with an angled outline painted on the ship's axial deck in 1952. Pilots made touch-and-go passes at the imitation angle, aligned five and a half degrees to port. That same year the Americans duplicated the tests with a far larger ship, USS *Midway* (CV-41), with similar encouraging results.

The limited offset on existing flight decks cramped available space for other purposes—taxiing, parking, and servicing. Therefore, British and American engineers expanded the angle to eight degrees, thanks in part to the influence of Commander Eric Brown, the foremost RN test pilot during an exchange tour at Patuxent ("Pax") River.

In early 1952, after experimenting with power-on and power-off approaches to a dummy deck, test pilots from Pax River adjourned to *Midway* and *Wasp* (CV-18), flying angled approaches in the Douglas F3D Skyknight, Grumman F9F Panther, and McDonnell F2H Banshee jets, plus a piston-driven AD Skyraider. The consensus favored a power-on approach to touchdown and the trap, so the Navy Bureau of Aeronautics approved a million-dollar conversion of USS

Antietam (CV-36) with suitable modifications at the Broo... Yard. The portside aircraft elevator was fixed in the "up" position, and the vacant space aft received an extension tapering to the fantail. A landing area seventy-five feet wide was marked on the deck, canted eight degrees port, and six arresting wires were installed to match the angle. The conversion was completed in December 1952.

Preliminary testing by Patuxent River pilots included 272 day and twenty-one night touch-and-go landings, followed by seventy-eight day and five night landings in four types of jets and four prop types. The path was clear for a carrier air group to determine the feasibility for fleet aviators. Air Group Eight ("CAG-8"), recently formed at Norfolk, Virginia, under Commander Robert B. Wood with only a handful of experienced pilots, would determine how well "nugget" aviators could manage the angled deck with as little as fifty hours of jet time.

Antietam left for Cuban waters in mid-January 1953. There were some in-flight engagements with the hook snagging a wire before the plane's wheels reached the deck, and one pilot sustained a back injury. But overall the least experienced pilots had little difficulty making repeated landings on the angled deck, and Wood's confidence grew to the point that several pilots became night qualified with four traps each.

Based on the Cuban cruise, *Antietam* tweaked the angled deck. The cant was increased to ten and a half degrees, setting the norm for future generations of carriers.

TESTING THE ANGLE

During the 1952 *Antietam* tests, Commander Harold Buell led VF-84. Buell was a highly experienced dive bomber pilot of 1942–44 vintage. His squadron had recently learned to fly the F9F-5 Panther, the final straight-wing model of the pioneering Grumman fighter. In 1987 he described some of the challenges of proving the "canted" flight deck.

The way VF-84 became a jet squadron was typical. In September 1952 two pilots were assigned who were jet qualified. They picked up the squadron's first two F9Fs and we began our own pilot checkouts. Two days later I flew my first jet flight—a 1.5-hour local "fam" around NAS Oceana.

Jet familiarity required a pilot to master new methods—higher speeds on takeoff and landing, climb schedules, how-goes-it fuel monitoring, weather penetration letdowns, emergency engine relight procedures, and the ejection seat, to name a few. Almost every flight required some actual instruments. One developed a new awareness of time. Getting lost or missing a field or carrier deck on penetration approach could become an immediate crisis from lack of fuel. Communications failures, especially loss of a nav aid such as a homer, were serious and might lead to a "dead" end. Adverse weather was a potential enemy to fear and respect. Jet flying was a new ball game.

To an experienced tailhooker, landing a jet on an angled deck was sheer bliss. The break and traffic pattern were basically the same as for a straight deck, with emphasis upon flying a pilot-controlled approach. The LSO was still in the approach circuit and made the landing or wave-off decision as always, but most of the apprehension at the cut for a straight deck no longer existed. With no barriers to hit, or possible crash into the pack, two of a tailhooker's deepest fears were banished forever.

A missed wire or hook "bolter" were the same as a touch-and-go; you simply applied full power and went around for another pass.

Hal Buell retired in 1962, earned a Ph.D., and died in 2014, age ninety-five.

Postwar changes to the Essexes came from the Ship Characteristics Board, mainly based on the belatedly completed *Oriskany*. Beginning in the late 1940s the SCB-27A configuration featured a reinforced flight deck and streamlined island. It was a significant project, usually requiring two years per ship.

Next came SCB-27C with steam catapults to handle increasingly heavy aircraft. Further modifications in the SCB-125 version included an angled deck, mirror landing system, and enclosed "hurricane" bow, retroactively applied to most previously modified Essexes. When aviators and sailors speak of "27 Charlies," they most often mean SCB-125, the final configuration. Work was completed on fourteen carriers between 1955 and 1959.

The last straight-deck carrier in U.S. service was *Lake Champlain* (CV-39), which her crew called "the Champ." After antisubmarine duty and recovery of spacecraft, "the straightest and the greatest" was decommissioned for the second and final time in 1966. She was the last U.S. carrier to employ LSOs with hand-held paddles rather than a mirror landing system.

Meanwhile, ship design evolved worldwide, with angled-deck carriers becoming the norm. The first Royal Navy carrier constructed with an angled deck was HMS *Ark Royal*, the fourth British warship of that name. Commissioned in February 1955, "Ark IV" also featured steam catapults, first tested aboard HMS *Perseus* in 1951. They generated significantly more thrust than hydraulic "cats" and permitted launching the heavier jets that were becoming common in naval aviation.

Though angled decks vastly improved safety statistics, a problem remained. If an aircraft needed to land with a damaged or inoperable tailhook, the angle offered nothing comparable to the axial deck's woven-wire barrier or subsequent series of entanglements. The original axial-deck Davis barrier was attributed to a civilian engineer, S. V. Davis of the Naval Aircraft Factory in Philadelphia during the 1950s.

HMS *Ark Royal* (pennant number R09) was the second British carrier of that name. Commissioned in 1955, she was Britain's last conventional aircraft carrier when retired in 1979. *Courtesy David Reid.*

After multiple iterations, the optimum version was found, an arrangement of vertical nylon and/or canvas straps perhaps twenty feet high. On angled decks, the current barricade can be erected in a few minutes, suspended from deckside stanchions and safely snaring an errant aircraft.

FLYING THE MIRROR

Intimately related to the angled deck was the mirror landing system that replaced paddle-waving LSOs. Again, the Royal Navy took the first steps when, in 1951, Lieutenant Commander Nicholas Goodheart advocated a mechanical replacement for the LSO. According to legend, he borrowed his secretary's lipstick to inscribe a red dot with horizontal reference lines on her compact. He reasoned that if a concave mirror showing a reflected light were gyro-stabilized, it would appear constant to a landing pilot, automatically showing the proper glideslope.

As seen on USS *Lexington* (CVA-16) in 1956, the mirror landing system greatly improved carrier aviation's safety record by providing pilots with consistent, immediate feedback. *Courtesy Tailhook Association.*

Sea trials aboard HMS *Illustrious* in late 1953 proved Goodheart's concept. The Americans took note: between 1954 and 1957 carrier landing accidents were reduced by a stunning 80 percent.

The next progression came from the United States in the late 1950s, a product of the Naval Air Development Center in Pennsylvania. The gyro-stabilized Fresnel lens was made of glass six feet high and four feet wide, portside. The light source was one hundred feet aft of the mirror, projecting a red dot or "meatball" onto the vertical surface in the optimum glideslope for a given aircraft type. Green datum lights extended from each side of the mirror, giving pilots immediate feedback whether they were above, on, or below the desired flight path.

Pilots immediately took to the mirror and lens, for several reasons. The main advantage was consistency. The aviator monitored his own progress, doing whatever was necessary to keep the ball centered. There was no delayed reaction in responding to LSO paddles, as the pilot "flew the ball" almost intuitively—high or low—shaving seconds and fractions of seconds when they mattered most.

That was especially important due to the faster approach speeds in jets. As an attack pilot recalled, "The visual scan was meatball—lineup—angle of attack. You had to look at the deck but only for left-right lineup. If you looked for glide path, 'spotting the deck' usually incurred bad results."

However, LSOs still had a job. They stood on the same platform, portside aft, holding aloft the waveoff "pickle switch" in one hand and a radio-telephone in the other. If a pilot erred visibly, the "Paddles" (old words die hard in the Navy) could offer a verbal correction such as "A little power" or "Little low." After hundreds of approaches, LSOs knew a particular aircraft type's proper appearance and sound as it neared the ramp.

If for any reason the LSO wanted a waveoff—pilot error or a fouled deck—he pressed the button on his "pickle switch." That in turn flashed red lights on the mirror, mandating a go-around for another pass. As in the days of paddles, a waveoff carried force of law. To ignore it was the cardinal sin in carrier aviation.

In case the LSO had to abandon the platform due to an unsafe approach or crash, the pickle switch had a dead-man feature. One activation of the waveoff lights turned on the lights, which remained illuminated until a second squeeze.

The U.S. Navy's first mirror landing on a carrier was made by Commander Robert G. Dosé, a superb aviator commanding Developmental Squadron Three (VX-3) in August 1955. He recalled:

> I took great interest in the project and, being the skipper, to me fell the honor of trying for the first U.S. Navy carrier mirror landing. Not the first landing, but the first attempt. If I "bitched" it up, the guy behind me would have the chance to do it!
>
> The big day came on August 22. We flew out as a flight of six FJ-3 Furys from NAS Atlantic City to *Bennington*

(CVA-20) off the Jersey coast. En route I couldn't get my flaps up so I went out "dirty" and used up a lot more fuel than anticipated. We made it there about ten minutes late and, of course, by that time my fuel state was such that I couldn't have made it back to the beach, so I had to get aboard!

I was required to make one touch-and-go and then trap. I had never operated on an angle deck, so when I turned for my first pass I swung wide, anticipating that it would be necessary, but it wasn't. I had to skew back and make a left turn and a right turn in the middle of the approach, made one bounce and went around.

Next time I turned into the groove sooner with good lineup and made the constant speed, constant attitude, constant everything pass to hit the deck. I remember distinctly coming down the groove on the mirror thinking, "How easy. Why didn't we do this long ago? It's just a natural!"

Captain Dosé commanded *Midway* (CV-41) in 1961–62 and retired in 1968. He died in 1998 at age eighty-three.

MOVING ON

In the early 1950s the Navy and Marines sustained "near catastrophic accident rates," leading to angled decks, but safety remained a continuing concern. In 1954 the naval aircraft accident rate approached fifty-five major mishaps per 100,000 flying hours, with 775 aircraft and 535 pilots or aircrew killed. The next year the accident rate was "only" 33.5, with 406 men killed in 574 wrecks. Then in 1957 the Navy lost 613 aircraft with 358 deaths in 1,106 major accidents.

The future of carrier aviation lay in the balance. Drastic changes were needed, and the Navy found answers, both technical and organizational. Between 1958 and 1963 the golden wingers had turned things around. In those six years the major mishap rate was reduced by more than 50 percent. The replacement air group (RAG) concept, coupled with Naval Aviation Training and Operations Procedures Standardization (NATOPS), produced unprecedented levels of improvement in safety, with profound savings in lives and equipment.

In continuing proof of NATOPS success, the Navy had only eleven "majors" in 2009.

ROYAL NAVY: JETS AND SHIPS

Like the Americans, the British were eager to put jets aboard carriers. Among the earliest designs was the two-seat De Havilland Sea Venom, derived from the RAF twin-boom fighter. An adequate performer for the day, it was rated at 575 mph with a range of seven hundred statute miles. Though fewer than three hundred Sea Venoms were built, they served aboard five RN carriers as well as Australia's HMAS *Melbourne*, while Sud-Est produced 121 for the French Navy.

De Havilland's Sea Vixen, the Royal Navy's first swept-wing jet featured missile armament, here approaching HMS *Ark Royal* circa 1965. *Courtesy Tailhook Association.*

De Havilland's elegant Sea Vixen began in 1947 as the DH 110, a two-seat, twin boom, twin jet fighter-bomber. Its design continued de Havilland's configuration with the Sea Vampire and Sea Venom, with the pilot in a cockpit to port and the observer fully enclosed to starboard. The "Vix" was the RN's first swept-wing design with missile armament as an all-weather fighter-bomber. Intended to replace the Sea Venom, the Sea Vixen took a detour to the fleet. Though originally envisioned as serving the RAF and the Royal Navy, it lost the "light blue" contract to the cheaper Gloster Javelin. But de Havilland believed in its product and continued development, leading to a Navy contract for development.

When it was first flown in 1951, the Sea Vixen hit upon rocks and shoals. The prototype crashed spectacularly at the next year's Farnborough Airshow, killing the pilot and thirty spectators. Following lengthy redesign, another prototype flew in 1955.

Successful carrier trials aboard *Ark Royal* in 1957 led to squadron service two years later. Boasting a forty thousand-foot-per-minute climb and rated at 690 mph (600 knots), the "Vix" was the fastest RN aircraft of its era, capable of Mach one in a dive. Without a chance at combat, its operational use was limited to show-of-force missions on the periphery of the Middle East and Africa. Upon retirement from the fleet in 1972, the Sea Vixen had deployed in five carriers but sustained severe losses: fifty-four of 145 produced, or 37 percent.

The Blackburn Buccaneer entered fleet service in 1962, but its anemic engines led to serious problems, and the type was permanently grounded in 1970. The improved variant remained operational until *Ark Royal*'s retirement in 1978.

In the early 1960s the Royal Navy proposed building two modern fifty-three thousand-ton carriers, the CVA.01 class, with fifty-plane air wings. By 1963, however, severe budgetary concerns forced cancellation of one ship, leaving the project in a fatal crossfire from Whitehall, Treasury, and the RAF. According to British naval legend,

HMS *Hermes* and *Victorious* responding to the Aden crisis in May 1967, following violence against British officials. *Courtesy Tailhook Association.*

the air force "proved" that long-range missions could be performed by land-based aircraft by moving Australia four hundred nautical miles closer to Singapore on a map.

In a compromise of sorts, *Ark Royal* and *Eagle* were to be upgraded while *Victorious* and *Hermes* were beached.

GOING SUPERSONIC

The 1950s brought immense change to carrier aviation: angled decks, mirror landing systems, steam catapults, and supersonic aircraft. Many early jets exceeded Mach one (760 mph at sea level) in dives, but "busting the Mach" in level flight was another matter. The first naval aircraft to do so was Vought's sleekly elegant F8U-1 Crusader, which achieved the record on its first flight in March 1955. The Crusader was an all-or-nothing effort for the company, which had invested heavily in the previous F7U Cutlass, a notoriously poor performer. In fact, one test pilot of the Cutlass claimed to have written to Westinghouse, saying, "I have just flown the XF7U-1 Cutlass with your J34 engine and want you to know that your jets produce less heat than your toasters."

The Navy's first supersonic aircraft was Vought's F8U-1, operational in 1957. Though possessing exceptional performance, the Crusader incurred a spectacular accident rate as in this 1961 landing aboard USS *Franklin D. Roosevelt*. *Courtesy author's collection.*

The F-8 (redesignated from F8U in 1962) enjoyed a long if checkered career. Its blazing speed—ultimately Mach 1.8—lent it to reconnaissance as well as fighter missions, equipping more than thirty deployable Navy and Marine Corps squadrons, and it served in the French Navy from 1964 to 1999. Over Vietnam "the last gunfighter" rang up the best kill-loss ratio of the war. However, it was extremely demanding in the carrier landing pattern and had one of the highest accident rates in history—a point of perverse pride among surviving F-8 pilots. Of 1,266 Crusaders produced, 1,106 were involved in major accidents.

The U.S. Navy's other late 1950s fighter was the long-lived McDonnell F4H Phantom II. It began setting records from its first flight in 1958 and was adopted by the Air Force five years later. A powerful Mach two interceptor, its two-man crew was tasked with fleet defense, relying wholly upon heat-seeking and radar-guided missiles. In order to provide a balanced air group on Forrestal-class carriers, one fighter squadron usually flew Phantoms and the other Crusaders.

McDonnell merged with Douglas in 1967, a union that lasted thirty years (until "McDouglas" was absorbed by Boeing), so, through most of its career the F-4 (like the A-4 Skyhawk) was a McDonnell Douglas product. The F-4 became a cult machine with a global following. It was flown by nine other nations, with both the RAF and Royal Navy accepting the type. Extremely stable and well-behaved in landing configuration, the F-4 was popular with pilots flying "around the boat" in carrier approaches, but it required positive technique on catapult shots, where it was prone to over-rotation off the bow. It left the U.S. Navy in 1987, and the Marine Corps held its "Phantom Pharewell" in 1992.

THE COST OF DOING BUSINESS

Jet aircraft operating from aircraft carriers incurred enormous losses from the 1940s to the 1970s. In 1962 the Navy and Marines lost at least eleven Phantoms and more than fifty Crusaders—eight or more in carrier accidents.

Here are some of the more notable lifetime safety figures, expressed in major accidents per 100,000 flight hours.

VOUGHT F8U/F-8 CRUSADER	46.7
NORTH AMERICAN A5J/RA-5 VIGILANTE	42.0
MCDONNELL-DOUGLAS A4D/A-4 SKYHAWK	23.3
MCDONNELL F4H/F-4 PHANTOM II	20.1
GRUMMAN F-14 TOMCAT	9.3

THE FORRESTALS

In 2001 retired Vice Admiral Jerry Miller reflected, "If the *Forrestal* had not been successful, it is quite possible that the Navy would not have built another carrier." He probably did not exaggerate.

America's first angled-deck carrier built as such was the landmark USS *Forrestal* (CVA-59), named for the original secretary of defense. Commissioned eight months after *Ark Royal*, "FID" ("First in Defense") was then the largest ship ever built, some 990 feet in length, as big as the luxury liner SS *United States* and 150 feet longer than the Yamato-class battleships. She displaced nearly sixty thousand tons standard and more than eighty thousand full load. In contrast, the Midways originally displaced forty-five thousand tons.

The shape of things to come: USS *Forrestal*, the first super carrier, under construction in 1954. She was commissioned in 1955, serving until 1993. *Courtesy Tailhook Association.*

Forrestal was built in surprisingly little time, ordered in July 1951 and commissioned in October 1955. The others followed at regular intervals: *Saratoga* (CVA-60) in 1956, *Ranger* (CVA-61) in 1957, and

Independence (CVA-62) in 1958. All served nearly forty years, with *Independence* retiring in 1998.

Forrestal and her sisters were very much creatures of the Cold War, ready to fight Armageddon at sea. Her first full deployment in 1957 embarked Air Group One with three attack squadrons flying A3D-1 Skywarriors, F9F-8 Cougars, and AD-6 Skyraiders, plus fighter squadrons with FJ-3M Furies and F3H-2N Demons for day-night defense. The air group also included Skyraider early warning and night attack detachments, with F2H-2P Banshee photo recon and HUP-2 helicopter detachments.

As the world's first super carriers, the Forrestals set the pattern for later air group organization and shipboard procedures. Their layout, with four deck-edge elevators and three catapults, provided optimum operating efficiency, leaving room for larger aircraft to join the fleet in later decades. For instance, in more than twenty deployments CV-59 operated twenty-one aircraft types, including nine fighters, five attack aircraft, five special-mission planes, and two helicopters.

Twenty-two of FID's thirty skippers became admirals, with the first, Rudolph L. "Roy" Johnson, retiring as the four-star commander of the Pacific Fleet in 1967.

The Forrestals were followed by the similar three-ship Kitty Hawk (CV-63) sub-class, differing in greater length and location of aircraft elevators. "The Hawk's" sisters were *Constellation* (CV-64), also commissioned in 1961, and *America* (CV-66) in 1965.

Following the *Enterprise* (CVN-65) in 1961, costs for nuclear power soared, prompting cancellation of the six-ship class. But two hulls were under construction already, as CV-66 and -67 were to be nuclear powered, each with four reactors of greater power than *Enterprise*'s eight. The secretary of defense directed them to be built with conventional power plants, although the reactors were completed and sat "on the shelf." When *Enterprise* began her service-life extension in 1991, her existing plant was upgraded with equipment manufactured for CV-66 and -67. Furthermore, the fuel intended for those two ships allowed the Big E to operate beyond her fifty-year lifespan.

John F. Kennedy (CV-67), commissioned in 1968 and retired in 2007, was visibly distinguishable from the Kitty Hawks, with a shorter hull. She was the last fuel-fired carrier in the U.S. Navy.

NEW BIRDS IN THE BARN

Carrier sailors and aviators referred to their ships as "flat-roofed bird farms," and the 1950s saw record numbers of birds roosting in the nautical rafters. Sixteen fixed-wing aircraft entered service, including three flying boats and an astonishing seven helicopters. During the 1960s the fleet introduction was down to five new carrier types, falling to two in the 1970s, plus the AV-8 Harrier.

If there was a golden year in carrier aviation's golden decade, it was 1956. Five front-line aircraft went operational, Douglas sealing its hold on attack aircraft with two very different types: the huge twin-engine A3D Skywarrior and the small single-seat A4D Skyhawk. Both became naval aviation icons.

That same year three fighters entered service. The Douglas entry was the F4D Skyray, an interceptor with rocket-like acceleration that set speed and climb records. Grumman's F11F Tiger was small, fast, and agile, but as some pilots said, "It was out of gas just off the catapult." The Tiger was best known as the Blue Angels' mount from 1957 to 1968. McDonnell's F3H Demon was "an underpowered dog" that nevertheless afforded single-seat night intercept capability until 1964 when the successor Phantom was well established.

As America had done with the unworkable multi-service F-111, Britain fell prey to the alluring shibboleth of developing a single aircraft for the RAF and RN. They settled on Hawker's proposed P.1154 vertical takeoff and landing (VTOL) jet, which favored Air Force requirements over the Navy's. The project ended when both services opted for the Phantom, but additional time was lost. Eventually the vertical and short takeoff and landing jets (VSTOL) design evolved into the Harrier.

SIOP: PLANNING ARMAGEDDON

In 1960 the outgoing Eisenhower administration developed the basis of an overall policy in the event of nuclear war with the Soviet bloc. The Single Integrated Operational Plan (SIOP) emerged that year but was steadily refined, assigning specific targets to each part of the "nuclear triad"—manned aircraft, submarines, and ballistic missiles. The naval portion included carrier-based bombers and sub-launched missiles, beginning with the five-boat George Washington (SSBN-598) class of 1958–61.

The Navy's ultimate doomsday bomber was Douglas's large, capable A3D Skywarrior, redesignated A-3 in 1962. Affectionately called "the Whale" for its size (length and wingspan both exceeding seventy feet), it proved extremely versatile as a tanker and reconnaissance aircraft. The original specification called for 100,000-pound gross weight, but Edward H. Heinemann, master wingsmith responsible for the SBD Dauntless, delivered the Whale at barely two-thirds that figure. Still, the Skywarrior's size limited its use aboard Essex class carriers.

With rapid development of more efficient nuclear weapons, smaller aircraft took up much of the SIOP mission. Two other Douglas designs—the prop-driven AD/A-1 Skyraider and single-engine jet A4D/A-4 Skyhawk—were standard "special weapon platforms" through much of the Cold War. Subsequent types were Grumman's two-seat A-6 Intruder and Vought's single-seat A-7 Corsair II.

Attack pilots and aircrews usually deployed with at least one specific target assigned. Fliers were thoroughly briefed on routes and likely defenses, sometimes coordinated to clear a radioactive path for Air Force strikers. Senior aviators occasionally marveled at the naivety of "nugget" pilots. One Sixth Fleet veteran said, "They seemed to think they were going to fly an eight- or ten-hour mission, nuke their target, return to the ship and watch the movie while eating popcorn in the ready room that night!"

Nonetheless, nuclear delivery was taken extremely seriously. Even in the depths of the Vietnam War, attack carriers deployed with fully developed SIOP plans, remaining in range of designated launch points. All the while, aircrews continued preparing for Armageddon. A typical pre-deployment syllabus was 60 percent nuclear training, 40 percent conventional.

The carrier portion of SIOP ended in 1976, a welcome development for naval planners, carrier captains, and aviators. No longer chained to their strategic launch points, carriers were relatively free to steam beyond their previously assigned SIOP areas. However, contingency attack squadrons were required to remain proficient in nuclear delivery until the weapons were removed from carriers in 1992.

"MR. ATTACK AVIATION"

Edward H. Heinemann was chief designer of Douglas Aircraft for most of his career, producing classic carrier aircraft from the SBD Dauntless to the A-1 Skyraider, A-3 Skywarrior, and A-4 Skyhawk. He was highly regarded in the industry as a remarkable weight saver. He reflected:

> People asked me what airplane I was proudest of, and I would say the A-3 because of the weight saving.
>
> In 1948 North American seemed to reflect the views of those not wanting to bid on the (nuclear bomber) contract. They felt the plane simply could not be built for the mission assigned at 100,000 pounds. The competition was eventually reduced to Douglas and Curtiss-Wright.

We were determined to whittle away until a 68,000-pound design was achieved. Included in that figure were 10,000 pounds for the bomb. I tried vainly to get specifics on the atomic weapon; I was convinced that state-of-the-art technology could produce a much smaller one than was anticipated. But whenever I asked a Navy acquaintance for more details, I was advised to stop probing.

Both El Segundo and Curtiss made monthly progress reports to the Bureau of Aeronautics over the next six months. As the milestones progressed, our basic design and weight stayed the same.

In July 1949 Curtiss was eliminated from the competition, and we signed a contract to build three test articles— two flight and one static. The plane was designated the A3D Skywarrior.

We decided on wings swept back 36 degrees, intersecting the fuselage at its top. The engines were contained in nacelles hung from pylons on either wing low enough to permit servicing without platforms. The pressurized cockpit was configured for a bombardier-navigator in the right seat and a navigator-turret operator back to back with the pilot, who flew from the left front.

We calculated that each pound added in equipment cost 6.4 pounds due to the growth factor. That is, we would have had to make wing and tail areas bigger to accommodate the extra weight while retaining the performance requirements. We weren't about to do that.

The Skywarrior made its maiden flight on October 28, 1952, and we learned that the Westinghouse J40 engine was not powerful enough for the aircraft. It took many months...but the Pratt & Whitney J57 was ultimately installed, and the A3D entered service in 1956. It became not just a bomber but a reconnaissance platform and an aerial tanker.

Heinemann left Douglas in 1960, later worked with General Dynamics in developing the F-16 lightweight fighter, and retired in 1973. He died in 1991, the same year the Skywarrior left Navy service.

TANKERS: EXPENSIVE FUEL

Jet aircraft brought unparalleled performance to carrier aircraft, but at a price. Aside from the difficulty of landing aboard ship at higher speeds than propeller planes, jets consumed large quantities of fuel. According to Rear Admiral James D. Ramage, an early commander of the East Coast heavy attack wing, "Tanker fuel is the most expensive there is because you pay for it twice. But when you need it, you really need it!"

In-flight refueling thus became an early priority with specialized equipment and techniques, and the Navy began examining the potential from 1948.

Jets could fly close formation and, with a tanker trailing a hose with a "basket" receptacle, the recipient could hook up without a piston aircraft's whirling propeller intervening. From the mid-1950s an increasing number of carrier jets were equipped with refueling probes, either fixed in place as with the A4D (later A-4) Skyhawk or retractable as with the F8U (later F-8) Crusader.

The earliest airborne tankers were modified A2J Savages, no longer needed for nuclear attack. However, the bigger, faster Douglas Skywarrior offered greater options and was modified or built in the KA-3B version, capable of lifting more than twenty thousand pounds (nearly three thousand gallons) of JP-5 jet fuel off a carrier deck.

Tankers not only extended the range of fighter and attack aircraft, but could save fuel-starved planes with battle damage or nearly empty tanks over a fouled deck.

An alternative to dedicated KA-3s and smaller KA-6 Intruder tankers was "buddy pack" refueling. A-4 Skyhawks and A-7 Corsairs could fly with underwing tanks containing nine thousand pounds or more, enabling squadron mates to hook up and receive life-saving "plugs." KA-3s left the fleet in 1987 and Intruders in 1997, leaving antisubmarine Lockheed S-3 Vikings to provide organic air wing tanking.

Lockheed's S-3 Viking antisubmarine aircraft doubled as an in-flight tanker for much of its career, here refueling USS *Constellation* EA-6B Prowlers in 1988. *Courtesy R. L. Lawson Collection, National Museum of Naval Aviation.*

The perceived need was such that the sixteen Vikings modified from ASW to multi-use electronic warfare roles retained the tanker capability. Some aircrew were appalled: "It showed a lack of clear thinking. They should have been as far from the carrier as possible, listening and recording." The ES-3s were retired in 1999, and the last fleet Vikings departed a decade later.

Lacking an indigenous tanker, carrier air wings became heavily dependent upon the Air Force. Consequently, long-range strikes over

Afghanistan and elsewhere required even more interservice cooperation. Some equitability ensued after the Air Force grounded its EF-111 Raven radar jammers, however, leaving the Navy and Marines the electronic warfare mission with EA-6B Prowlers.

NUCLEAR POWER

Shortly after World War II the Navy began considering a revolutionary change: nuclear propulsion for carriers. It represented a quantum leap in technology and operating methods, capping millennia of seaborne propulsion, from oars to sail to coal to fuel oil. The concept languished for several years, but as carriers grew in size, the prospect of multiple reactors blossomed, especially when the first nuclear submarine, USS *Nautilus* (SS-571), was commissioned in 1954.

"Father of the nuclear Navy" was Admiral Hyman G. Rickover, a Polish-born engineering officer who spent sixty-three years on active duty. A noted taskmaster, Rickover was entirely about results. He told subordinates, "If you cannot do your job in a twenty-four-hour day, you'll just have to work nights." But results he produced in abundance.

The concept of a nuclear-powered task force seemed attractive at first, as "nuke" ships could maintain high speed without running short of fuel en route to a "hot" zone. But a CVN required nuclear-powered cruisers and destroyers, which were too costly to build in ample numbers. Originally the Navy envisioned six Enterprise (CVN-65) class carriers, ninety thousand-ton ships capable of more than 30 knots. However, costs proved prohibitive and only the lead ship was built. To power *Enterprise* the Navy installed eight Westinghouse A2W reactors with geared steam turbines turning four shafts for 280,000 shaft horsepower (SHP). The published top speed of 33 knots was probably conservative.

USS *Enterprise* (CVN-65), the world's first nuclear-powered aircraft carrier, during sea trials in 1962. She was decommissioned in 2012. *Courtesy USN.*

Enterprise was laid down at Newport News, Virginia, in February 1958 and raised her commissioning pennant in November 1961—a respectable construction period for so large and revolutionary a ship. Her commissioning skipper was Captain Vincent de Poix, who had flown Wildcats from CV-6 in 1942.

A MEMORABLE TOUR OF DUTY

Vice Admiral Peter M. Hekman Jr., was an Annapolis-trained engineering officer who spent nearly four years aboard the world's first nuclear-powered carrier. He recalled:

> I reported aboard USS *Enterprise* as a lieutenant commander in Norfolk, Virginia, one stormy night in January 1971, for duty as engineer officer. I served aboard her in that capacity until November 1974. In that period, the ship made three deployments to the Western Pacific and Indian Ocean, rounded the tip of South America en route from Norfolk to Alameda, and spent six months in Puget Sound.

I was home 52 days during those 46 months. In that period, the ship steamed over 252,000 nautical miles. I do not know the number of aircraft launches and recoveries, but I do know there were more launches than recoveries. We were in a war.

Forrest S. Peterson was the CO upon my reporting aboard. Peterson was relieved by Ernest Tissot in early 1972, and he was relieved by C. C. Smith in late 1973. Captain Smith was still the CO when I left the ship. All three were selected for flag rank while on *Enterprise*.

The most remarkable thing about *Enterprise* was not simply her amazing nuclear power plant—a first of its kind. The truly amazing characteristic was found in the crew and the Engineering and Reactor Department personnel in particular. The ship's entire plant was NOFORN—no foreign access. Thus, any maintenance and repair needed to the plant overseas had to be accomplished by ship's force. Those young men were exceptionally talented. They lifted main engine turbine casings while underway to repair leaks. They conducted numerous reactor plant repairs without incident. The machine and electrical shops could repair most everything, as could the catapult and elevator shop. If they did not have the right tools, they designed and fabricated them. Especially skilled were the nuclear welders. The sign on their shop door read, "We can repair everything—except a broken heart or the crack of dawn." A statement that truly defined the crew of "The Big E."

We also had some serious accidents back then and inadequate facilities. In 1972 the ship's force designed and built the most modern medical intensive-care facility on the west coast—all without official permission, using ship's funds. We saved a life the first day we had the facility in commission. I was honored to serve on *Enterprise*, with some of the Nation's finest officers and men. A most memorable tour of duty.

Vice Admiral Hekman's commands included a destroyer escort, a guided missile destroyer, and a nuclear-powered cruiser. He retired as chief of Sea Systems Command in 1991.

NUKE ADVANTAGES AND DISADVANTAGES

Like every other invention, nuclear-powered carriers involve advantages and disadvantages. The advantages are obvious: almost unlimited range, greater internal space for aviation fuel and ordnance otherwise used by fuel bunkers, a cleaner operating environment, greater electrical power, and more water for steam and habitability. Greater capacity for aviation fuel and ordnance means more combat sorties between replenishments.

There are a number of disadvantages, however. Nuclear carriers are designed for an interim maintenance period every five years, and for a refueling and modernization overhaul every fifteen years, producing a fifty-year service life. Their entire operational cycle is based on that routine. They can spend three or four years laid up for overhaul and refueling their reactors, and they require far more support facilities ashore, with far more training needed for their engineering divisions.

Purely on a fiscal basis, CVNs proved inordinately more costly than oil-fired carriers. The typical fifty-year life of a warship involved 35 percent more expense for CVNs versus CVs, a factor of multiple billions of dollars. That does not include the huge effort and cost of disposing of nuclear waste and reactors—a consideration that became reality with *Enterprise*'s dismantling beginning in 2013.

Naval nuclear power plants have little in common with their civilian counterparts. Expended Navy cores are sent to a joint Navy and Department of Energy facility in eastern Idaho. There the cores are cooled and dissolved, radioactive material is extracted for industrial and medical applications, and the unused fuel is recycled for use in new cores.

Despite the complexity and expense, the Navy proceeded with nuclear carriers, acquiring ten Nimitz (CVN-68) class ships between 1975 and 2009. Typically they displace more than 100,000 tons with 5,600 personnel. Excepting the lead ship, all were named for presidents and politicians—to the lasting displeasure of naval purists.

THE LONGEST-LIVED CARRIERS

The ten-ship Nimitz class likely will be the longest-lived carriers ever. They are listed by year of commissioning.

NIMITZ (CVN-78)	1975
DWIGHT D. EISENHOWER (CVN-69)	1977
CARL VINSON (CVN-70)	1982
THEODORE ROOSEVELT (CVN-71)	1986
ABRAHAM LINCOLN (CVN-72)	1989
GEORGE WASHINGTON (CVN-73)	1992
JOHN C. STENNIS (CVN-74)	1995
HARRY S. TRUMAN (CVN-75)	1998
RONALD REAGAN (CVN-76)	2003
GEORGE H. W. BUSH (CVN-77)	2009

While *Enterprise* employed eight reactors, *Nimitz* had two West-inghouse A4Ws with four shafts of 260,000 SHP. Therefore, the Big E's reactors averaged thirty-five thousand SHP and *Nimitz*'s 130,000 each—more than three and a half times as much.

One widely appreciated aspect of nuclear power was the desire to eliminate oil-fired plants' need to "blow stacks." In order to lessen the accumulation of excessive soot, engineers periodically have to force air through the smoke stack. The result is appalling—a malodorous sulfurous, toxic excretion that can cause vomiting. Aircrews in particular detested the process, which often occurred during recoveries. For decades air wing commanders feuded with engineers over timing of blowing stacks, usually without satisfaction.

"WHERE ARE THE CARRIERS?"

Throughout the half-century Cold War, international crises erupted around the globe. Frequently they involved a naval response, nearly always featuring carriers. Presidents, prime ministers, and premiers recognized the carrier's invaluable advantage of "territorial independence"—the ability to deploy significant airpower without basing concerns with wavering allies.

For ten days in October and November 1956, the world's attention focused on the Suez Canal, which Egyptian President Nasser had nationalized in July. He also closed the vital waterway to Israel. Consequently, Israeli forces invaded the Sinai Peninsula and quickly were joined by Britain and France. Anglo-French aircraft then bombed Cairo.

The Royal Navy committed *Eagle*, *Albion*, and *Bulwark*. The resulting operation was the first ship-based helicopter assault ever conducted. *Eagle*'s air group was an eclectic combination of jet de Havilland Sea Venoms and Hawker Sea Hawks with turbo-prop Westland Wyverns and reciprocating Douglas Skyraiders. Meanwhile, *Theseus* and *Ocean* operated as helicopter carriers deploying Royal Marine commandos.

HELICOPTER CARRIERS

The U.S. and Royal Navies deployed several classes of carriers classified as Landing Platform Helicopter (LPH). They included conversions beginning with USS *Block Island* (CVE-106/LPH-1) and three modified Essex class carriers: *Boxer* (CV-21/LPH-4), *Princeton* (CV-37 and LPH-5), and *Valley Forge* (CV-45/LPH-8).

USS *Iwo Jima* (LPH-2) was the first ship designed for the role of amphibious assault. At eleven thousand tons light load, she could operate two dozen helicopters. Completed in 1961, she led to six sisters commissioned through 1970. They cost less to maintain than a modified Essex class ship, and Marines preferred the new design's greater capacity for a large battalion landing team. The last, *Inchon* (LPH-12), was retired in 2002.

Tarawa (LHA-1) class assault ships combined helicopter and landing-craft capability, the latter via a stern gate. At nearly forty thousand tons and 834 feet long, the Tarawas were close in size to Essex class carriers. They could embark nineteen CH-53 Sea Stallions or twenty-five CH-46 Sea Knights, or a combination. Provisions also were available for as many as six Harriers. Four Tarawas were commissioned from 1976 to 1979, with *Peleliu* (LHA-5) retiring in 2015.

Britain's first two LPHs were HMS *Theseus* (R64) and *Ocean* (R68), Colossus-class ships drafted as commando carriers for the 1956 Suez crisis. Three Centaur-class light carriers were converted in the 1960s and 1970s with *Albion* (R07) and *Bulwark* (R08) operating ASW and assault helicopters, while *Hermes* (R12) flew both helos and Sea Harriers. *Hermes* continued operating Harriers after transfer to India in 1987.

France's *Aeronavale* committed *Arromanches* (R95), formerly HMS *Colossus*, and *La Fayette* (R96), formerly USS *Langley* (CVL-27) operating F4U-7 Corsairs (specific to the French Navy) and TBM Avengers. Their brief combat included bombing and strafing Egyptian bases on November 3.

The episode ended when the United States and Russia arranged a diplomatic settlement, requiring the Anglo-French to withdraw. Israeli troops remained until 1957, however, the year the canal reopened.

British carriers provided support in the Middle East a few years later during the Kuwait Crisis. In June 1961 the Baghdad strongman, General Qasim, announced his intention to annex his oil-rich neighbor thirty years before Saddam Hussein's similar effort. Kuwait, still a British protectorate, applied for assistance, which was immediately granted. Royal Navy ships in the Persian Gulf sent Royal Marine commandos ashore, protected by *Victorious* with Sea Vixen all-weather fighters. *Victorious* was relieved by *Centaur* in late July, with Supermarine Scimitars. One *Centaur* pilot lamented, "We sat off Kuwait for weeks and the Iraqis did not advance." The crisis was resolved in October, as friendly Arab forces sided with Kuwait.

At the time the Iraqi Air Force flew a mixture of British and Russian aircraft, but Qasim, sympathetic to communists, subsequently obtained newer Soviet jets including MiG-19s. However, none of the Iraqi armed forces were up to invading Kuwait, and Qasim's bluster evaporated in the face of uncontested sea and air power.

CARIBBEAN CRISES

Meanwhile, carrier activity shifted to a very different locale. The Eisenhower administration's ill-conceived contingency plan to liberate Cuba from Fidel Castro's tyranny was revived by newly elected President John F. Kennedy. In 1961 he approved a doomed campaign to force an amphibious landing on Cuba's southern coast at the Bay of Pigs. On April 17 free Cuban forces with minimal air support from Central American bases were overwhelmed while *Essex* (CVA-9) aviators orbited offshore, unable to intervene. An Attack Squadron 34 Skyhawk pilot deterred one Castro bomber by flying close formation and casting "a steely-eyed Blue Blaster stare." Otherwise, the defenders had things entirely their way, and the invasion collapsed in a rubble of embarrassment for the United States.

The following fall brought a bone-chilling situation in the same venue. In response to Soviet nuclear missiles in Cuba in October 1962, the Kennedy administration declared a "quarantine" of ships bound for Cuba. The Navy deployed three attack carriers and six antisubmarine ships in three task groups, in a legally questionable blockade judged necessary to defend the continental United States. The most powerful was Task Group 135.2 with *Enterprise* (CVAN-65) and *Saratoga* (CVA-60), while 135.1 was built around *Independence* (CVA-62). TG-136.2 unified the ASW flattops *Essex* (CVS-9), *Randolph* (CVS-15), and *Wasp* (CVS-18).

Though Soviet submarines cruised Caribbean waters, there was little contact. The Russians removed their missiles in return for the United States pulling missiles out of Turkey.

A typical antisubmarine air group aboard USS *Wasp* (CVS-18) in 1957 with Grumman S2F-1 Trackers and Sikorsky HSS-1 Seabat helicopters. *Courtesy Tailhook Association.*

Nevertheless, antisubmarine warfare remained a significant carrier mission throughout the Cold War. Eighteen Essexes were employed as ASW ships, mainly redesignated between 1953 and

1959, with the last four converted through 1969. Throughout most of their ASW careers, the ships operated dedicated air groups with varying combinations of Grumman S2F/S-2 Tracker squadrons (operational from 1954) and Sikorsky HSS/SH-3 helicopter squadrons (operational from 1961). However, most embarked an airborne-early warning detachment, and a few—such as *Intrepid*—flew A-4 and F-8 units during Vietnam deployments.

RUNUP TO VIETNAM

Following President John F. Kennedy's assassination in November 1963, the Lyndon Johnson administration continued Washington's policy of increasing military commitment to Southeast Asia.

Veterans of the Korean War had labored under onerous political constraints, and many of the same pilots who flew there returned to fight in Southeast Asia a decade or more later. Some of the same ships and aircraft served in the second "cold war." *Bon Homme Richard* (CVA-31) and *Oriskany* (CVA-34) would steam in the Tonkin Gulf,

One of the most elegant carrier aircraft was North American's RA-5C Vigilante, a bomber successfully modified for photo reconnaissance. "Viggies" served from 1961 to 1979, flown by crews known for stratospheric morale. *Courtesy USN via R. R. Powell.*

and the AD Skyraider (redesignated A-1 in 1962) remained in Navy combat units until 1968.

Meanwhile, two of the most remarkable carrier aircraft of the era entered service: North American's RA-5C Vigilante and Grumman's A-6A (and later E model) Intruder. The "Viggie" was conceived as the A3J before the Department of Defense adopted a unified aircraft designation system in 1962. First flown in 1958, the twin-engine Vigilante was a supersonic nuclear delivery aircraft intended to spit out the weapon from its tail. However, the concept encountered numerous technical problems that ended the A-5A version, leading to the RA-5C reconnaissance aircraft. With extraordinarily sleek lines, the "Vige" looked as if it was doing 400 knots on the catapult. From 1963 ten fleet squadrons flew the type which, despite holding the Navy's second-worst safety record (just behind the F-8 Crusader), engendered stratospheric morale among pilots and reconnaissance navigators.

The Intruder was a vastly more successful attack aircraft. First flown as the A2F in 1960, it was a twin-engine, all-weather bomber with pilot and bombardier-navigator sitting side by side. The Intruder was subsonic (other aviators joked about bird strikes on the wing's trailing edge) but featured an advanced navigation-attack computer that became the world standard at the time. Nearly seven hundred were built, with squadron service extending to the Marines in 1993 and the Navy in 1997—a thirty-four-year career. The A-6 became known to the public via former attack pilot Stephen Coonts's 1986 novel, *Flight of the Intruder*, and the 1991 movie of the same name.

A late arrival in Vietnam was Grumman's EA-6B Prowler, a dedicated jamming aircraft that proved invaluable for more than four decades. With a pilot and as many as three electronic-warfare officers, the Prowler could defeat enemy air defenses by jamming radar and communications while firing antiradar missiles for "hard kills."

Reflecting their value, the Vigilante, Intruder, and Prowler were never exported, in contrast to many other carrier aircraft such as the A-4, F-4, F-8, E-2, and FA-18.

A DECADE IN ASIA

In early 1964, increasing American concern over events in Laos led to "Yankee Team" reconnaissance flights over communist-controlled areas. From May the Plaine des Jars and the nation's panhandle were crisscrossed by naval and Air Force planes monitoring communist activities. Navy and Marine Corps photo-recon aircraft flew repeated sorties from carriers in the Tonkin Gulf, originally from *Kitty Hawk* (CVA-63), with others following. The Douglas RA-3Bs and Vought RF-8As launched from "Dixie Station" about 115 miles off South Vietnam, occasionally drawing gunfire. One Crusader was shot down on June 7, Lieutenant Charles Klussmann being captured by the Pathet Lao and surviving two months in captivity before escaping. Klussmann's Crusader was the first naval fixed-wing aircraft lost in Southeast Asia. Nearly one thousand would follow.

Tensions heightened in the Tonkin Gulf. On the afternoon of August 2, 1964, three North Vietnamese torpedo boats clashed with the American destroyer *Maddox* (DD-731) patrolling the coast. Gunfire and torpedoes were exchanged while F-8 fighters from USS *Ticonderoga* (CVA-14) raced to the scene. Led by Commander James B. Stockdale, the four Crusaders strafed one of the boats, claiming it sunk, though in fact one was severely shot up and two damaged.

Two nights later the destroyer *Turner Joy* (DD-951) joined *Maddox* to enforce right of passage. Radar and sonar operators reported aggressive Vietnamese PT boats, leading to a four-hour live-fire exercise again involving Jim Stockdale. From his vantage in the dark sky he saw U.S. gunfire and ships' wakes but no hostile vessels. Again the Americans claimed a sinking, but Hanoi denied that any action had occurred.

As it turned out, the communists were right. But the Johnson administration, only ninety days from a presidential election, chose to believe the confused, contradictory, uncertain accounts of "The Second Tonkin Gulf Incident." The next day Lyndon Johnson ordered "retaliatory" air strikes against North Vietnam. Sixty-four aircraft from *Ticonderoga* and *Constellation* (CVA-64) bombed naval and petroleum targets. Two planes were downed with one pilot killed and one captured. The polls showed a fourteen-point jump in public approval, and in November Johnson won a decisive victory.

However, the Washington politicians refused to allow airpower to attempt a decision in Vietnam. Worried about encouraging Chinese or Soviet involvement—when in fact both were actively involved from before the beginning—the Johnson administration adopted halfway measures. During a Tonkin Gulf tour Secretary of Defense Robert S. McNamara—previously a Ford Motor Company executive—told aircrews to expect "unlimited losses in pursuit of limited goals."

Decades later Jim Stockdale reflected upon "Washington's second thoughts, the guilt, the remorse, the tentativeness, the changes of heart, the backout. And a generation of young Americans would get left

An F-4B Phantom off USS *Enterprise* rockets Viet Cong positions in South Vietnam during 1966 operations. *Courtesy USN.*

holding the bag." He paid a bitter price himself: shot down in September 1965, he spent seven years in Hanoi's extortionist torture chamber.

While the generals and admirals in Washington feuded over turf wars in Vietnam, tactical aircrews found ways to support one another, much as Navy, Marine, and Army fliers had done at Guadalcanal. Because the Navy possessed SAM warning gear before the Air Force, some Tonkin Gulf A-4 squadrons sent single Skyhawks to F-105 wings in Thailand. The process had begun early, resulting in a notable mission during October 1965.

Lieutenant Commander Trent Powers, executive officer of *Oriskany*'s VA-164, flew with the 355th Tactical Fighter Wing at Takhli, leading eight F-105s against two SA-2 sites north of Hanoi. The Skyhawk-Thunderchief team covered strikes by two carrier air wings, which escaped unharmed. The SAMs all missed, and Powers pressed his attack to extreme low level in bombing one of the sites. Flak tore his Skyhawk apart and he ejected into captivity. At some point he died in prison, receiving a posthumous Navy Cross.

THE SAGA OF CAPTAIN HOOK

On July 23, 1966, Commander Wynn F. Foster was an attack aviator flying the second combat cruise of his second war. Leading the "Saints" of VA-163 off *Oriskany*, "Old Salt One" led four A-4E Skyhawks against a petroleum target near Vinh on the North Vietnam coast. He recalled:

> I sighted the target and ran through the three-dimensional attack problem: roll in at 8,000 feet.... establish a 45-degree dive; track the sight pipper to the target; check the crosswind drift; "pickle" the bombs at 4,500 feet; pull out at 4 G; no lower than 2,000 feet; turn hard left; keep jinking; head back to the Gulf. Twenty seconds in and out.
> BA-LAM!

Suddenly the foggy mist of an explosive decompression swirled around me. The 400-knot slipstream blasted through the cockpit. My helmeted head bounced against the headrest. I looked up. The Plexiglass canopy over my head and part of the windscreen were gone! I was flying an open-cockpit Skyhawk. My oxygen mask, tightly cinched, was still in place. My helmet visor was down. I felt no immediate discomfort, but the deafening roar of high-speed air enveloped me. My jet had been hit...but how badly? There was a mild stinging sensation in my right elbow, but my attention was still outside. The plane appeared to be flying OK, except the left wing was dropping slowly. I moved my hand to the right to level the wings. Nothing happened. *What the hell?*

I glanced at the instrument panel and did a double take. An electric hot flash jolted through me, and for what seemed an eternity I stared in disbelief. The wall of instruments before me was a bloody mess. I glanced down. My right arm was missing! My gloved right hand lay like a macabre display atop the radio console on the right side of the cockpit. Stunned, I looked outside the cockpit as if that would dismiss the awful spectacle from my mind. When I looked again I realized that I was not hallucinating. But I still did not believe my eyes. I could feel the stick gripped in my right hand. But there was no right hand on the stick! Again, I moved my right arm to move the stick, but nothing happened. Reality banged at my brain. I had no right arm!

"My God," I thought. *"This can't be happening to me!"*

Foster flew to the northern search-and-rescue ship in the Tonkin Gulf. There he ejected and was rescued. He waged a two-year battle with the naval bureaucracy to remain on active duty with a prosthetic and retired a captain in 1972. Widely admired, "Captain Hook" died in 2013.

FIRE AT SEA

After World War II, twenty-one years passed without anything comparable to the horrific beatings sustained by *Bunker Hill* and *Franklin* in 1945. Then the Navy suffered three catastrophic carrier fires during the Vietnam War, none caused by enemy action.

Off Vietnam on October 26, 1966, *Oriskany*'s hangar deck crew was storing ordnance when two men mishandled a flare. It ignited, and rather than throw it overboard the panicked sailors tossed it into a locker with flares and rockets, then dogged the hatch. The resulting explosion tore through the hangar, spreading to the flight deck. Forty-four men died, 156 were injured, and six aircraft were destroyed or damaged. Five men were court martialed but none were convicted. The standard flare was redesigned to reduce chances of a repetition.

Nine months later, on July 29, 1967, *Forrestal* was preparing to launch aircraft from "Yankee Station" off North Vietnam. Stray voltage ignited a weapon pod on a Phantom, sending a Zuni rocket slashing across the flight deck and striking a Skyhawk. Ten A-4s loaded with fuel and ordnance erupted. Seconds later a 750-pound bomb exploded, sweeping the first fire-fighting crew.

Explosions continued for several minutes with ten more bombs "cooking off" in the heat. *Forrestal*'s determined crew fought fires for ten hours, sustaining 134 fatalities and 161 injured. Sixty aircraft—most of the air wing—were destroyed or damaged.

On January 15, 1969, *Enterprise* steamed south of Hawaii preparing for a practice mission. An auxiliary power unit was negligently turned on a Phantom's rocket pod, detonating the five-inch warheads. The explosions punctured the F-4J's fuel cells, igniting the JP-5 and blowing holes in the flight deck. Then a bomb exploded, starting a violent chain reaction of ordnance and fuel. A KA-3 Skywarrior tanker exploded with thousands of gallons on board, sweeping the deck in a churning fireball. The Big E's men fought the conflagration for three hours, feeling their way around eighteen holes in the deck

In January 1969 USS *Enterprise* suffered the third major carrier fire of the Vietnam War, attended by the destroyer USS *Rogers* (DD-876). *Courtesy USN.*

including one twenty-two feet across. *Enterprise* sustained more than 370 casualties, including twenty-eight dead with thirty-two aircraft destroyed or damaged.

Subsequently the Naval Ordnance Systems Command established a panel to recommend improvements in handling weapons and fire-fighting.

SMART BOMBS

The Navy entered the modern precision munition age in 1967 with the television-guided Walleye bomb. When the attack pilot designated the aim point, the TV seeker remained focused on that area and the unpowered AGM-62 flew itself to the target—a "fire and forget" weapon. The seeker did best against high-contrast targets, optimally hitting a designated window in a target building. After four years of development, Walleye was first deployed to combat aboard *Bon Homme Richard*. Attack Squadron 212 flew a successful mission against the Hanoi Thermal Power Plant on May 19, 1967, with a follow-up strike on the notorious Thanh Hoa Bridge two days later.

The first Walleye carried a relatively small 250-pound warhead, so the Navy upgraded to a longer-ranged one-ton weapon in Walleye II, which entered combat in 1972. The precision revolution begun in Southeast Asia would peak in the Iraqi desert a quarter century later.

VIETNAM END GAME

Beset at home and abroad, in 1968 Lyndon Johnson decided against running for re-election. In March he banned bombing north of the twentieth parallel, leaving most of North Vietnam a sanctuary. He was succeeded by Republican Richard M. Nixon, who largely limited offensive air operations over the North for nearly four years. One example will suffice: from 1965 through 1968 Navy aircrews downed thirty-three enemy aircraft, but over the next three years tailhookers splashed only one. Meanwhile, "peace talks" trickled out in Paris.

Then, on March 30, 1972, Hanoi launched a full-scale conventional attack against South Vietnam, shattering the dead-end Paris "peace talks." American airpower responded massively.

Leading *Constellation*'s Air Wing Nine was Commander Lowell "Gus" Eggert, a cheerful aviator who enjoyed partying with his aircrews. Eggert's keen intuition told him the 1971–72 cruise might be different from the previous three years. He began training his squadrons for large "Alpha" strikes in addition to the usual close air support in South Vietnam and Laos.

"Connie" completed her six-month deployment, and on April 1 she was in Japan preparing to return to California, when the North Vietnamese spring offensive rolled south. Sailors and aircrews hastily offloaded their new purchases—notably motorcycles—and began loading ordnance. The ship was back in the Tonkin Gulf five days later, joining *Hancock*, *Coral Sea*, and *Kitty Hawk*. By then the communists had beefed up their air defenses, and on one mission over South Vietnam an Intruder pilot had to abort his attack because a cloud of tracers obscured the reticle of his bombsight.

After further delay, Nixon finally loosed the airmen. A Phantom pilot recalled, "We had reports of 168 SAMs on the first night after Nixon got serious in May. But that was coordinated with massive B-52 raids supported by three carrier air wings."

On May 9 a handful of aircraft demonstrated the carrier's potential for strategic effects with extreme economy of force. While *Kitty Hawk* provided a diversionary strike, *Coral Sea* launched nine jets that turned the war around in two minutes: six Navy A-7Es and three Marine A-6As laid three dozen mines in Haiphong Harbor. The weapons were time-delayed to allow ships to leave North Vietnam's major port. During the next three days, thousands more mines were sown in Hanoi's coastal waters, effectively blockading the communists from seaborne replenishment. Commander Roger Sheets's Air Wing Fifteen, on its seventh Vietnam deployment, shut down Haiphong for almost a year—well beyond the impending "peace" treaty.

The mines were frequently replenished, eventually totaling more than eleven thousand weapons. Sometimes the "reseeding" involved unconventional tactics, as when *Saratoga*'s Air Wing Three employed Phantoms flying formation on Intruders and Corsairs in what one F-4 pilot called "a one-potato, two-potato" drop sequence, based on when the attack jets released.

Finally Phantom crews could ply their trade again. From January 1972 through January 1973, carrier-based F-4s claimed twenty-five aerial kills—nearly as many as the Navy total in the first six years of the war. The tailhookers' best day was May 10. That morning a two-plane VF-92 section off *Constellation* trolled Kep Airfield and caught two MiG-21s taking off. The high-speed, low-level chase ended with one MiG destroyed which, with the Air Force bombing the Paul Doumer Bridge in Hanoi, sparked an exceptional response.

That afternoon "Connie" launched thirty-two planes against Hai Duong logistics, producing one of the biggest combats of the war with Phantoms, Corsairs, and MiGs embroiled in a "furball" of maneuvering jets. When it was over, two F-4s fell to flak and SAMs while VF-96 claimed six kills, producing the Navy's only ace crew of the war. In all, the Navy and Air Force downed a dozen MiGs, which remains an unsurpassed one-day total more than forty years later.

During Operation Linebacker—the final air campaign over North Vietnam—American aircrews claimed seventy-two aerial kills versus twenty-eight known losses to MiGs, an overall exchange ratio of 2.5–1. However, the Navy's intensive fighter training program from 1969 onward produced exceptional results. "Topgun" graduates and doctrine yielded twenty-four MiGs against four carrier planes lost, including a lone Vigilante escorted by fighters. In contrast to the Navy's 6–1 kill ratio, the Air Force figure was closer to 2–1, approaching parity in some months.

The disparity between the two services was dramatically illustrated in August 1972, when four F-8E Crusaders from *Hancock* deployed to Udorn, Thailand, to update Air Force Phantom crews on air combat maneuvering. The senior Navy pilot was already a MiG killer, Commander John Nichols, who noted, "My biggest challenge was keeping my guys from lording it over the blue suiters."

Throughout the war, naval aviators shot down sixty enemy aircraft—all by carrier pilots. It was a stark contrast to Korea when barely a dozen communist planes were credited to tailhookers among fifty-four total by Navy and Marine pilots.

In fact, the reason for carrier-based fighters was to establish air superiority so the attack planes could perform their vital mission. Skyraiders, Skyhawks, Intruders, and Corsairs seldom worried about enemy aircraft while placing ordnance on target the length and breadth of Indochina. Few aircrews and probably few admirals realized how far carrier aviation had come since the start of World War II. Long gone was the era when airpower theorists insisted that sea-based aircraft could not compete with land-based planes. If nothing else, Vietnam confirmed that naval aviation was a world-class organization.

On two days in October 1972, Commander Donald Sumner led USS *America* (CVA-66) A-7 Corsairs against Thanh Hoa Bridge, a vital communist transportation target. One of his pilots, Lieutenant Commander Leighton Smith, had first bombed the bridge as a *Coral Sea* A-4 pilot in 1966. The Air Force had badly damaged "The Dragon's Jaw," but spans remained intact. With a combination of two thousand-pound TV-guided weapons and conventional one-ton bombs, the naval aviators finally slew the long-lived dragon, more than seven years after the first U.S. efforts.

During the eleven-day "Christmas War" of 1972, carrier aircraft again supported B-52s in bombing an intransigent Hanoi back to the bargaining table. By then Hanoi was nearly out of SA-2 missiles.

The Paris accords among Washington, Saigon, and Hanoi took effect January 27, 1973. On that day Commander Harley Hall, a former Blue Angel leader and the commander of an *Enterprise* F-4 squadron, became the last naval aviator shot down in the long war. His Phantom fell north of the Demilitarized Zone, and though his back-seater survived captivity, Hall did not. Long thereafter his widow learned that he had probably lived two or more years in captivity, abandoned by his government with unknown numbers of other men.

VIETNAM DEBRIEF

The nine-year Asian morass left a generation of aviators disgusted with their leaders who, in attack pilot Stephen Coonts's words, "lacked the wisdom to win or abandon" the effort.

A high-time Crusader pilot, Commander John Nichols, explained the prevailing attitude: "Professionalism was a dominant motivation. We had accepted the king's shilling for years, and now we were expected to pay back the investment. It was not only expected of us; we expected it of ourselves."

Perhaps there exists no better example of tailhookers' devotion to each other than a rescue attempt over North Vietnam in July 1967. Two *Oriskany* Skyhawks were shot down about thirty miles south of Hanoi, well inland and within the envelope of multiple defenses.

Leading the rescue CAP was Lieutenant Commander Richard Schaffert of VF-111, a talented, aggressive Crusader pilot. After forty minutes on station, dodging AA and occasional SAMs, he knowingly overstayed his time until a relief arrived. Perilously low on fuel, he probably could not even reach the enemy coast.

Meanwhile, Lieutenant Commander Thomas Maxwell of *Oriskany*'s tanker detachment orbited offshore. Hearing Schaffert's call for help, Maxwell quickly checked with his two crewmen, who knew the risk. They readily consented, realizing that standing orders prohibited tankers from going "feet dry" (over land).

The ungainly KA-3 motored through flak, hearing SAM calls, while steering to intercept Dick Schaffert. There was no margin for error.

With exquisite timing, Maxwell turned ahead of the F-8, streamed the hose, and Schaffert established an overtake. His fuel gauge almost read empty—he probably had time for only one try. From long experience he knew the technique: make minute control inputs and "Don't fence with the basket."

He nailed it.

The Whale began pumping life-saving JP-5, permitting Schaffert to recover aboard *Oriskany.*

Another Skyhawk was lost in the rescue attempt, but two of the three downed A-4 pilots were picked up.

Medals of Honor have been awarded for less than what Maxwell and his two crewmen did that day. By Vietnam War standards they deserved a Silver Star or better, but because they busted regulations, their skill and heroism received no official recognition. However, they and their shipmates knew their value.

Small wonder that the original title of Stephen Coonts's smash bestseller was *For Each Other.*

USS *Kitty Hawk's* Air Wing 11 in 1974 after its seventh Vietnam deployment, parading A-6 Intruders, A-7 Corsairs, and F-4 Phantoms in formation. *Courtesy National Museum of Naval Aviation.*

THE NINE-YEAR SCHEDULE

From 1964 to 1973, seventeen attack carriers logged seventy-one Tonkin Gulf cruises. Regardless of the class of ship—Essex, Midway, Forrestal, or Enterprise—the crews and fliers maintained a rigorous schedule without interruption. Men and machines wore out, but the pace was maintained.

Typically, carriers alternated on a noon-to-midnight and midnight-to-noon schedule, sustaining cyclic operations on a "one plus forty-five" basis, or three deckload Alpha strikes, four hours apart. But for "the gang on the roof," sixteen-hour days were common. Amid the unrelenting noise and bustle, muscular sailors strained on "hernia bars" to hoist bombs for ordnance men to attach weapons to ejector racks before threading in nose and tail fuses. Plane handlers maneuvered ten-ton jets around a crowded four-acre area via mechanical mules, while purple-clad "grapes" refueled planes scheduled for the next launch.

Throughout the Vietnam "conflict," carrier air wings lost 530 aircraft to known or suspected enemy action and 329 operationally. The A-4 bore the brunt of the offensive missions and suffered accordingly, with 282 carrier-based losses, while air wings wrote off 138 Phantoms and 118 Crusaders. Of 704 carrier personnel who died in the Pacific area during the Vietnam War, some six hundred were aircrew.

One of the Yankee Station survivors was Jack D. Woodul, who finished his career as a Reserve commander. In 2013 he wrote, "I flew airliners for thirty years and I never think about it. I flew combat from an aircraft carrier for six months and I think about it every damn day."

In the galling wake of Vietnam, the Navy adjusted its carrier basing policy. During 1973 *Midway* with Air Wing Five moved permanently to Yokosuka, Japan, remaining the forward-deployed flattop until relieved by *Independence* in 1992. Subsequently "Indy" was relieved by *Kitty Hawk* seven years later. "The Hawk" returned to San Diego in 2008, awaiting decommissioning.

WHITE LIGHTS

Captain Lonny McClung enjoyed a richly varied career, flying E-2 Hawkeyes and F-4 Phantoms, becoming an LSO, and commanding the Naval Fighter Weapon School. But he recalls a flight-deck innovation as one of the most memorable aspects of his career.

One of the great improvements in carrier aviation safety arrived in 1966. The advent of the white flight deck flood lights was a most welcome improvement for pilots and plane handlers alike. The tactical thought left over from World War II had been that red lights made the carrier harder to see for any threat platform to visually locate the target. While that was essentially true, enhancements in the electronic spectrum during the late '50s and early '60s had replaced visual locating and targeting of ships. Therefore, by the time a threat platform was in visual range, the electronic spectrum had long since located and targeted the carrier.

Before white flood lights, the flight deck lighting was red with dustpan lighting at the arresting gear for visual reference to aid prop planes in establishing the proper attitude after being cut by the LSO. In late summer 1966 USS *Kitty Hawk* did the initial certification with the Naval Flight Test Center conducting the testing. Captain Martin "Red" Carmody was the ship's CO. Interestingly enough, the initial night landings under the white floods were made by the Pax River C-1 Trader carrier onboard delivery aircraft (COD). Policy was that the COD did not operate at night, but it was the perfect platform for the first looks due to its closure rate and two pilots to help with the evaluation.

Jet operations followed the initial C-1 testing. It was immediately obvious that the dramatic improvement in situational awareness for both pilots and the flight deck crew was here to stay. The speed and ease of flight deck movements and launch sequence improved significantly. Flight deck "crunch" events were reduced. Incidents of injuries on the flight deck also decreased. It was definitely a win-win. When we look back now, it is amazing that it took that long for this innovation to find its way into carrier flight operations.

Captain McClung retired in 1992 with over seven thousand flight hours and more than one thousand carrier landings. In civilian life he continues flying everything from seaplanes to tactical jets.

244 ON WAVE AND WING

INDIA-PAKISTAN

India's first carrier was the British-built HMS *Hercules*, with construction suspended in 1946. Sold to India and completed in Belfast, she was commissioned as *Vikrant* (Courageous) in 1961. Ten years later she participated in the second Indo-Pakistani war, part of the broader Bangladesh Liberation War. Her air group consisted of Hawker Sea Hawks, Breguet Alizes for ASW, plus Aerospatiale-designed Alouette and Sikorsky Sea King helicopters. Captain Swaraj Prakash was not an aviator, but his Commander (Air) was R. S. Grewal, who oversaw flight operations.

On December 4, 1971, from sixty miles offshore, Lieutenant Commander S. K. Gupta led eight Sea Hawks against Chittagong Airfield and Harbor. After bombing and rocketing, the fighter-bombers returned to refuel and rearm. The aviators were back that afternoon, again attacking the airfield and Pakistani shipping.

Insufficient wind prevented air operations on December 5, but Sea Hawks logged two missions on December 6, while the ungainly but capable Alizes contributed bombing sorties over Chittagong for two nights.

Admiral Elmo Zumwalt, the U.S. Chief of Naval Operations, was directed to send the *Enterprise* task group from the Tonkin Gulf to the Bay of Bengal without a stated mission. The Indians noted the approach of the world's largest warship and four escorts with some concern, but the American group withdrew after two days. However, the Big E spent ninety-eight days in the Indian Ocean without seeing a port, refueling her escorting destroyer as required.

Between December 4 and 14, *Vikrant* launched Sea Hawks at least twice a day, except when insufficient wind prevented catapulting with a useful ordnance load. The ASW Alizes took up the slack, flying day and night.

Hostilities ended with Pakistani forces surrendering in East Pakistan on December 16. No Indian naval aircraft were lost, though

Seahawks sustained minor battle damage while one Alize barely made it back. In return, *Vikrant*'s air group claimed sinking or beaching eight merchant vessels, eight gunboats, and two landing craft.

Vikrant was auctioned in 2014, and was scrapped the following year.

AFTER VIETNAM

For more than two decades the U.S. Navy distinguished between attack carriers (CVAs) and antisubmarine carriers (CVSs). That ended in June 1975 with the arrival of the Lockheed S-3 Viking, providing indigenous ASW within attack air wings. Consequently, dedicated antisubmarine ships disappeared and CVs became standard.

The most significant aircraft of the immediate post-Vietnam period was Grumman's two-seat F-14 Tomcat, featuring variable-sweep wings. Optimized for fleet defense, like the Phantom its crew was a pilot and radar intercept officer (RIO). The "Tom" entered service in 1974, with the first two squadrons embarked in *Enterprise*, covering the American abandonment of South Vietnam in April 1975. Unfortunately, the ultimate fleet-defense fighter suffered from inadequate engines, as the Pratt & Whitney TF-30 lacked sufficient power for the heavy airframe and required careful handling. The limited-acquisition F-14B and D models achieved the Tomcat's potential with GE's F-110 engine providing 60 percent more thrust.

Despite new equipment, funding lagged, including maintenance support. During the Carter administration a fearless F-14 squadron commander said, "When I was a boy growing up in North Carolina I wanted to command a fighter squadron and run a junk yard, and now I'm doing both." Despite his candor, Monroe "Hawk" Smith retired as a captain.

The Phantom logged its last trap in 1987, a Reserve F-4S aboard *America*. Meanwhile, the future of carrier aviation became clear in 1983, when McDonnell-Douglas FA-18 Hornets joined a Marine squadron, VMFA-314, shortly followed by the Navy's VFA-25, which logged the Hornet's first cruise aboard *Constellation* in 1985. The Hornet's versatility earned it a new designation in naval aviation: strike fighter, or VFA. It was highly capable both for air-to-air and air-to-surface, but suffered from short range, requiring significant tanker support.

Meanwhile, carrier aviation kept an eye on NATO's northern flank. Navy Secretary John Lehman—a qualified bombardier-navigator—recalled the transition from Annapolis graduate Jimmy Carter's administration to that of former cavalryman Ronald Reagan:

> Nine months after the President's inauguration (in January 1981), three U.S. and two Royal Navy carriers executed offensive exercises in the Norwegian Sea and Baltic. In this and subsequent massive exercises there and in the northwest Pacific carried out every year, carrier aircraft proved that they could operate effectively in ice and fog, penetrate the best defenses, and strike all of the bases and nodes of the Soviet strategic nuclear fleet. Subsequent testimony from members of the Soviet General Staff attested that this was a major factor in the deliberations and the loss of confidence in the Soviet government that led to its collapse.

Air wing cruise reports also reflected adverse operating conditions in the Northern Pacific. Flying in all weather, pilots described LSOs' sardonic radio calls: "You sound good, keep it coming." Russians on the Kamchatka Peninsula could not help but take note.

MELEES IN THE MED

In the wake of the Vietnam debacle, the United States armed forces worked hard to absorb new equipment and doctrine as

America sought to reassert itself internationally. Most of the opportunities came in the Mediterranean.

From 1973 Libyan strongman Colonel Muammar Gaddafi—a longtime supporter of global terrorism—had claimed the Gulf of Sidra as territorial waters, far beyond the internationally recognized twelve nautical miles. In August 1981 President Reagan dispatched naval units to reinforce the right of navigation, resulting in a brief aerial combat on August 19. Two Tomcats from USS *Nimitz* (CVN-68) clashed with two Libyan Sukhoi 22 fighter bombers, destroying both.

In 1983 Reagan sent a Marine landing team to Beirut in an ill-advised effort to interpose "peace keepers" between warring factions. But on October 23 an Iranian-sponsored suicide bomber drove a large truck past ill-prepared sentries at the Marine barracks, detonating one of the largest non-nuclear blasts to date, destroying the building and killing 141 Americans.

A-6E Intruders and A-7E Corsair IIs from USS *Forrestal* flying over Lebanon during the 1981–82 Beirut crisis. *Courtesy Tailhook Association.*

Six weeks later, in December, U.S. carrier aircraft attacked Syrian antiaircraft positions that had fired upon U.S. planes flying reconnaissance missions. The Reagan administration dictated an early-morning attack, which aircrews attributed to the U.S. news cycle. Thus, the retaliation was planned in extreme haste, under orders from Washington that foolishly required the aircrews to attack with the early morning sun shining in their eyes. An A-6E off *John F. Kennedy* was shot down with the pilot killed and the navigator briefly captured, while the *Independence*'s air wing commander ejected from his crippled A-7.

France's *Foch* (R99) alternated with *Clemenceau* (R98) contributing to the allied effort, launching Crusaders and Etendards against Iranian targets within Lebanon. Absent the political agenda driving U.S. operations, the *Aeronavale* squadrons sustained no losses.

Then it was back to Libya.

On April 5, 1986, Libyan agents exploded a bomb in a Berlin night club, killing three people including two U.S. servicemen. President Reagan ordered Operation El Dorado Canyon, a response by the Navy and Air Force.

Air Force F-111 fighter-bombers launched from England, flying around the periphery of Western Europe to avoid involving NATO allies. Most of the U.S. response came from the sea, with air wings aboard *Coral Sea*, *Saratoga*, and *America*. It was the first combat for most of the Navy aircrews; one flier said, "The briefing was really serious. Nobody was joking."

Strike planners compressed the twenty-seven Navy and eighteen Air Force planes into a twelve-minute window, seeking to saturate the defenses at Benghazi and Tripoli while USAF EF-111 Raven jamming aircraft orbited offshore. Time over target was 2:00 a.m., but the Libyans, alerted by anti-American Italians, shot down an F-111 on the ingress.

Coral Sea and *America* launched fifteen A-6E Intruders, six A-7E Corsair IIs, and six McDonnell Douglas F/A-18A Hornets. All struck their targets—army barracks, Benina Airfield, and air defense networks. All returned to their ships.

El Dorado Canyon was a tactical success, but it did not cure Muammar Gaddafi's offensive behavior. Three years later Libya repeated its territorial claim, drawing another U.S. response. The *John F. Kennedy* battle group arrived on station, resulting in an aerial engagement on January 4, 1989. Two F-14s maneuvered against two Libyan MiG-23s, destroying both. The two Libyan engagements ended the Navy Tomcat's record at 4–0, although Iran's F-14s saw extensive combat during the 1980–88 war with Iraq.

THE DISAPPEARING RUSSIAN THREAT

During the Cold War the Soviet Navy was caught between communist dogma and nautical reality. Though Russia had castigated the carrier as "the principal instrument of aggression" at a time when Moscow had no carriers, eventually a building program arose on the Baltic.

In 1967 the Soviets launched *Moskva*, a helicopter carrier, followed by her sister *Leningrad* two years later. They were twelve thousand-ton antisubmarine ships typically embarking fourteen Kamov helicopters. Both were retired in the 1990s.

Next came the more ambitious four-ship Kiev class, commissioned between 1975 and 1987. Classed as "heavy aircraft carrying cruisers," they displaced 30,500 tons with Yak-38 "jump jets" and updated Kamov helos. But they were also surface combatants, packing long-range cruise missiles. Most frequently they were assigned to the Mediterranean and Northern Fleets, none achieving much distinction.

In 1993 *Kiev* and *Minsk* were sold to China, becoming tourist attractions, while *Novorossiysk* was sold for scrap. *Admiral of the Fleet Gorshkov* (formerly *Baku*) went to India in 2004, becoming

INS *Vikramaditya*. In that role she became a genuine carrier with a "ski jump" bow, embarking navalized MiG-29Ks in 2010.

The Red Navy's architect, Admiral Sergei Gorshkov, recognized big-deck carriers as the measure of great fleets, and he backed a construction scheme. In the early 1980s U.S. analysts projected a class of perhaps four Soviet carriers operating MiG and Sukhoi fighter bombers modified for fleet use. A summary in 1983 stated, "Our opponents will field their first genuine CV in 1988 or 1989 with task force organization on the horizon (probably employing multiple CVs) by the end of the next decade."

The American projection proved significantly wrong. The two-ship Admiral Kuznetsov class began with the name ship commissioned in 1991, joining the Black Sea Fleet late that year. However, the forty-three thousand-ton carrier only began jet operations in 1993 with Sukhoi 33s. She fell in and out of commission for many years but remained deployable as of 2016.

Kuznetsov's sister *Varyag* was laid down at Riga in the Ukraine in 1985 and was two-thirds complete when construction was canceled in 1988. A decade later she was sold to communist China, where she was commissioned in 2012. Christened *Liaoning*, she has become a learning platform for the Peoples' Liberation Army Navy. She flies Chinese-built Su-33s with helicopters.

Four years before *Liaoning* was commissioned, Major General Quian Lihua of the Chinese Defense Ministry's Foreign Affairs Office stated, "The navy of any great power…has the dream to have one or more aircraft carriers. The question is not whether you have an aircraft carrier, but what you do with your aircraft carrier."

That statement indicates an awareness of reality. Merely possessing a carrier does not a carrier navy make, as combat operations require sustainability that one hull cannot deliver. Single-carrier navies must either remain satisfied with the perceived prestige of a "showboat," or recognize that a first flattop must lead to others.

HARRIER CARRIERS

In 1957 the British began a prolonged development program for vertical and short takeoff and landing jets (VSTOL). Hawker's prototype P.1127, which debuted in 1960, emerged as the Harrier in 1967, flown by the RAF and the Royal Navy. The latter's Sea Harrier showed enough promise to convince the U.S. Marine Corps to acquire the AV-8A beginning in 1971, followed by the B model in 1985.

The Royal Navy's three Invincible class "Harrier carriers" were twenty-two thousand-ton *Invincible* (R05), *Illustrious* (R06), and *Ark Royal* (R07), collectively in service from 1980 to 2014. Though their Harrier jump jets received most of the attention, the class was largely intended for helicopter ASW. *Invincible* was sold for scrap in 2005 and *Ark Royal* six years later. *Illustrious* was retired in 2014 with intentions to make her a museum ship.

FALKLANDS/MALVINAS: UNLIKELY CONTEST

London's folly in retiring the previous *Ark Royal* (R09) became evident four years later, when Argentina seized the British-held Falklands/Malvinas Islands on April 2, 1982. Within days London dispatched the South Atlantic Task Force including *Hermes* and *Invincible*, with twenty Sea Harriers between them, reinforced en route by twenty-two Royal Navy and RAF Harriers. They were opposed by some 120 Argentine Air Force and Navy fighter and strike aircraft based on the mainland, but the Super Etendards, Skyhawks, and Mirages operated at extreme range, four hundred nautical miles from the Malvinas.

The air war was joined on May 1 when the first Argentine strike reached the task force, inflicting no damage. But a trend was established that day when *Invincible* Sea Harriers shot down three Argentine attackers and mortally damaged another. Despite the Harriers' success, it was apparent that the British needed more fighters.

On May 2 a British submarine sank Argentina's *General Balgrano*—a former U.S. cruiser and survivor of the Pearl Harbor attack. The loss forced the Argentine command to recall the carrier *Veinticinco de Mayo* with its A-4s. She was another World War II ship, originally HMS *Venerable* and previously the Netherlands' *Karel Doorman*. A potential landmark event was thus foiled, as it would have been the last time aircraft carriers attacked each other.

Arriving in mid-month, the British container ship *Atlantic Conveyor* flew off fourteen Harriers and Sea Harriers shortly before the amphibious landing. The timing was fortuitous. On May 25 two Argentine Navy Super Etendards destroyed the vessel with Exocet cruise missiles. The British lost ten valuable helicopters, including heavy-lift U.S. Chinooks.

Throughout the two-month campaign, Sidewinder-armed Sea Harriers downed twenty Argentine jets without loss in air combat. Timing was fortunate for the Royal Navy, as the Sea Harrier had only entered service in 1978, the year *Ark Royal* was retired. The RAF Harriers flew ground-support and strike missions ashore.

Weather in the South Atlantic that spring was typically terrible. Some ships reported "excursions" of eighty feet or more in tossing seas, but aviators flew despite low ceilings and reduced visibility. Harriers thus proved more adaptable to poor sea state than most conventional carrier aircraft.

Important as *Invincible* and *Hermes'* Sea Harriers were to task force defense, the helicopters proved crucial. Sikorsky Sea Kings provided airborne early warning and ASW patrol, but they also transferred equipment between ships and from sea to shore.

Many of the "Argie" aviators were skilled and aggressive. The naval Skyhawks and Super Etendards were especially effective, sinking four British warships and a logistics vessel.

The land campaign progressed through the Falklands bogs, and British forces raised the Union Jack throughout the islands by June 20, bringing to an end one of the least likely and most bizarre wars of the sanguinary twentieth century.

Illustrious (R06) was commissioned at sea during the Falklands/ Malvinas war, but too late for combat. She returned to Britain and was formally commissioned in 1983, serving another thirty-one years.

HMS *Ocean* (L12), designed as a commando carrier, was commissioned in 1998, operating a wide variety of helicopters.

PRAYING MANTIS

Western and allied navies participated in the Persian Gulf "tanker war" during the mid to late 1980s, protecting oil tankers from attack by Iranian small craft. In April 1988 the frigate *Samuel B. Roberts* (named for one of the destroyers lost at Leyte Gulf) hit a mine, sustaining heavy damage but no casualties. Physical evidence proved what was already apparent—the mine came from Iran.

In response, *Enterprise* and her escorts with a surface action group launched Operation Praying Mantis, attacking Iranian facilities in the gulf on April 18—the forty-sixth anniversary of the Doolittle raid.

Primary targets were two Iranian oil platforms that offered a base for Revolutionary Guard speedboats harassing reflagged Kuwaiti tankers. Marines helicoptered onto one platform, leaving explosives to disable the facility. In response, the Iranians deployed Swedishbuilt Boghammer speedboats threatening transiting tankers. Two *Enterprise* Intruders intercepted the boats, dropping Rockeye cluster bombs that destroyed one Boghammer and holed others.

Meanwhile, one of Iran's fast La Combattante class frigates exchanged missiles with two U.S. ships, coming off second best. Iran's *Joshan* sank with heavy loss of life.

Shortly thereafter an Iranian frigate sortied, firing SAMs at nearby A-6s. The Intruders combined with a destroyer to smother 1,100-ton *Sabalan* with Harpoon missiles and laser-guided bombs. She drifted away on fire and was towed to port for repair.

During the day the Iranian air force launched two pair of F-4 Phantoms, but neither could intervene. The first two diverted when illuminated by a destroyer's fire-control radar; the second set was engaged by a guided missile cruiser, damaging one of the American-made fighters and forcing its withdrawal.

In all, Praying Mantis destroyed an Iranian frigate, a gunboat, three speedboats, and damaged another frigate. A Marine Corps helicopter crashed during the operation with two fliers killed in the accident.

Then, in 1990 naval aviation faced the challenge of multi-carrier operations for a sustained air campaign.

DESERT STORM

On August 2, 1990, Saddam Hussein's Iraqi regime invaded Kuwait, seeking to secure a greater share of Mideast petroleum. Aside from blatant aggression, the West could not tolerate a despot's hand on more of the world's oil taps. A U.S.-led coalition began Operation Desert Shield, building up forces in the region prior to forcibly ejecting Iraq from Kuwait. A Navy operations officer later quipped, "Saddam won the toss—and elected to receive."

First on the scene was *Independence*, arriving in the Gulf of Oman on August 5. Carriers became critically important, with Coalition airpower crowding ashore until there was little remaining ramp space in the Arabian Peninsula. News crews, needing footage of current air operations, cycled through "Indy" for several days, prompting Air Force partisans to describe CNN as "Carrier News Network."

The naval aviation planning cell took an unusual approach. "We looked at D.C. and asked ourselves what targets should we hit to shut down this place?" Turning that equation inside out, strike planners established targeting priorities for Baghdad. Command and control centers, government offices, bridges, and power plants all made the list.

Before the air war lifted off, the Navy had positioned *America*, *John F. Kennedy*, and *Saratoga* in the Red Sea. *Midway* and *Ranger* steamed in the Persian Gulf. The latter were joined by *Theodore Roosevelt* (CVN-71) in late January. In all, the carriers deployed thirty-four attack or fighter squadrons plus electronic warfare, early warning, and antisubmarine/tanker units. Before returning home, *Eisenhower* (CVN-69) steamed the Red Sea, prepared to defend against an Iraqi offensive into Saudi Arabia.

Operation Desert Storm began on January 17, 1991, with coordinated attacks on Iraqi air defenses and headquarters. EA-6B Prowlers were especially important in neutralizing Saddam's extensive radar network, while E-2C Hawkeyes provided airborne command and control in airspace clogged with aircraft from multiple nations.

One of the aviators flying that night was Commander Mark Fitzgerald, skipper of the VA-46 "Clansmen" aboard *John F. Kennedy*. Though the tartan-painted squadron had been transitioning to FA-18 Hornets, Fitzgerald took his command to war in its familiar A-7 Corsair IIs with sister squadron VA-72 on merely four days' notice.

On opening night Air Wing Three launched from the Red Sea, 860 statute miles from Baghdad. Fitzgerald's flight carried High-Speed Anti-Radiation Missiles (HARMs) to destroy enemy radars.

And the defenses were up: threat warning lights strobed in American cockpits, indicating Iraqi MiGs airborne and SAMs active as the Corsairs pushed through weather toward the target.

Fitzgerald later recalled:

> About 70 miles from Baghdad the weather broke and the sight was impressive. There was literally a dome of lead over the city with missiles popping out the top. Decoys, bombs and Tomahawks had brought every SAM system on line. Each HARM aircraft fired two missiles from pre-determined launch positions, and the third missile was fired at targets of opportunity against any emitting sites that were left.
>
> I fired my first HARM. We were all warned, don't look as the missile plume is blinding. Of course, I looked and had stars twinkling in my eyes. Next missile, I didn't look until it had climbed to its perch at 80,000 feet. The flight was increasingly exciting. The prebriefed shots could be fired outside missile range, but targets of opportunity were much closer.
>
> My scope had a symbol I had not seen before—a blinking "six." Fascinated, I studied it a bit too long only to look up to see an SA-6 missile pitching over and heading my direction. I quickly shot my HARM and hit my chaff switch. But the chaff was gone, emptied during a MiG encounter. I executed a very hard break turn to escape. A satisfying explosion of my HARM and a disappearing SAM warning indicated that the missile had done its job.

Meanwhile, air combat was brief for the tailhookers. On the first night, an Iraqi MiG-25 shot down a *Saratoga* Hornet, apparently due to confusion over the Foxbat's identity. The next day the pilot, Lieutenant Commander Scott Speicher, was written off by the U.S. Defense Department, though his death was not confirmed until 2009.

Later that day, two of Speicher's squadron mates quickly engaged MiGs during an airfield attack, shot down both "bandits," and continued to hit the target.

Iraq's Al Basra power plant was one of many targets struck by USS *Ranger's* A-6E Intruders in February 1991. *Courtesy USN.*

Carrier air wings deployed with laser guided bombs (LGBs) and the new Standoff Land Attack Missile (SLAM), which had not completed operational testing. But Intruders and Hornets employed SLAM against precision targets, continuing the trend begun over Vietnam a quarter century before.

Supporting the ground offensive beginning February 24, aviation ordnance requirements more than doubled, reaching 116 tons per carrier per day. But Washington called off the war after four days, leaving the carriers' magazines well stocked.

After Iraq was ejected from Kuwait, aircrews sometimes contended with reduced visibility from the smoke from hundreds of burning oil wells—the residual of Saddam's vindictiveness. Some of his retreating troops set fire to Kuwaiti wells in a calculated policy of spite. But in the desert, under clear skies, the Iraqi army had nowhere to hide and was battered relentlessly.

The Navy had not performed sustained strike operations in almost twenty years, but procedures and logistics were up to the task. In both the Persian Gulf and the Red Sea, carriers received additional aviation fuel every three days via underway replenishment. Carriers in the Gulf maintained the same rate for ordnance while Red Sea air wings needed more "bombs and bullets" as often as every one or two days, being closer to their operating areas. Even during heavy operations, no individual ship used more than 5 percent of its ordnance capacity per day, leaving ample reserves.

The four-carrier battle force in the Persian Gulf during Desert Storm. Clockwise from upper left: *Midway*, *Theodore Roosevelt*, *America*, and *Ranger*. *Courtesy USN.*

When a cease-fire took effect on February 28, the Gulf-based ships had accounted for about two-thirds of the eighteen thousand carrier sorties because the Red Sea station lay four hundred to six

FLIGHT OF AN INTRUDER

Then-Lieutenant Steve Snyder was an A-6E pilot in VA-35 aboard *Saratoga* during Desert Storm. In 1991 he penned this whimsical account published in *The Hook* magazine, the journal of carrier aviation—a combat sortie as told by his veteran airplane, born in 1969.

In the clear, black night the desert slips by below as we conclude our top-off from the airborne tankers en route to the Iraqi border. My lights and radar off, we enter enemy airspace undetected and proceed toward the target. I am equipped with a sophisticated navigation and targeting system that allows me to deliver a variety of weapons day or night, in any weather.

After 20 minutes we hit the initial point and commence the attack run. The pilot turns me toward the target as the BN uses the radar to fine-tune my navigational system. Both crewmen recheck all switches and, as the pilot commits, I am cleared to release the weapons to hit the target defined by the bombardier. Thirty seconds prior to weapons release, anti-radiation missile impact the enemy SAM sites. As a result, the sky is alive with enemy AAA directed at us. The air beneath us boils and we are rocked in the turbulent air caused by the exploding flak. My wings rumble as the weapons are ejected from their racks and within three seconds my "complete" light indicates the release of all 20 bombs. The pilot snaps my airframe to the egress heading and, as both crewmen continued to scan the night sky for enemy missiles or aircraft, my infrared sensor tracks the target until my weapons hit the target. As the thousands of bomblets detonate, the ground glitters and an occasional tremendous plume indicates a secondary explosion.

After receiving another fuel top-off, we proceed back to the ship. Five hours after the catapult shot, my engines once again scream to full power as my wheels slam onto the flight deck. My hook snags the third of four arresting wires and we come to a wrenching stop. The final act is complete and I am parked into my spot with engines shut down. I am old, but once again I have proven my worth in combat.

hundred nautical miles from its targets. But carrier aviation's overall contribution was substantial, running some 420 sorties per day.

Among seventy-five Coalition aircraft lost, sixty-three were American. Carrier losses were three Intruders, two Hornets, and a Tomcat with six fliers killed.

The G. H. W. Bush administration, eager to disengage, allowed the Middle East's most accomplished dagger man to remain in power. Some junior officers recognized the folly: during the Tailhook symposium that summer, a Tomcat RIO said, "We'll have to go back and do it again in ten years."

He was only two years off.

SIX

AFTER THE STORM

1991–2017

USS *John C. Stennis* and *John F Kennedy* plus France's *Charles de Gaulle* steam with ships from Britain, Italy, and the Netherlands in the Arabian Sea supporting Afghanistan operations in 2002. *Courtesy USN.*

FOR NAVAL AVIATION—AS FOR THE ENTIRE U.S. MILITARY— AMERICA'S avowed victory in Desert Storm acted as a needed salve to the lingering frustration over U.S. involvement in Vietnam involvement two decades earlier.

Meanwhile, additional tasking drove operational tempos far beyond the "peace dividend" expected by presidents and politicians after the collapse of the Soviet Union. In the words of one aviator, equipment and people had been "rode hard and put up wet." In 1989 nine carriers plus Japan-based *Midway* were deployed, but from 1992 to 1997 only five or six carriers deployed, dropping to an appalling four in 1999.

Yet tasking continued. In the sandy wake of Desert Storm, Operation Southern Watch trolled Iraqi airspace from 1992 to 2003, often involving carrier aircraft. NATO's 1995 Operation Deliberate Force in Bosnia was followed by Operation Allied Force in the spring of 1999, with *Theodore Roosevelt* (CVN-71) diverted there for two months before returning to Southern Watch.

Many operators as well as pundits chafed at the assignments. Few of the post-Desert Storm operations seemed directly tied to American national interests, and aircrews grew restive at the relative inactivity. Still, the deployments accumulated. In 1996 alone *America*, *Nimitz*, *George Washington*, *Carl Vinson*, *Enterprise*, and *Kitty Hawk* monitored the no-fly zone.

WOMEN AND CARRIERS

While the world's navies wrestled with new carrier concepts, the U.S. Navy accepted female flight school applicants, winging its first women aviators in 1974, but not for carrier service. Later Congress changed the law to permit females in most positions aboard surface ships. Women began serving aboard auxiliary vessels in 1978, and finally aboard carriers and other warships in 1993. The submarine community, however—long a noncombatant but jealously guarding its fiefdom—held out for almost forty years before admitting women.

Driven by political agendas, and following an extremely rough and lengthy transition period, women aircrew gained more acceptance by their male counterparts. However, committing young male and female sailors to the confined spaces of a warship produced inevitable problems that consistently—almost humorously—surprised the civilian and naval leadership. Perhaps the ultimate statement came from the executive officer of a Sixth Fleet carrier, who said, "My job is basically entertainment director on a love boat with jets. The biggest problems start when we're westbound out of Gibraltar because that's when the cruise romances start breaking up."

Decades later the Navy remains engaged in a continuing effort to deal with "gender issues," not confined to fraternization between senior male officers and female subordinates. There are also technical difficulties to surmount. To take one example, when *G. H .W. Bush* (CVN-77) was commissioned in 2009, her new waste-management system was quickly rendered inoperable, partly due to "inappropriate objects" being flushed down toilets by women crew members.

The British Royal Air Force winged its first female pilots in 1989, and the Navy permitted women aboard warships the following year. France's *Marine* already had a lead. An American aviator with a 1980s exchange tour was impressed with what he found aboard *Clemenceau*: despite wine available at most meals, he saw no abuse. But more memorably he said, "Their female sailors look like Catherine Deneuve in fitted fatigues." The French naval academy accepted females in 1993.

THE LONG WAR

Following Islamic terrorists' stunning airliner attacks on New York and Washington on September 11, 2001, carriers entered "The Long War."

First engaged was *Enterprise*, preparing a launch against Taliban targets in Afghanistan on October 7. As she plied the darkness of the Arabian Sea, ordnance was elevated from below-decks magazines to the flight deck where bombs were loaded. Red-shirted ordnance men chalked heartfelt messages on Mark 80 series weapons: "Hijack this," and cryptically "NYPD" or "FDNY" in tribute to first responders who died in the World Trade Center.

As related by Lieutenant Commander Thomas J. Cutler of the U.S. Naval Institute *Proceedings*:

> There was no wild cheering as the first aircraft rocketed down the catapult track and roared into the black sky. There were no high fives as, one after another, Hornets and Tomcats took to the air and headed for the enemy's territory far to the north. Instead, there was an almost palpable sense of relief as the observers felt the dissipation of the feeling of helplessness that had gripped them since they first stared, horrified, at televisions screens, watching airliners full of innocent people forced to crash into buildings full of more innocent people. Unlike the vast majority of Americans who could do little more than seethe or grieve, the men and women of USS *Enterprise* were striking back. And as many would attest, it felt very good indeed.

In the months that followed, carriers rotated in and out of "Operation Enduring Freedom," the open-ended campaign in Afghanistan.

Distances from the Arabian Sea to targets in Afghanistan required Air Force tankers to refuel carrier aircraft, as these FA-18 Hornets in 2010. *Courtesy USN.*

Air wings committed to the campaign after *Enterprise* then launched from *Carl Vinson* (CVN-70), *Theodore Roosevelt* (CVN-71), and *George Washington* (CVN-73) through 2002. Carriers were especially valuable before U.S. and NATO air forces arrived in-theater, though tailhookers often flew one thousand-mile round-trip missions from the North Arabian Sea to strike Taliban targets.

The F-14 "Bombcat" was a valuable player, given its range after the Bush administration's ill-advised, premature retirement of the A-6 Intruder. As one Tomcat aviator recalled, "The F-14 was a wonderfully stable platform for dropping stuff." But even with carrier-based S-3 Viking airborne refuelers, Air Force tanker and E-3 AWACS support was essential.

Over the years, inevitably stagnation set in. During *Carl Vinson*'s six-month deployment in 2011–2012, her air wing dropped merely 7,283 pounds (3.6 tons) of ordnance while firing just 1,717 rounds of 20mm ammunition. Assuming one-quarter of the 1,085 sorties went "over the beach," they averaged thirty pounds of bombs or rockets and seven rounds of cannon ammunition per launch. Even die-hard navalists questioned the efficacy of deploying a nuclear-powered carrier with sixty-five aircraft, five thousand personnel, and six or more escorts for so little return.

When the last Tomcat squadrons stood down in 2006, the U.S. Navy took itself out of the deep-strike mission. Not even the improved FA-18E Super Hornet (operational in 2002) had the legs to make up the deficit.

IRAQ AGAIN

In March 2003 the George W. Bush administration launched the highly controversial "Operation Iraqi Freedom," following "Bush 41's" liberation of Kuwait twelve years before—which had left Iraqi despot Saddam Hussein in power. This time Washington invaded

Iraq on the basis of disputed reports about Baghdad's weapons of mass destruction.

Five carriers supported the invasion, operating in the Mediterranean and Arabian Seas: *Kitty Hawk*, *Constellation*, *Theodore Roosevelt*, *Lincoln*, and *Truman*. A notable feature of the campaign was heavy reliance upon precision-guided munitions (PGMs) far more than conventional ordnance. Partly because much of Saddam Hussein's defense infrastructure was sited in populated areas, PGMs were even more valuable to operations planners.

The ground phase of OIF was brief, with U.S. forces entering Baghdad on April 9. But that summer the resistance turned into irregular forces relying on explosive devices and ambush.

On May 1, the day after major ground combat ended, President George W. Bush flew aboard *Abraham Lincoln* off San Diego to proclaim the end of offensive operations. "Abe" had just completed a ten-month deployment—the longest by a carrier since Vietnam. A large banner proclaiming "Mission Accomplished" waved over the president's head as he delivered a victory speech. That photo-op would become a supreme embarrassment to the administration, as the Iraqi resistance extended several more years. The Obama administration officially ended U.S. involvement in Iraq in December 2011, though in fact American forces remained long after.

END OF AN ERA

An era ended when *Kitty Hawk* (CV-63) was decommissioned in May 2009. After a forty-eight-year career she finished her fleet service as the forward-deployed PacFleet carrier in Japan. Her last skipper, Captain Todd "Zeke" Zecchin, was a history-oriented officer who rode a C-2 Greyhound in the *Hawk*'s last arrested landing, number 407,511—a total only surpassed by *Lexington* (CVT-16) with 493,028 landings at the end of her operational and training career in 1991.

Enterprise (CVN-65) is the only other flattop to log more than 400,000 traps.

On a grander scale was the de facto end of U.S. carrier presence in the Mediterranean. The Sixth Fleet—a cornerstone of U.S. naval policy throughout the Cold War—gradually lost its carrier clout. After about 2003 the few carriers plying the Mediterranean were, in one flier's words, "drive by" appearances en route to the Persian Gulf. While carriers had once been front-row center in "the Med," operating against Libya throughout the 1980s, their absence was keenly felt in the new century.

The United States was briefly engaged in NATO air strikes in Operation Odyssey Dawn during the last two weeks of March 2011. (NATO, the United States, Britain, and Canada all had different titles for the operation.) Behind an opening barrage of 112 Tomahawk cruise missiles on March 19, nine allied nations supported Libyan rebels opposing longtime strongman Muammar Gaddafi. Washington's goal in Odyssey Dawn was murky, as conflicting statements alluded to protecting civilians or effecting Gaddafi's overthrow.

No fixed-wing carriers were engaged, but new EA-18G Growlers—active tailhook aircraft—provided electronic warfare support from Italy, plus P-3 Orion patrol planes.

Despite absolute air supremacy, the coalition air forces were hard-pressed to affect events on the ground. Gaddafi was killed in October, and though widely unmourned, his vacancy left Libya a failed state. The leadership void led to the 2012 Islamist assault on the U.S. consulate in Benghazi, which left the U.S. ambassador and four staffers dead under controversial conditions.

In mid-June 2014 *George H. W. Bush* was diverted from the North Arabian Sea to conduct reconnaissance and surveillance sorties over Iraq and Syria from the Persian Gulf. American leaders had largely ignored the growing strength of the Islamic State (ISIS/ISIL) forces, but by August the threat was obvious. Air Wing Eight began selectively bombing Islamic State targets a week before land-based aircraft. Hornet pilots subsequently reported that weapons release required White House approval, but even thereafter many jets returned with 70 percent of their ordnance, lacking timely permission to expend "kinetic weapons."

The operation—with the typically grandiose name "Inherent Resolve"—appears open-ended.

FRANCE—AGAIN

After a long absence from new carrier construction, France's *Marine Nationale* returned in strength with the nation's first nuclear-powered flattop. *Charles de Gaulle* (R91) was laid down in 1989 and launched in 1994. But funding lagged, with work suspended on four occasions during the 1990s before commissioning in May 2001, five years late. Displacing forty-two thousand tons, her original air wing included Super Etendard and Rafale M strike aircraft, and E-2 Hawkeyes, respectively flying attack and reconnaissance missions over

NATO partners USS *Enterprise* and newly-commissioned FS *Charles de Gaulle*, France's nuclear-powered carrier, steaming together in 2001. *Courtesy USN.*

Afghanistan in support of Operation Enduring Freedom through 2006.

In February 2015 France committed *Charles de Gaulle* against ISIS forces in Iraq and Syria—the first nation to join U.S. military operations against the Islamic State.

A tentative second French carrier designated PA2 (*Porte-Avions 2*) was based on Britain's new Queen Elizabeth class carriers. PA2

THE WORLD'S AIRCRAFT CARRIERS

Deployable "tailhook" carriers completed as of 2015
(*Definitions of CV, CVL, and CVE vary*)

NATION	CV	CVL	CVE	TOTAL
UNITED STATES	54	11	124*	189
GREAT BRITAIN	17	16	16	49
JAPAN	12	7	5	24
FRANCE	4	0	0	4
RUSSIA	1	0	0	1
CHINA	1	0	0	1
INDIA	1	0	0	1
TOTALS	90	34	145	269

*Includes those built for Britain.

Of 269 conventional aircraft carriers built or modified as such since 1917, 204 (76 percent) were completed from 1939 through 1945.

was intended as a seventy-five-thousand-ton ship with a forty-plane air wing. Propulsion was alternately considered for conventional and nuclear power, but budgetary problems intruded, and she was cancelled in 2013.

CARRIERS TODAY

The follow-on to the highly successful Nimitz class CVNs is the three-ship Ford (CVN-78) class, subject to repeated scrutiny due to high cost over-runs. The average price of the three ships has been calculated at more than twelve billion dollars (22 percent over budget), not counting the air wings, which are expected to include the enormously expensive, controversial F-35C stealth aircraft.

The Ford design has similarities to the Nimitz class hull but otherwise relies heavily on new technology. Its two new-generation reactors are expected to produce 250 percent more electrical power than the Nimitzes while embarking only three-fourths as many personnel.

The 110,000-ton CVN-78 was laid down in November 2009 and launched four years later. Advances include electro-magnetic catapults and arresting gear, which ease strain on aircraft and require fewer sailors. But the program lagged badly, mainly due to systems slippage. The new multi-function, dual-band radar was more than four years late, while the arresting gear and catapults were delayed between two and three years. However, program defenders note that the lead ship's high cost will be amortized in its two sisters.

As of this writing, *Ford* is expected to commission in 2017.

Meanwhile, carriers have a key role to play in protecting the vital sea lanes of commerce that benefit so many industrialized nations. Though the Persian Gulf frequently sees carriers, other potential choke points often go lacking. Trillions of dollars in commerce— including most of the oil to China, Korea, and Japan—come through the South China Sea. As a retired admiral and carrier captain noted, "We are currently not minding that store well."

STEALTH ON DECK

In 1983 the U.S. Navy made the extraordinarily poor decision to follow the Air Force down a treacherous technological path. Because the Air Force was investing heavily in stealth, from the "F"-117 attack aircraft (incapable of defending itself) to the ghastly expensive B-2 bomber, aviation admirals feared losing roles and missions. The Navy's first abortive step was the McDonnell Douglas A-12 Avenger II, a program expected to run $4.8 billion. Ultimately it was cancelled in 1991 to avoid wasting more funds, but the Navy had already doomed itself to decades of extremely costly aircraft that could not meet the most basic requirements. Aviators cited the two-man Avenger II as an example of design philosophy gone wild, as every tradeoff was made in favor of "low observable" technology over operational capability.

Big and black, the A-12 was subsonic and mainly limited to operating at night in good weather, as rain could degrade the stealth coating, which was irreparable at sea. Composite materials in the airframe failed to meet standards, resulting in excess weight beyond design specifications. With weapons carried internally, the A-12 could not immediately jettison ordnance in a marginal catapult shot or sudden engine problem, likely causing loss of the aircraft. Furthermore, the cockpit geometry ignored decades of carrier aircraft design. Pilots could barely see over the nose in a landing approach, and the colossal eighty-foot wingspan made lineup exceptionally difficult. It also limited the number of stealth bombers that could be launched simultaneously. According to one critic, "We ended up with a mini B-2 with a tailhook."

Retired Captain Lonny McClung said in 2013:

> I was at OP 74 (strike warfare) in the early 90s. We were
> selling our soul for stealth. The attitude in the Pentagon
> was that if we did not come up with stealth (read: A-12),
> we would be out of the strike business and USAF would
> own the mission. I kept saying that somewhere in some
> dark basement room in Eastern Europe was a group of
> guys wearing glasses about as thick as Coke bottles who
> were figuring out how to defeat stealth. I was for more
> performance and getting as much stealth as we could get—
> once we had a platform that would perform in com-
> bat. A-12 was in the black world. You could not take the
> material to your desk. You had to read it in a vault. The
> airplane had a lot of problems. Cancelling the thing saved
> the Navy from itself.

Before cancellation, McDonnell Douglas and its partner General
Dynamics only built one mockup, and ultimately each paid the Navy
two hundred million dollars or equivalent in products and services.
However, the carrier stealth bomber refused to die for another twenty-
three years. Litigation between Boeing and the Navy finally ended in
early 2014.

Following cancellation of the failed A-12, the Navy suddenly was
left with no deep strike capability. Because Defense Secretary Dick
Cheney had killed the A-6 and F-14—apparently in a snit aimed at
the New York congressional delegation—carrier air wings were left
with the relatively short-ranged FA-18 Hornet, leaving the Navy heavily reliant on Air Force tankers. Additionally, absent new airframes,
the Tomcat dead-ended, becoming unsupportable with forty-five
maintenance man-hours per flight hour.

Meanwhile, the Department of Defense compounded its problems by selecting the Lockheed-Martin F-35 over Boeing for the joint strike fighter (JSF) contract. The Lightning II became the most expensive military program in history, and immediately ran into severe problems. Despite the example of the 1960s F-111 failure of a single aircraft for multiple services, the naval-political-industrial establishment pressed ahead. Neither the Air Force, Marine Corps, nor Navy F-35 variants lived up to "the brochure," each running years late and hundreds of millions over budget.

Lockheed-Martin's F-35C is the carrier variant of the Joint Strike Fighter, which passed carrier qualification tests aboard USS *Nimitz* in late 2014. *Courtesy USN.*

Worst of all was the Navy's C model, intended to replace Hornets in carrier air wings. Although the Navy had been putting tailhooks on airframes since 1922, Lockheed-Martin and the naval test establishment managed to produce its only fifth-generation carrier aircraft—the future of naval aviation—that could not reliably catch an arresting wire even in shore-based "roll-in" tests. Some analysts noted that Lockheed had only built one carrier type in the company's seventy-year history—the S-3 antisubmarine aircraft—and had never produced a naval fighter. After a prolonged period of redesign and experimentation (two years or more) the C model successfully landed aboard USS *Nimitz* in November 2014. Other problems remained to be solved, however, including shipboard aircraft support and handling, maintaining the stealth coating at sea, flight deck effects, and JSF-specific ordnance storage.

The program went through numerous on-again, off-again evolutions, repeatedly hitting the "reset button" to declare the long-delayed program "on schedule." The Navy version originally was expected in fleet service in 2012; the VSTOL F-35B in 2010. Apparently for political purposes the Marines declared their version operationally capable in 2015, though still unable to meet significant mission requirements. As of this writing in 2016, the C model is expected to arrive in 2018 or 2019.

The Navy continues low-rate acquisition of Hornets, a tacit acknowledgement of F-35's perennial failings. But the Marine Corps lacks that wisdom, insisting on an all-or-nothing approach with F-35B, to the exclusion of additional FA-18s. It could prove an extremely myopic decision, prompting some observers to fear that F-35B might be the end of Marine Corps fixed-wing strike. Those concerns are piled on top of the dubious wisdom of assigning a stealth aircraft to expeditionary missions where its sensitive covering could be degraded, and the counter-intuitive expectation that a high-cost aircraft will perform close air support—Marine aviation's primary *raison d'etre*—in a low-level, visual combat environment.

A seldom-discussed question is whether the stealth role might be accomplished by electronic countermeasures (ECM) at vastly lower costs. "Low observability" will remain a consideration, but active electronic warfare is always available as a cost-capability tradeoff. Electronic warfare officers still note that few stealth aircraft has crossed the beach into hostile airspace without jammers in attendance. The cost differential between stealth and EW is enormous, but the Pentagon continues to ignore that fact.

Another futuristic program is Northrop-Grumman's subsonic X-47B "unmanned combat air vehicle," first flown in 2011. Its mission is defined as "unmanned carrier-launched surveillance and strike" (UCLASS), stated to enter fleet service in 2019. It launched and recovered from *George H. W. Bush* in May 2013. Originally funded at $638 million, UCLASS expanded to $813 million. However, the Navy opted for a non-stealthy UCLASS that could only operate safely in uncontested airspace, apparently influenced by perennial F-35 cost over-runs. UCLASS's main mission likely will be surveillance rather than combined with a strike potential, but the ability to refuel the drone in flight should extend its range and endurance.

HOW MANY DECKS?

In 1959 the world carrier census was pegged at one hundred, down about a dozen decks from the immediate post-Korea period. Thereafter the figure never reached eighty. As of 2016, six navies own fifteen conventional fixed-wing carriers in commission, depending upon definitions.

Britain, France, Russia, China, and India possess one carrier each, though not all are deployable at a given time. Thus, America's historic carrier dominance remains unapproachable by any combination of prospective opponents. The likelihood of a sixth carrier battle is so remote as to appear microscopic. Meanwhile, critics ask whether America can continue maintaining eleven nuclear carriers.

The future is uncertain, for multiple reasons.

First, the eleven figure is decades old, based on Cold War requirements. Carriers have been diverted to noncombat roles such as disaster relief, without unduly upsetting deployment schedules.

Secondly, the U.S. Navy is running out of carrier aircraft. The Marines Corps bought its last F/A-18s in 1997, starting the clock for the Hornet, and leaving the trouble-plagued F-35B VSTOL model as

THE MAX TRAPPERS

In carrier aviation the aviators and aircrew with the most arrested landings are reckoned "max trappers" or "master baggers" for "bagging" an extraordinary number of traps. Some have gone out of their way to accumulate one thousand or more landings, while others achieved that mark as part of their ordinary career paths.

By far the most prolific carrier aviator was Captain Eric M. Brown, who flew Royal Navy aircraft from 1941 onward. After swimming away from the first escort carrier, HMS *Audacity*, he drew plumb assignments evaluating new carriers and conducting an eye-watering variety of flight tests. In 1942–43 he logged about 1,500 landings on most of Britain's U.S-built escort carriers, which required multiple landings by fighter and attack aircraft to certify each ship's arresting wires. When he retired in 1970, "Winkle" Brown had 2,407 shipboard arrested landings, beyond any of his Fleet Air Arm contemporaries.

Brown's closest competitor was Lieutenant Commander J. S. Bailey, who logged his two thousandth arrested landing in 1950. He died in a traffic accident, but no one else approached his figure. In 2011 Brown recalled that the next highest RN figure was something over six hundred.

The first American member of "the grand club" was Captain George Watkins, a noted bagger who flew an exceptional variety of tailhook aircraft. In an A4D Skyhawk, he made the first launch and landing from the then-new USS *Constellation* in February 1962, and three months later he made "Connie's" one thousandth landing in an AD-6 Skyraider. He logged his one thousandth personal trap in May, piloting an F11F Tiger. When he retired from the Navy to take up soaring, Watkins had some 1,400 landings on an incredible thirty-seven flight decks.

The American record for pilots belongs to Captain John "Lites" Leenhouts, primarily an A-7 pilot and strike leader in

Captain John "Lites" Leenhouts, the leading American carrier pilot with 1,645 arrested landings. *Courtesy John Leenhouts.*

Desert Storm. Between 1975 and 1995 he logged 1,645 landings on sixteen carriers, including ten deployments. In eight thousand hours of Navy flying he also became a world-recognized aerial photographer and author. Close behind is Captain Dennis "Dizzy" Gillespie, with 1,601 shipboard landings.

The outright U.S. record for carrier landings is held by a naval flight officer, Vice Admiral Walter E. "Slapshot" Carter, who became superintendent of the Naval Academy in 2014. He was an F-4 and F-14 RIO with 2,016 landings on nineteen aircraft carriers to compile his record number of "traps." Another NFO, the late Commander Arthur Critser, accumulated nearly 1,900 landings.

As of 2016 the Tailhook Association counted nearly 350 pilots and almost 130 NFOs as Grand Club members.

the only option. Even if the scandalous Lightning II does become fully operational, it cannot possibly be purchased or maintained in numbers comparable to Hornets.

Nor are aircraft the only problem. As lead ship of her class, the *Ford* has been plagued with system problems and massive cost overruns that remain to be corrected after she is commissioned.

The mundane can overwhelm operational capability in new weapon systems, and perhaps no better example exists than *G. H. W. Bush*. She was built with a waste-product vacuum system collection that malfunctioned almost immediately. Commissioned in 2009, most of her "heads" were inoperable, and on two occasions none were available. Male sailors were able to relieve themselves over the side or into bottles, while females had fewer options. Some ten thousand man hours were spent trying to correct the egregious system, with 250 miles of waste collection pipes.

Meanwhile, Congress continues to require eleven carriers, with ten rated as deployable at any one time. In 2012, however, the Navy intended to stand down Air Wing Fourteen, which last deployed with USS *Ronald Reagan* (CVN-76) in 2011. After subsequent reversals of policy, "CAG-14" may finally be disestablished in 2017. Thus, until *Ford* enters service, the U.S. carrier fleet will remain below mandated levels to meet any new contingencies.

More than ships and aircraft, carrier aviation is people. That includes the "snipes" down in the engineering spaces, maintainers on the hangar deck, and "the gang on the roof" who shoot airplanes off the flight deck and recover them at the blunt end.

The ambience—the culture—of aircraft carriers was well described by attack pilot-turned-novelist Stephen Coonts in 2016:

> The men I met in the Navy (the squadrons were all male then) were universally interesting. A few were assholes, a few were super technocrats, but most were extremely competent young men somewhere on the spectrum between those poles. These were men to fly with. These were men

to fight with. And if necessary, these were men to die with. They were good friends and good companions for life's journey.

Walking out onto a flight deck, manning up, taking the cat shots, flying around awhile and dropping some bombs (without getting shot at), doing a few whifferdills on the way back to the boat, then catching a wire (hopefully the third one) and strolling into the ready room to laugh and scratch with my shipmates—yes, I'd love to do that one more time. Or two.

Hell, I'd pay to go on another A-5 cruise. I remember poker in the JOs' bunkroom, mid-rat leftover "sliders," liberty in Hong Kong and Singapore. It certainly wasn't all fun and games, but life never is. Naval aviation was dangerous; people died doing it; combat was insanity. At times I was so scared that even today, all these years later, I remember the fear. And yet...That was Life with a capital L, the 200-proof stuff; the pure, raw essence.

EPILOGUE

QUO VADIS CARRIERS?

In December 2012 five active aircraft carriers were docked together probably for the first time since 1945, though *Enterprise* was being decommissioned. Left to right: *Dwight D. Eisenhower*, *George H.W. Bush*, *Enterprise*, amphibious assault ship *Bataan*, *Harry S. Truman*, and *Abraham Lincoln*. Courtesy USN.

IN THE TWENTY-FIRST CENTURY'S SECOND DECADE, aircraft carriers maintain their pride of place among warships, with more under construction or on order in the world's admiralties. Their design, technology, aircraft, and employment continue to evolve as their cost grows exponentially. But carrier cost is only one side of the equation. The other is need, and it is becoming a hard sell in some quarters. Skeptics and budgeteers alike are inclined to ask: "How big a navy do we need, and for what purpose?"

With the collapse of the Soviet Union, America and the world entered the post-naval era. For centuries, fleets existed to maintain freedom of the seas and, if necessary, to engage opponents in naval combat, but that contingency has nearly vanished. After 1945 naval combat has mainly occurred on the peripheries with minimal losses, such as India-Pakistan in 1965 and 1971, and Britain-Argentina in 1982, which saw the destruction of the seven thousand-ton cruiser *General Belgrano* by a British submarine. No other post-1945 loss comes close.

Demise of the Red Fleet relieved the United States and NATO from realistic concerns about maintaining sea lines of communication. The remaining rare threats to navigation resulted from sporadic efforts at mine warfare, as during Iran's 1980s "tanker war" in the Persian Gulf.

As for war at sea, nothing remotely like Leyte Gulf can happen again. Then, some 360 combatant vessels engaged in a three-day clash of giants, ending with nearly three dozen ships sunk. But the three hundred-plus American ships engaged at Leyte easily exceeds the size of today's entire U.S. Navy.

However, other operations besides fleet actions could place carriers in harm's way. Increasingly long-ranged cruise missiles—including those launched from land bases or aircraft—pose a growing threat. With constantly improving targeting data from satellites, carriers face a drastic reduction in their traditional ability to hide in an oceanic expanse.

Moreover, the U.S. Navy still finds itself relying upon Air Force tankers for the range needed for many missions. Organic air wing tankers have entered a descending graveyard spiral: from the classic KA-3 Skywarrior (retired in 1987) to the less capable but useful KA-6D Intruder (killed by Dick Cheney in 1997) to the marginal S-3 Viking.

In 2016 a fleet-experienced naval flight officer said, "The Navy has painted itself into a corner with Super Hornet tankers. The mission eats up fatigue life at a ridiculous rate, and there is something really,

really stupid about using your most capable strike platform as a tanker." Because "classic" Hornets, through the FA-18D, did not carry a "buddy store" refueling pack, later-model Hornets are required. But the tanker mission badly eroded the Super Hornet's six thousand-hour airframe life, further reducing availability, since FA-18Es typically spend 25 percent of their time tanking.

As always, aircraft availability affects carrier availability. According to fleet operators and industry sources alike, in 2016 deploying three carriers with complete air wings was reckoned "a real stretch," and four was thought practically impossible. Flight hours—which equals readiness—depend upon Hornet airframe hours, which likely would be extended to eight thousand or even ten thousand. But that means less structure tolerance, both in carrier landings and hard maneuvering. With mandated limits on aerodynamic loads, pilots would have fewer options in combat, and more than one aviator has said, "I don't want to cross the beach in a five-G airplane."

Also in 2016, the Navy expanded the prospect of carrier-based drones as tanker aircraft. Previously called the Unmanned Carrier Launched Airborne Surveillance and Strike system (UCLASS), the

A pioneering program in naval aviation is the unmanned Carrier Based Aerial Refueling System, here being tested with a civilian tanker in 2015. *Courtesy USN.*

Carrier Based Aerial Refueling System (CBARS) would free five or six strike-fighters per air wing. Therefore, a dedicated tanker drone could address the more immediate problem of the Hornet's relatively short legs, leaving the intelligence and surveillance roles to other platforms.

Even assuming that CBARS proceeds with congressional approval, the most optimistic estimate is four years to fleet service. Based on decades of institutional experience, best-case scenarios can prove 50 to 100 percent optimistic. There are few better examples than the F-35, which despite being declared "operational" by the Marine Corps is still unable to match stated requirements. As of early 2016 more than two hundred Lightning IIs had been delivered to the three services, logging fifty thousand hours since 2008—and apparently none were fully combat capable.

Looking farther downrange, the UCLASS concept may emerge as a significant player in air wing composition. In the 1980s the Naval Strike Warfare Center generated doctrine that included, "Never send a man where you can send a bullet." At the time the mantra alluded to standoff weapons—air-launched missiles that extended the tactical reach of the launching aircraft. But in the twenty-first century, armed drones operating off carriers could augment manned aircraft, and may well supplant them in some cases.

Meanwhile, the U.S. Navy plans to continue purchasing carriers. The current twenty-year plan expects to add four new decks through 2035 and two more over the subsequent decade. Placed in context, America's fleet would increase from the current 272 ships (including seventy-one submarines) to something over three hundred in 2035, maintaining the congressionally mandated eleven flattops. At the same time, the U.S. Navy has some three hundred admirals—more than one per active ship. By comparison, the ratio during World War II was approximately one admiral per ten ships.

The U.S. government's perennial tolerance of scandalous military programs assures that increasingly costly carriers and questionable new-generation aircraft will dominate the future. The political clout inherent in military procurement is well known, if reluctantly acknowledged, but inevitably it drives acquisition policy rather than fiscal responsibility, operational efficiency, or even national interest. Perhaps no better example exists than the overall Lockheed-Martin F-35 program, whose three versions are represented by contractors in forty-six states and some 80 percent of congressional districts.

Foreign navies face similar problems, most notably Britain's plan for two Queen Elizabeth-class ships. *Queen Elizabeth* was launched in 2014 despite deep uncertainty as to its viability, especially with lingering problems of the F-35B VSTOL jet replacing the Harrier. If the B model fails, the options are limited, including converting the ships to conventional carriers or selling them to other nations.

The French Navy remains active with the long-delayed, nuclear-powered *Charles De Gaulle*, completed in 2001, still the flagship of the *Marine Nationale*. At forty-two thousand tons she is far smaller than her American counterparts, flying Rafale fighters, Super Etendard strike fighters, E-2 Hawkeye AWACS, and helicopters.

Communist China demonstrates continued interest in carriers—an ironic development considering Mao Tse Tung's reputed assertion that the carrier was "an instrument of imperialism." In 1985 China purchased Australia's HMAS *Melbourne* for dissection and study. China also obtained the former Soviet carriers *Minsk* and *Kiev*, which operated Yak 38 jump jets. Both ships became tourist attractions.

Far more serious was acquisition of *Varyag*, sold while two-thirds complete in 1995. She was finished as the Peoples Liberation Army Navy's first carrier, *Liaoning*, in September 2012. Classified as a training ship, she represents a fifty-three thousand-ton *Langley* or *Hosho*, permitting the PLAN to learn carrier basics, flying a nominal forty-eight conventional jets as well as helicopters.

China's first carrier, *Liaoning*, was begun as Russia's *Varyag*, purchased from Ukraine in 1998, and completed in 2012. *Wikimedia.*

HOW BIG?

After decades of controversy, the argument regarding optimum carrier size continues strong. Advocates of relatively small conventionally powered carriers note—correctly—that apart from affordability, they would provide more deployable ships to meet widespread contingencies.

Yet how likely is the need for multi-carrier battle groups in different theaters of operation? America has long since abandoned the strategic concept of two major wars fought simultaneously, though the hard-pressed armed forces have been engaged in Afghanistan and elsewhere in the Middle East for more than a decade.

A carrier is not simply a huge, expensive ship. It is a platform for launching strike aircraft, and the air wing will always remain the vessel's *raison d'etre.* But that includes the support infrastructure ashore and afloat to keep a carrier on station, wherever that may be. Operational analysts typically estimate that three fifty thousand to sixty thousand-ton conventional carriers would be needed to match the capabilities of a ninety thousand-ton nuclear-powered ship. Both types of flattops need underway replenishment, but the CVN requires less because it does not use fuel oil.

Meanwhile, carrier designers and strategists face a daunting challenge. With ship lives running fifty years or more, and classes of ships extending far longer, planners need a finely tuned crystal ball as well as drafting paper or 3D computer programs. It may have been a more difficult task eighty years ago when, for example, the Yorktown (CV-5) class ships were designed. In the mid-1930s biplanes were standard, and monoplanes were barely on the naval horizon. In that era, military aircraft often progressed from first flight to squadron service in two years or less, requiring planners to anticipate successive generations of hardware. Today, stealth aircraft gestation is measured in a decade or more.

Additionally, smaller carriers lack the growth potential or "stretch" of CVNs. New aircraft and new or improved shipboard systems are inevitable requirements, forcing engineers back to the three-dimensional Rubik's Cube of cramming aircraft, fuel, ordnance, berthing, and people into a given volume of space. Therefore, CVNs will remain the U.S. configuration, and abroad only France deploys a nuclear carrier. But as noted, the enormous price tag dangling from a nuke means a limited number.

Moreover, what happens if the unthinkable occurs? In the age of global terrorism, a single carrier could offer a tempting target to well-prepared, highly motivated attackers. Whether at sea or in port, one of the world's most lucrative targets might prove irresistible.

No aircraft carrier has come under attack since 1945. The appalling damage inflicted on such victims as *Franklin* and *Bunker Hill* demonstrated their survivability, but they did not return to combat. Today, carriers may be increasingly vulnerable to evolving anti-ship missiles that cost less than two million dollars. The ability of carrier forces to defend against determined submarine attack remains to be seen—it has not been seriously tested since World War II.

What would the U.S. Navy do if a Nimitz class carrier were badly damaged—or even sunk?

Much would depend upon the circumstances—the strategic context. If it occurred during combat operations, the decision to retain carriers within reach of hostile forces likely would rely upon the risk-benefit equation. Does the presence of the onsite air wing offset the continuing threat to an irreplaceable asset? What are the national priorities—strategic, military, and diplomatic? Damage to a second CVN would almost certainly force withdrawal—especially in the absence of adequate land-based aerial tankers.

LATIN BEAT

South America has long been a minor player in the aircraft carrier league. The *Armada de la República Argentina* commissioned its first carrier in 1959, when Canada's former eighteen thousand-ton HMCS *Warrior* began operating piston aircraft as ARA *Independencia* (V-1). She was retired in 1970.

Subsequently Argentina obtained the twenty thousand-ton HMS *Venerable* via the Netherlands, recommissioning her as ARA *Veinticinco de Mayo* (V-2) in 1968. She put to sea briefly with McDonnell Douglas Skyhawks and Grumman Trackers during the 1982 Falklands-Malvinas war but launched no strikes. Later engineering problems sidelined the aging ship, which became undeployable circa 1990. She was decommissioned in 1997 with some of her parts going to her Colossus class sister, Brazil's NAeL *Minas Gerais* (née HMS *Vengeance*). When the latter was decommissioned in 2001, she was the oldest deployable carrier on earth, dating from 1945. *Minas Gerais* was sold for scrap in 2004, fifty-nine years after completion.

Cooperation between the two Latin Navies sometimes allows Argentine aviators to fly from *Marinha do Brasil*'s French-built NAe *São Paulo* (A-12, née *Foch*) in her rare periods of availability.

Brazil's *São Paulo* (formerly France's *Foch*) operating A-4 Skyhawks and S-2 Trackers in 2003. *Wikimedia.*

Additional training sometimes is available with touch-and-go landings aboard American carriers transiting the Argentine coast during Gringo-Gaucho maneuvers.

CARRIERS IN PERSPECTIVE

The eminent military historian Sir John Keegan (1934–2012) ventured offshore in his 1990 treatise, *The Price of Admiralty*, examining naval warfare from Trafalgar (1805) to Midway (1942). Against all evidence, he declared the submarine the dominant warship of the twentieth century. His claim flies in the face of the facts: U-boats were decisively defeated in both world wars; unlike aircraft, submarines' capabilities ended miles offshore in both global conflicts; and after 1945 the world's submarines sank, at most, perhaps three warships. Missile-armed subs played a role in the Cold War, but only as one-third of the "nuclear triad" deterrent with bombers and ICBMs.

We need to put aircraft carriers in their proper perspective.

Certainly flattops earned their keep in World War II and Korea. Imagine the Pacific War without carriers: from Pearl Harbor onward, the essential nature of the conflict would have been vastly different. In fact, there would have been no Pearl Harbor attack, and it is possible that without the stunning Sunday surprise—with the Japanese hoping to shock America into a negotiated truce—Tokyo might not have gone to war in the first place.

Once the bloodletting began, however, carriers formed the tip of the trident. The Pacific campaigns progressed at an astonishing pace, best exemplified in the world-altering six months between Pearl Harbor and Midway. Shortly thereafter carriers enabled America's first offensive of the global war at Guadalcanal. Later they permitted oceanic strides in seven-league boots, providing air superiority wherever amphibious troops splashed ashore. The island-hopping footfalls begun in the Solomons trod Nippon's shore almost exactly three years later—beneath a blue umbrella of carrier-based airpower.

American and British escort carriers were vital to the Atlantic victory in World War II, defeating the U-boats. Absent an uninterrupted flow of men and material eastward from the U.S. East coast, the transatlantic convoy routes could not have sustained the immense effort prior to D-Day.

Yet how quickly things changed. Merely five years after V-J Day, America's strategic dominance had dissipated to the point that a third-rate military power very nearly pushed U.S. and allied forces off the Korean peninsula. With most U.S. Air Force units withdrawn to Japan, Pyongyang's aggression likely would have succeeded except for a handful of U.S. and British carriers in the crucial three months before the Inchon landing. Naval airpower supporting allied ground forces made all the difference between June and September, offsetting communist superiority in men and firepower, and again with the massive year-end Chinese intervention.

In short: South Korea almost certainly would have been lost except for blue airplanes with tailhooks.

Throughout the rest of the Cold War, carrier airpower formed a crucial part of U.S. and NATO strength, especially in the Atlantic and Mediterranean. The twin missions of power projection and sea control forced the Soviet Bloc to consider placement of carriers in a variety of scenarios for nearly half a century.

Yet there were limits, most notably in Southeast Asia from 1964 to 1973. National policy—merely avoiding defeat could hardly be called a "strategy"—placed onerous burdens on American warfighters for most of a decade. Naval aviation contributed more than half the U.S. sorties over North Vietnam, but ultimately lack of political willpower in Washington overrode the sacrifice of aircrews launching from flight decks in the Tonkin Gulf.

Elsewhere, carriers demonstrated their historic advantage of territorial independence. When erratic allies might withdraw basing rights, international waters provided navies with other options. From the 1950s onward, American and other flattops benefited from freedom of the seas in conducting operations as far-flung as North Africa, the Indian subcontinent, and the Falklands.

Whatever their future, however many carriers the world's admiralties may procure, one fact remains inescapable: as long as they exist, aircraft carriers will remain the most prestigious targets afloat.

ACKNOWLEDGMENTS

CONTRIBUTORS

+ Deceased

Mark Aldrich

Ray Bean

Captain Eric M. "Winkle" Brown, RN (Ret) +

Commander Harold E. Buell, USN (Ret) +

William Casey

John Cassidy

Commander Pete Clayton, USN (Ret)

Rear Admiral Ernest E. Christensen, USN (Ret)

Commander Stephen P. Coonts, USNR (Ret)

Captain J.R. Davis, USN (Ret)

Captain Dave "Dollar" Dollarhide, USNR (Ret)

Commander Curtis R. Dosé, USN (Ret)

Captain Robert G. Dosé, USN (Ret) +

Vice Admiral Robert F. Dunn, USN (Ret)

Commander William G. Esders, USN (Ret) +

James H. Farmer

Captain Wynn F. Foster, USN (Ret) +

Charles Haberlein

Vice Admiral Peter Hekman, USN (Ret)

Mark Herber

Sean Hert

Mark Horan

Captain Dennis W. Irelan, USN (Ret)

Larry Lassisse

Captain John "Lites" Leenhouts, USN (Ret)

Rick Leisenring

Captain Lonny K. "Eagle" McClung, USN (Ret)

Vice Admiral Jerry Miller, USN (Ret) +

Lieutenant Commander Rick Morgan, USN (Ret)

Jon Parshall

Lieutenant Commander Dave "Hey Joe" Parsons, USN (Ret)

Norman Polmar

Commander Robert R. "Boom" Powell, USN (Ret)

Rear Admiral James D. Ramage, USN (Ret) +

David Reid

Commander Douglas Siegfried, USN (Ret)

Captain Steve Snyder, USN (Ret)

Osamu Tagaya

Commander William F. Tobin, USN (Ret) +

Captain T. Hugh Winters, USN (Ret) +

Commander Jack D. Woodul, USNR (Ret)

Yatsushi Yamashita

APPENDIX ONE

NOTABLE CARRIER VETERANS

THE FOLLOWING IS A PARTIAL LIST OF AMERICANS KNOWN for career achievements after serving aboard aircraft carriers.

Neil A. Armstrong (1930–2012). Aviator, F9Fs, USS *Essex* (CV-9), Korea. X-15 test pilot, astronaut. Commanded Gemini 8 in 1966 and Apollo 11 in 1969. First person to walk on the moon. Retired as a commander.

George H. W. Bush (1924–). Aviator, TBMs, USS *Langley* (CVL-30), WW II. U.S. president 1989–93.

Eugene Cernan (1934–). Aviator, FJs and A-4s. Aeronautical engineer and astronaut. Three space flights and the last man to walk on the moon during Apollo 17 in 1972. Retired as a captain.

John B. Connally (1917–93). Fighter director, USS *Essex* (CV-9), WWII. Secretary of the Navy 1961, governor of Texas 1963–69, treasury secretary 1971–72.

Stephen P. Coonts (1946–). Aviator, A-6s, USS *Enterprise* (CVN-65), Vietnam. Bestselling author. Retired as a commander.

Jeremiah A. Denton (1924–2014). Aviator, A-6s, USS *Independence* (CVA-62), Vietnam POW 1965–73. Retired as a rear admiral. Alabama senator 1981–87.

Gerald R. Ford (1913–2006). Assistant navigator, USS *Monterey* (CVL-26), WWII. Michigan congressman 1949–73; U.S. vice president 1973–74; and president 1974–77.

James A. Lovell (1928–). Aviator, test pilot, astronaut. Four space flights including Apollo 13, subject of the movie of that name. Retired as a captain.

John S. McCain III (1936–). Aviator, A-4s, USS *Forrestal* (CVA-59) and *Oriskany* (CVA-34), Vietnam. POW 1967–73. U.S. congressman and senator since 1983, presidential candidate in 2008.

Bert DeWayne Morris (1914–1959). Aviator, F6Fs, USS *Essex* (CV-9), WWII. Movie actor pre- and postwar, best known for *Kid Galahad* and *Paths of Glory*. Died visiting USS *Bon Homme Richard* (CVA-31).

Donald H. Rumsfeld (1932–). Aviator, 1954–57, S2Fs. Reserve captain. Defense secretary 1975–77, 2001–2006.

Alan B. Shepard (1923–1998). Aviator, test pilot, astronaut. First American in space, 1961. Commanded Apollo 14 moon landing, 1971. Retired as a rear admiral.

Walter M. Schirra (1923–2007). Aviator, test pilot, astronaut. Only person to fly on all three of America's first manned space programs: Mercury, Gemini, Apollo. Retired as a captain.

James B. Stockdale (1923–2005). Aviator, F-8s and A-4s, USS *Ticonderoga* (CVA-14) and *Oriskany* (CVA-34). Vietnam POW. Retired as a vice admiral. Vice presidential candidate under Ross Perot, 1992.

Richard H. Truly (1937–). Aviator, F-8s *USS Intrepid* (CVA-11) and *Enterprise* (CVN-65), test pilot, astronaut. Manned Orbiting Laboratory and pilot of space shuttle *Enterprise*. Retired as a vice admiral. First astronaut to become NASA administrator.

Byron White (1917–2002). Intelligence officer, USS *Lexington* (CV-16), WWII. Prewar college and professional football standout. Served on the U.S. Supreme Court 1962–93.

Charles "Bud" Wilkinson (1916–1994). Hangar deck officer, USS *Enterprise* (CV-6), WWII. Minnesota football star prewar, coach at Oklahoma 1947–63, three national championships.

John W. Young (1930–). Aviator, test pilot, astronaut. Four Gemini-Apollo and two space shuttle flights. Retired as a captain.

APPENDIX TWO

AIRCRAFT CARRIER MOVIES

Silent screen idol Ramon Novarro in 1929's *The Flying Fleet*, filmed aboard USS *Langley* (CV-1). *Courtesy James H. Farmer via John Cassidy.*

SINCE THE 1930S AT LEAST TWENTY ENGLISH-LANGUAGE films have been built around aircraft carrier themes. The first list below describes the most notable movies, in chronological order of the plot, while the others are similarly listed for readers who may want to view them.

MOST NOTABLE CARRIER FILMS

Hell Divers (1931)—directed by George W. Hill, starring Clark Gable, Wallace Beery, and Conrad Nagel.

Probably the first aircraft carrier movie, *Hell Divers* remains a classic of the genre for its depiction of 1930s naval aviation. It is also notable as an early "talkie," filmed just three years after the first full-length movie sound track.

In the film, rival chief petty officers are played by old salt Wally Berry, who won the 1931 Oscar for *The Champ*, and up-and-coming Clark Gable, who appeared in thirteen films that year. Their competition for the top non-commissioned slot in the squadron forms the basis of the plot, written by former naval aviator Frank "Spig" Wead.

Aviation highlights include flight deck footage of USS *Saratoga* (CV-3), then only four years old, and the rigid airship *Los Angeles*. The title is based on Fighting Squadron One's two-seat Curtiss F8C aircraft, dubbed "Helldivers" (normally rendered as one word).

Security concerns are evident in the movie, with the lower part of the screen blacked out when aircraft catch an arresting wire.

Hell Divers was released in January 1932, early in the Great Depression, before Hollywood increasingly produced escapist fare such as comedies and musicals.

Best line: "Say, if them was real bullets we'd be hitting you in the face with a spade." (Chief Riker [Beery] to Steve Nelson [Gable] after camera-gun practice)

Dive Bomber (1941)—directed by Michael Curtiz, starring Errol Flynn, Fred MacMurray, and Ralph Bellamy.

Another buddy-rivalry film, *Dive Bomber* had box office star power with Errol Flynn at the height of his career, ably supported by Fred MacMurray and Ralph Bellamy. The tyrannical Michael Curtiz directed—his twelfth pairing with Flynn—two years before his enduring classic, *Casablanca*.

Flynn and Bellamy are Navy flight surgeons trying to solve altitude sickness while veteran stick-and-rudder man MacMurray is assigned to assist. Regarding all doctors as the natural enemies of fliers, MacMurray is skeptical but eventually helps the medicos devise a fanciful solution resembling a deep-sea diving suit.

Filmed in glorious Technicolor, *Dive Bomber* received an Oscar nomination for photography. Period aircraft such as Brewster Buffalos, Vought Vindicators, and N3N trainers are seen in magnificent prewar livery, afloat, ashore, and aloft. Several scenes were shot aboard USS *Enterprise* (CV-6) at San Diego, augmented by USS *Saratoga* (CV-3) aircraft.

Enterprise veterans recall that Vice Admiral William F. Halsey resented the "Big E" losing valuable training time to support the movie, and on the last day he shouted from the flag bridge, "Now get the hell off my ship!" According to legend, Flynn obliged with a parting gesture—and dived overboard.

Released in August 1941, the film's timing could hardly have been better, and reportedly it earned a stunning one million dollars overall (roughly fifteen million dollars in 2015).

Best line: "Remember you? Honey, you're a window in the house of my life!" (Lieutenant Doug Lee [Flynn] to Linda [Alexis Smith])

The Fighting Lady (1944)—directed by Edward Steichen and William Wyler, starring Robert Taylor, Charles Boyer, and Joseph J. Clark.

A pace-setting documentary, *The Fighting Lady* presents a generic view of a wartime Essex-class carrier, mainly USS *Yorktown* (CV-10), but footage also came from her sister *Ticonderoga* (CV-14).

Part-time flight instructor Robert Taylor narrates the hour-long film, tracing the "Fighting Lady" from stateside training to Pacific combat. Footage includes carrier strikes at Kwajalein, Truk, and the Marianas.

The color film and intimate look at officers and sailors resonated with wartime audiences, who never seemed to get enough information about the subject. Realism was enhanced when some of the fliers introduced in the movie are reported killed or missing at the end.

Released in December 1944, *The Fighting Lady* won the Oscar for best documentary at the 1945 Academy Awards. Its rival was an Army training film, *Resisting Enemy Interrogation.*

In the seven decades since its release, *The Fighting Lady* has provided innumerable examples of combat and operational footage for television programs. Some of the most memorable scenes are overhead views of Japanese carriers off Saipan in June 1944. Though most segments feature Hellcats, several portions depict Dauntlesses, Avengers, and Helldivers.

The World War II documentary spawned a Korean War offspring, *Men of the Fighting Lady* (1954), featuring Van Johnson.

Task Force (1949)—directed by Delmer Daves, starring Gary Cooper, Jane Wyatt, and Wayne Morris.

Gary Cooper stars as the fictional retiring Rear Admiral Jonathan L. Scott, who reflects upon a career that took carrier aviation from biplanes to jets. His former commander and mentor, played by Walter Brennan, seems loosely based on Admiral Marc Mitscher. Scott's wife, Mary (Jane Wyatt), a prewar aviation widow, encourages him through peacetime, politics, and fighting for Navy Air.

In the film prewar actor Wayne Morris (who became a World War II fighter ace flying Hellcats) plays a torpedo pilot who survives the Battle of Midway.

Scott's unnamed ship is based on USS *Franklin* (CV-13), which suffered catastrophic damage off Japan in March 1945, steaming to New York for repair.

The Navy charged Warner Brothers twenty-four thousand dollars a day for access to facilities and ships at San Diego, with much of the carrier footage filmed aboard USS *Bairoko* (CVE-115) and *Antietam* (CV-36).

Aircraft range from a replica Vought VE-7 during USS *Langley* (CV-1) trials, to a Boeing 100 representing a 1930s F4B fighter, to a WWII Dauntless and Wildcat. A realistic mockup represents Douglas TBDs at Midway.

Task Force remains one of the most authentic carrier movies, but it faced tough competition with other 1949 top earners, including *Twelve O' Clock High*, *Battleground*, and *Sands of Iwo Jima*.

Best line: "Do you know any satisfyin' profanity?" (Rear Admiral Pete Richard [Walter Brennan] awaiting a contact report during the Battle of Midway)

The Bridges at Toko-Ri (1954)—directed by Mark Robson, starring William Holden, Grace Kelly, and Fredric March.

James Michener scored a major hit with his fact-based novella, *The Bridges at Toko-Ri*, published by *Life* magazine in July 1953, the month of the Korean armistice. Paramount Pictures immediately scooped up the rights, and the movie debuted only seventeen months after publication.

Michener had reported from Task Force Seventy-Seven in 1951, obtaining much of the background and realism evident in the book and film. The fictional Toko-Ri attack was based on "Carlson's Canyon," a target of USS *Princeton*'s (CV-37) Commander Harold G. Carlson.

Paramount Pictures won the 1956 Oscar for special effects in *The Bridges at Toko-Ri*. Wire-mounted Panther jet models were filmed outdoors for enhanced realism. *Courtesy James H. Farmer via John Cassidy.*

William Holden had a personal connection to the subject, as his younger brother, Lieutenant (jg) Robert W. Beedle, had been killed in action flying a Hellcat in 1944.

The film was a Christmas 1954 release, receiving the special effects Oscar at the ensuing Academy Awards dinner.

The novel was built around an F2H Banshee squadron, but the movie spotlights Grumman F9F-5 Panthers, Douglas AD-4 Skyraiders, and a Sikorsky HO3S-1 helicopter. In the bridge scene the jets are the only ones to attack, when in fact Skyraiders and Corsairs were the main carrier-based bombers.

"Bridges" was mainly filmed aboard USS *Oriskany* (CVA-34) in 1954, where the cast was warmly received. The air group commander, James D. Ramage, recalled, "The guys loved meeting Mickey Rooney but they would have preferred more time with Grace Kelly." That year "the O boat" also hosted a film crew for a lesser-known movie, *Men of the Fighting Lady*.

Best line: "You can say anything you want to an officer as long as you put 'sir' on it." (Chief Petty Officer Mike Forney [Mickey Rooney])

Lieutenant Harry Brubaker (William Holden) abandons his downed F9F Panther in the Korean War film *The Bridges at Toko-Ri*, based on James Michener's novel. *Courtesy James H. Farmer via John Cassidy.*

Wings of Eagles (1957)—directed by John Ford, starring John Wayne, Maureen O'Hara, and Dan Dailey.

Commander Frank "Spig" Wead was a pioneering naval aviator medically released after a 1926 accident. He turned to writing successful movie scripts and stage plays, and recovered enough to return to active duty during World War II. Wead died in 1947, prompting his friend and colleague John Ford to film a "biopic" a decade later.

At the heart of *Wings of Eagles* is the erratic relationship between Wead (John Wayne) and his wife (Maureen O'Hara), following Wead's career through the war and overcoming serious disability along the way. The plot includes a movie within a movie, as the fictional "John Dodge" (Ward Bond, playing a Ford stand-in) is shown directing *Hell Divers*. Actually, Ford appears in none of the credits.

A key plot point is the moment when an ailing Wead is visited by Rear Admiral John Dale Price (Ken Curtis), who remarks, "I have a jeep outside." Wead seizes upon the term as a way to solve the Navy's carrier shortage, equating "jeep carrier" with "escort carrier." The scene is wholly fictional but entered naval lore, as Wead sometimes is credited with devising the CVE concept. In fact, USS *Long Island* (CVE-1) was commissioned before Pearl Harbor.

One of the few aircraft in the film is a Burgess N-9 floatplane that crashes an admiral's party (reputedly a true event). Wartime carrier operations are represented aboard USS *Philippine Sea* (CV-47) with a few outdated Grumman Hellcats and Avengers.

MGM reported a loss of eight hundred thousand dollars on the film.

Best line: "I don't want a story just about ships and planes. I want it about the men who run them—how they live and think and talk. I want it from a pen dipped in salt water, not dry martinis." (Director John Dodge [Ward Bond] to Wead)

Midway (1976)—directed by Jack Smight, starring Charlton Heston, Henry Fonda, and James Coburn.

Though a box-office success, *Midway* remains one of the worst naval aviation films of all time. A far, far better depiction of the pivotal 1942 battle is found in 1949's *Task Force*.

The script is a convoluted mixture of fact and fiction. Knowledgeable viewers counted seventy or more factual and historical errors, including extending the June 4 carrier battle into the following day. An irrelevant romance between a Wildcat pilot and a Japanese-American girl in Hawaii only detracts from the flow of the narrative.

The film editing is atrocious. (Among other things, Charlton Heston—a captain in the movie—crashes in a Grumman F9F jet.) Most of the stock footage of ships is anachronistic, extracted from 1944–1945 films. However, one brief snippet appeared to show a Forrestal-class carrier.

Some of the performances are laughable. Hal Holbrook, previously known for his one-man Mark Twain act, plays intelligence genius Commander Joseph Rochefort as a corn-fed hayseed bumbling toward victory. While Heston, Henry Fonda, and Glenn Ford deliver credible performances, they cannot retrieve the effort from an avoidably flawed script and egregious editing.

The one benefit of the movie, released in America's bicentennial year, is that it introduced a younger audience to the most significant naval victory in American history.

Best line: there isn't one.

Top Gun (1986)—directed by Tony Scott, starring Tom Cruise, Tim Robbins, and Kelly McGillis.

One of the most successful recruiting films of all time, *Top Gun* was based on the Naval Fighter Weapon School (actually Topgun) at NAS Miramar, California. Reportedly Air Force recruiters set up booths in some theaters to capitalize on the glamor of jet fighters. Probably no USAF movie has ever generated such enthusiasm.

The plot is a routine service rivalry between two hot F-14 pilots, Tom Cruise ("Maverick") and Val Kilmer ("Iceman"), vying for top honors in their weapon school class. Anthony Edwards steals the film with his portrayal of Cruise's RIO, "Goose," whose death gives the rebellious "Maverick" the focus he needs to succeed. Love interest

Kelly McGillis is improbably cast as an astrophysicist consulting for Topgun.

The movie generated dozens of interview requests with Fighter Weapon School instructors. One pilot said, "Well, Maverick had the right stuff but with his attitude we wouldn't let him in the back door."

Spectacularly filmed, the aerial sequences feature F-14s engaging adversary trainers, A-4s and F-5s. Some of the low-level shots remain among the most memorable ever seen, and flight-deck operations aboard USS *Enterprise* (CVN-65) also are well photographed.

Best line: "Do some of that pilot stuff!" (Lt(jg) Nick "Goose" Bradshaw [Anthony Edwards] to Maverick)

Flight of the Intruder (1991)—directed by John Milius, starring Danny Glover, Willem Dafoe, and Brad Johnson.

Grumman A-6 pilot Stephen Coonts's debut novel benefited from personal experience as an attack aviator aboard USS *Enterprise* (CVN-65) in 1970–72. His 1986 book defied the conventional wisdom about a saturated Vietnam market, becoming a major motion picture five years later.

The story revolves around an A-6 crew played by pilot Brad Johnson and bombardier-navigator Willem Dafoe. Their disaffection with the Navy and America's no-win Vietnam policy prompts them to bomb a SAM storage area in Hanoi—a forbidden target. When their offense is revealed, they face serious charges.

In the film the miscreants' CO, Commander Frank Camparelli, is depicted as an African American, although the Navy had no black squadron commanders until after the war.

Some of the flying sequences are exceptional, with A-6s, F-4 Phantoms, and A-1 Skyraiders. Milius oversaw two weeks of filming aboard USS *Independence* (CV-62), providing an authentic look at period carrier operations. Additionally, some of the computer-generated imagery is unusually good for the early 1990s.

Box office receipts amounted to about twenty million dollars for a thirty-five million dollar budget, although Milius said he could have made "FOTI" for five million dollars less. Subsequent video and DVD sales boosted earnings.

However, the film's main problem was timing, as it debuted in mid-January 1991, competing with live coverage of Operation Desert Storm, which kicked off the day before.

Best line: "Fighter pukes make movies. Bomber pilots make…history!" (Lieutenant Jake Grafton [Brad Johnson])

SHORT SUMMARIES

Flight Command (1940)—directed by Frank Borzage, starring Robert Taylor, Ruth Hussey, and Walter Pidgeon.

Future Navy flight instructor Robert Taylor in the 1940 movie *Flight Command*, playing the newest pilot in the fictional Hell Cats, the hottest squadron in the fleet. *Courtesy James H. Farmer via John Cassidy.*

Taylor plays a new pilot joining the hottest squadron in the fleet, trying to fit in with the old salt F3F pilots.

Flight Command was partly filmed aboard USS *Enterprise* with Grumman F3Fs of "The Big E's" Fighting Squadron Six. *Courtesy James H. Farmer via John Cassidy.*

Ships with Wings (UK 1942)—directed by Sergei Nolbandov, starring John Clements, Leslie Banks, and Jane Baxter.

An undisciplined prewar Royal Navy pilot is dismissed from the service, but after 1939 fetches up in the Mediterranean, where he has an opportunity to redeem himself. Contains excellent footage of HMS *Ark Royal*.

Tora! Tora! Tora! (1970)—directed by Richard Fleischer, Kinji Fukasaku, and Toshio Masuda, starring Martin Balsam, Sô Yamamura, and Jason Robards.

A docudrama following American and Japanese officers leading up to the Pearl Harbor attack with better than average special effects and attention to detail. Several sequences depicting Imperial Navy flight deck action.

Pearl Harbor (2001)—directed by Michael Bay, starring Ben Affleck, Kate Beckinsale, and Josh Hartnett.

Nowhere near as good as *Tora! Tora! Tora!*, this sixtieth anniversary release has minimal carrier content, mainly focusing on two Army pilots. Casting Alec Baldwin as Jimmy Doolittle outraged everyone who ever met Doolittle.

Wing and a Prayer (1944)—directed by Henry Hathaway, starring Don Ameche, Dana Andrews, and William Eythe.

A fictional version of Midway made memorable by excellent contemporary footage of Essex-class carriers and their squadrons.

The Eternal Sea (1955)—directed by John Auer, starring Sterling Hayden, Alexis Smith, and Ben Cooper.

The story of Captain John Hoskins of USS *Princeton* (CVL-23), sunk at Leyte Gulf, and his determination to remain on active duty despite loss of a foot.

Men of the Fighting Lady (1954)—directed by Andrew Marton, starring Van Johnson, Walter Pidgeon, and Louis Calhern.

Partially the story behind the story of researching James Michener's *The Bridges at Toko-Ri*, focusing on a blinded pilot's attempt to return to his ship.

Flat Top (1952)—directed by Lesley Selander, starring Sterling Hayden, Richard Carlson, and William Phipps.

A film within a film, set in Korea and largely told in World War II flashbacks via the tough-as-nails squadron commander.

The Final Countdown (1980)—directed by Don Taylor, starring Kirk Douglas, Martin Sheen, and Katharine Ross.

An atmospheric anomaly sends USS *Nimitz* (CVN-68) back in time to December 6, 1941, posing a variety of dilemmas for the crew.

F-14 squadrons exulted "Tomcats 2, Zeroes 0."

Hot Shots! (1991)—directed by Jim Abrahams, starring Charlie Sheen, Cary Elwes, and Valeria Golino.

With tongue firmly planted in cheek, this romp pokes fun at *Top Gun* while never taking itself seriously.

Stealth (2005)—directed by Rob Cohen, starring Josh Lucas, Jessica Biel, and Jamie Foxx.

A futuristic look at carrier aviation featuring the mythical "F-37" stealth fighter controlled by artificial intelligence gone wrong.

APPENDIX THREE

THE FOLLOWING IS EXCERPTED FROM *HELLCAT: THE F6F IN* *World War II* (1970, Naval Institute).

In the centenary of aircraft carriers, let a glimpse of the 1940s represent all that came before and since because, in a period of less than four years, carriers mattered as never before or since.

During World War II the big, handsome Essex-class ships, accompanied by their Independence-class team mates, made an unforgettable sight steaming under the topic sky as they prepared to launch full deck loads.

Gaily-colored signal pennants snapped from their halyards as the diamond-design Foxtrot flag was hoisted to signal commence of flight operations. As the carriers turned smartly into the wind, trailing thirty-knot wakes, aviators rushed from their ready rooms. Each flier was loaded with Mae West, parachute harness, pistol and survival knife, helmet and goggles with oxygen mask, and the pilots' ever-present plotting boards. They trooped up steep companion-ways, emerging topside where the ship's island, top-heavy with radar antennae, looked incongruously narrow compared to the width of the flight deck.

The Douglas Fir decks became a pandemonium of organized confusion as khaki-suited fliers climbed into their aircraft while plane directors in yellow jerseys shouted orders to deck hands who pushed planes into position, unfolded and locked wings, or removed wheel chocks. Red-shirted ordnance men removed safety wires from bomb and torpedo fuses; asbestos-suited fire fighters stood by while catapult crews in green jerseys waited to see if the wind would remain strong enough for an unassisted launch.

The aircraft themselves—with Hellcats in front, as they needed less deck room than the strike planes—were no less colorful. Three-tone or dark gloss blue paint schemes vividly offset white geometric air group symbols boldly emblazoned on tail surfaces.

But it wasn't only color and salt spray. There was noise, too. The incomparable sound of perhaps forty radial engines turning over, forming the bass chorus for the high-pitched whine of inertia starters, and the punctuation of shotgun-type cartridges kicking over pistons in Pratt & Whitneys or Wrights, was deafening. Three-bladed Hamilton-Standard propellers on blunt-nosed Hellcats and big-bellied Avengers, and four-bladed Curtiss Electrics on round-tailed Helldivers, jerked into motion by fits and starts, then blurred into invisibility. The clouds of light blue smoke that seemed to hang over the flight decks never stayed long, for they were swept away in the relative wind and ever-increasing prop wash.

BIBLIOGRAPHY

Battle of Midway Roundtable. http://www.midway42.org

Brown, David. *Carrier Operations in World War II. Volume I: The Royal Navy*. Annapolis: Naval Institute Press, 1974.

Brown, Eric. *Wings on My Sleeve*. UK: Airlife, 1978.

Cox, Sebastian, and Peter Gray. *Air Power History: Turning Points from Kitty Hawk to Kosovo*. London: Frank Cass Publishers, 2002.

Cutler, Thomas J., Lieutenant Commander. "Retribution." Naval Institute *Proceedings*, February 2016.

Fitzgerald, Mark, Admiral, USN (Ret). "Remembering Desert Storm." *Wings of Gold*, Spring 2016.

Flying Magazine. Special Issue. *U.S. Naval Aviation at War*. Chicago: Ziff-Davis Publishing Company, February 1943.

Fontenoy, Paul E. *Aircraft Carriers: An Illustrated History of Their Impact*. ABC-CLIO, 2006.

Foster, Wynn. *Captain Hook: A Pilot's Tragedy and Triumph in the Vietnam War.* Annapolis: Naval Institute Press, 1992.

French Fleet Air Arm 1910–2010. http://www.ffaa.net/version-english.htm

Friedman, Norman. *Aircraft Carriers: An Illustrated Design History.* Annapolis: Naval Institute Press, 1983.

Fuchida, Mitsuo. *For That One Day: The Memoirs of Mitsuo Fuchida, Commander of the Attack on Pearl Harbor.* Translated by Douglas T. Shinsato and Tadanori Urabe. Waimea: eXperience, inc, 2011.

Go Navy. *Carrier Air Wings and Aircraft Carrier Deployments.* http://www.gonavy.jp/AirWingsf.html

Goodspeed, M. Hill. *U.S. Navy: A Complete History.* Washington, D.C.: Naval Historical Foundation, 2003.

Grossnick, Roy A. and Mark L. Evans. *United States Naval Aviation 1910-2010.* Washington, D.C.: Department of the Navy, Naval History and Heritage Command.

Hallion, Richard P. *The Naval Air War in Korea.* Baltimore: Nautical & Aviation Publishing Company, 1987.

Hatch, Alden. *Glenn Curtiss, Pioneer of Aviation.* Guilford: Lyons Press, 2007.

Hearn, Chester G. *Carriers in Combat: The Air War at Sea.* Mechanicsburg: Stackpole Books, 2007.

Heinemann, Edward H. with Rosario Rausa. *Ed Heinemann: Combat Aircraft Designer.* Annapolis: Naval Institute Press, 1980.

Horan, Mark. *"With Gallantry and Determination." The Story of the Torpedoing of the Bismarck.* http://www.kbismarck.com/article2.html.

Jones, Ben (ed.). *The Fleet Air Arm in the Second World War, 1939-1941: Norway, the Mediterranean and the Bismarck.* Farnham: Ashgate, 2012.

Labs, Eric J. "A Fiscal Pearl Harbor." U.S. Naval Institute *Proceedings*, February 2016.

Lawson, Robert L. *Carrier Air Group Commanders: The Men and their Machines*. Atglen: Schiffer Military History, 2000.

Lundstrom, John B. *The First Team: Pacific Air Combat from Pearl Harbor to Midway*. Annapolis: Naval Institute Press, 1984.

———. *The First Team and the Guadalcanal Campaign*. Annapolis: Naval Institute Press, 1994.

Mark, Eduard. *Aerial Interdiction in Three Wars*. Washington, D.C.: Center for Air Force History, 1994.

Miller, Jerry. *Nuclear Weapons and Aircraft Carriers*. Washington, D.C.: Smithsonian Press, 2001.

Morison, Samuel Eliot. *History of U.S. Naval Operations in World War II* (15 volumes). Edison: Castle Books, 2001.

National Museum of Naval Aviation. Emil Buehler Library. http://www.navalaviationmuseum.org/education/emil-buehler-library/

Naval History and Heritage Command. Allowances and Location of Navy Aircraft, various dates. http://www.history.navy.mil/research/histories/naval-aviation-history/allowances-and-location.html

———. *Naval Aviation News*, various dates. http://www.history.navy.mil/research/histories/naval-aviation-history/naval-aviation-news/back-issues.html

Nichols, John B. and Barrett Tillman. *On Yankee Station: The Naval Air War Over Vietnam*. Annapolis: Naval Institute Press, 1987.

Nihon Kaigun: The Imperial Japanese Navy Page. http://www.combinedfleet.com

Parshall, Jonathan, and Anthony Tully. *Shattered Sword: The Untold Story of the Battle of Midway*. Dulles: Potomac Books, 2005.

Pattie, D. A. *To Cock a Cannon: A Pilot's View of WW II*. Privately published, 1983.

Peattie, Mark R. *Sunburst: The Rise of Japanese Naval Air Power, 1909–1941*. Annapolis: Naval Institute Press, 2001.

Polmar, Norman. *Aircraft Carriers* (two volumes). Dulles: Potomac Books, 2006, 2008.

Reynolds, Clark G. *The Fast Carriers: The Forging of an Air Navy*. New York: McGraw-Hill, 1968.

Royal Navy Fleet Air Arm Museum. http://www.fleetairarm.com

Tillman, Barrett. *Clash of the Carriers*. New York: Caliber, 2005.

Warner, Guy. *World War One Aircraft Carrier Pioneer. The Story & Diaries of Jack McCleery, RNAS, RAF*. Great Britain: Sword & Pen, 2011.

Wildenberg, Thomas. *Billy Mitchell's War with the Navy*. Annapolis: Naval Institute Press, 2014.

INDEX

A

Aeronautique Maritime, 28
Aeronavale, 6, 225, 248
Afghanistan, 219, 261, 263–64,
   269, 286
Africa, 6, 51, 54, 65, 76–77,
   153, 207, 291, 308
Aichis, xxii, 108, 114, 122
aircraft, xi, xiii, xvi, xxi–xxii,
   4–8, 10–11, 13–28, 30–31,
   33–40, 42–49, 51, 53–55, 57,
   59, 64, 66, 68–78, 80–81, 83,
   88–89, 92, 96, 98–100, 102,
   114, 117–20, 123–25,
127–31, 133–34, 136, 138,
142–43, 145–49, 152, 154–
55, 157–58, 161–62, 164–66,
168, 170, 173–75, 177, 180–
83, 185–86, 191–93, 197–99,
201–5, 207–8, 210, 212–18,
221, 224, 226, 228–31, 234–
39, 242–46, 248–52, 255–
56, 259–60, 262, 264–65,
268–71, 273–78, 281–89,
300–1, 303, 306, 314
   front-line, 84, 213
   stealth, 270, 274, 287
   supersonic, 208–9